PENGU

Bliss t

Gavin Hills was one of the most influential and original journalists of his generation, and died tragically in May 1997, just shortly after his thirty-first birthday. He was a journalist for the *Face*, the *Observer*, the *Idler* and the *Manchester United* magazine, among many others.

Sheryl Garratt was editor of the *Face* between 1989 and 1995 and then went on to edit the *Observer Life* magazine. She is currently a staff writer for the *Observer*. Her book on dance culture, *Adventures in Wonderland*, was published in 1998.

Bliss to be Alive

The Collected Writings of Gavin Hills

EDITED BY SHERYL GARRATT

PENGUIN BOOKS

PENGUIN BOOKS

Published by the Penguin Group
Penguin Books Ltd, 27 Wrights Lane, London w8 5tz, England
Penguin Putnam Inc., 375 Hudson Street, New York, New York 10014, USA
Penguin Books Australia Ltd, Ringwood, Victoria, Australia
Penguin Books Canada Ltd, 10 Alcorn Avenue, Toronto, Ontario, Canada m4v 3b2
Penguin Books India (P) Ltd, 11 Community Centre,
Panchsheel Park, New Delhi – 110 017, India
Penguin Books (NZ) Ltd, Cnr Rosedale and Airborne Roads, Albany, Auckland, New Zealand
Penguin Books (South Africa) (Pty) Ltd, 5 Watkins Street,
Denver Ext 4, Johannesburg 2094, South Africa

Penguin Books Ltd, Registered Offices: Harmondsworth, Middlesex, England

First published by Penguin 2000
1

Copyright © Gavin Hills, 2000

Introduction copyright © Sheryl Garratt, 2000
All rights reserved

The moral right of the author has been asserted

Grateful acknowledgement is made to Small Wonder Music for permission to
reproduce lyrics from 'Police Car' by the Cockney Rejects; to Notting Hill Music
UK Ltd for permission to reproduce lyrics from 'It's On' by Flowered Up; to Dells/
De Wilde/De Coster/Slijngard for permission to reproduce lyrics from 'No Limits'
by 2Unlimited © Universal/MCA Music Ltd, 1993.

Set in 11/13 pt PostScript Monotype Dante
Typeset by Rowland Phototypesetting Ltd, Bury St Edmunds, Suffolk
Printed in England by Clays Ltd, St Ives plc

Except in the United States of America, this book is sold subject
to the condition that it shall not, by way of trade or otherwise, be lent,
re-sold, hired out, or otherwise circulated without the publisher's
prior consent in any form of binding or cover other than that in
which it is published and without a similar condition including this
condition being imposed on the subsequent purchaser

To the author's parents, Helen and John, and to his brother Fraser and sister Rona. And to everyone else who misses him – whether or not they ever met him

Contents

Contents

Introduction

The night after Gavin Hills died, a few of his friends gathered in his flat in Hackney, with its varnished yellow walls painted to look like those of a nicotine-stained pub, its giant portrait of Sir Matt Busby, its kitchen bar dispensing vodka, the little office where he worked and his abysmal music collection. We got drunk there one last time, we cried, and we all told our favourite Gavin stories – which meant that we laughed a lot, too.

But we also laughed, I think, because none of us quite believed it. It seemed so unreal, so senseless that he should die this way. Gavin, who was full of energy and life, always taking off on new adventures, always getting into scrapes. He'd travelled as a reporter to Beirut, Somalia, El Salvador, he'd been on Army manoeuvres in the Belize jungle and, like many of us, he'd clubbed and consumed above and beyond the call of duty or even sanity. He caught tropical diseases in Angola. He was shot at by snipers in Sarajevo. He was clumsy, always falling off or over things: stairs, tables, railway bridges. That he should die this way – in England, on holiday, while perfectly straight and sober – is something many who knew him still struggle to come to terms with.

Gavin Hills died on 20 May 1997, three days after his thirty-first birthday. He was washed off a rock by a wave while fishing at the foot of a cliff on the coast of Cornwall. The sea was deep, the current heavy and, despite his friends, Tom Hodgkinson, and his brother-in-law, Alex Smith, and the coastguard trying everything possible to save him, he drowned.

I wanted to say all this first, because his death is sad but it is not what makes him interesting. If Gavin were still alive today, a collection similar to this would have been published anyway. He was one of the strongest voices of his generation, and his work explains what it meant to be young in the Nineties – a record of confused but often exhilarating times.

I was editor of *The Face* from 1989 to 1995. I was interviewed a lot during this period, and one of the issues that often came up during the early years was that although the magazine had successfully reinvented itself, shaking off its image as an Eighties style bible, it no longer had a star writer, a journalist with a voice and an attitude as strong as that of earlier contributors Julie Burchill or Robert Elms. Then Gavin Hills started writing for the magazine, and that subject didn't come up any more. After that, the main question was: *what is he like?*

What was he like? Gavin got more fan letters than all of *The Face*'s other writers put together. He even got a few marriage proposals. His writing was sharp, funny, original, opinionated, analytical without ever being pretentious. The readers liked him, they trusted him, and so they read his views on Angola or Sarajevo as avidly as his pieces on clubs, drugs, trainers or football.

He had an absurd, loud laugh that sounded like a cross between a donkey in pain and a hysterical hyena. He had a winning smile. He was losing his hair, although every time he went to the chemist's to buy Regaine, he would insist – loudly, deliberately drawing the attention of the whole store – that it wasn't for him but for a follically challenged friend. He was utterly charming, even when incoherently drunk. He was a terrible dancer, a clumsy sportsman and had the worst taste in music ever known. Most people who met him fell in love with him, instantly. The rest took a week or two longer.

Everyone who ever met him has a Gavin tale to tell. Gavin serving spam to his guests on VE Day. Gavin trying to get into Wembley for an England match dressed as St George, then riding up in a stretch limo to dance at the Liverpool superclub Cream – still dressed as St George. Gavin at EuroDisney, with pâté smeared all over his face, trying to ambush boats on the Pirates of Penzance ride. Gavin turning up at a party dressed as a cat, and sitting in a corner telling fortunes all night as Mystic Mog. Gavin organizing parties, trips, sports days, ice sculptures, costumes, scams. Gavin taking his clothes off, forming a band, acting in a movie . . . He never stayed still, never wasted a minute. He always had a new idea, a new friend, a new cause, a new scam to share.

But he was more than just a party animal. There are other stories, too. Little acts of kindness, generosity, compassion. Well-placed words of advice or encouragement. Gavin was a good friend, and he worked hard at it. He was more sensitive than his smile sometimes showed, and there were hidden scars left by some of the things he'd seen while reporting in Africa and the former Yugoslavia: bad dreams, depression, guilt. This depression deepened with the breakdown of his marriage in 1993, which ended after less than a year when his wife moved in with his best friend – a double loss he found hard to come to terms with.

As he wrote in *Elle* in 1994, 'It's hard being wrong. Not just niggly wrong. Not just the wrong that sends you back from the shop with Bovril instead of Marmite. But the *really* wrong. The wrong that means you've made completely false assumptions about life, love, friends and the huge great cosmos. Things have been hard recently. I was wrong. I thought the myth and magic of romantic love would protect me from the evil spirits that wreck lives and loves. A faith that was destroyed when my eyes were burnt open by marital fall-out.'

He was a romantic who believed marriage was for ever and, for someone who captured his time so perfectly, he could be curiously old-fashioned in other ways, too. Concepts like honour, loyalty, truth, patriotism and idealism were important to him. He was comfortable with all kinds of different people and made them feel at ease with him. He knew a High Court judge and one of the Great Train Robbers. He knew pop stars and comedians, low-life and dealers. He treated them all pretty much the same. He was, in his own eccentric way, a true gentleman.

Gavin grew up in the village of Headley near Leatherhead in Surrey, the youngest of three children. When he was twelve or thirteen, he started going to Tottenham Hotspur matches with his older brother Fraser and became a member of that large and largely undocumented Eighties youth cult of casual. He was soon travelling the country doing what young men did in those days around football matches: dressing up, milling about, doing a lot of running, a bit of fighting and a bit of thieving.

Later he went to take his A Levels and study fashion at Epsom School of Art, although according to his brother he was a lousy designer. His graduating collection was menswear with a heraldic twist: Arthurian legend was a lasting obsession. By 1988, he was living in Camden, north London, and had become involved in the skateboard scene. He turned out be a lousy skateboarder, too. But he discovered a different talent: he could write. He began contributing to the skate magazine *RaD* (*Read and Destroy*) and quickly became a staff writer. He wrote the children's bestseller, *Skateboarding is Not a Book* (Fantail, 1988), and another, less successful, book, *Street Skating* (Wayland, 1989).

Gavin started writing just as the Eighties finally began to grind to an end. Celebrated by some as the designer decade, a time of stylish clubs, glitzy pop and big City bonuses, for the majority of youngsters coming of age in that era, it was a grim, grey decade. For most, the hip clubs of Soho were as inaccessible as a job that paid a good wage. Children born in the Sixties grew up with a whole raft of rights and expectations, assuming they'd get a university education if they were smart enough, state benefits if they needed them. Children born in the Seventies came of age in a time when all of these things had been cut away, when demos and protests no longer changed anything – after Live Aid, after AIDS, after all the old comforting beliefs and 'isms' had begun to wither away.

And then along came acid house and Ecstasy, and for a while it seemed like anything was possible. These were heady times: suddenly the fantasy world of clubs was open to all who had the price of a ticket and a pill, and the illegal raves of 1989 and 1990 saw young people dodging the police and defying the law on a scale never seen before, all for the right to dance. Many of those involved really did believe, at least for a while, that it would change everything. And meanwhile, the world *was* changing, at a dizzying pace: communism crumbled, the Cold War ended, the Berlin Wall came down, Nelson Mandela walked free, new countries were formed and began fighting, the Internet began connecting us all with a speed previous generations could never have imagined.

Gavin's work documents these times. It charts the demise of the soccer hooligan and the changing face of football (in his 1991 *Face* feature, 'Whatever Happened to the Likely Lads?', and later in his short story 'White Burger Danny', published in the hugely successful 1997 anthology *Disco Biscuits*). It records the emergence of the chemical generation, for which drugs are a normal leisure activity and clubbing a means of escape. It records the merging of youth tribes and fashion. Dole culture and the blag economy. Worries about technology, about information overload, about the ever-accelerating rate of change. It aimed to redefine / explore ideas about being British, being male, being left wing or liberal at a time when there was deep uncertainty about such things. It is about a generation which has lost the old certainties of religion and politics but which is still desperately searching for something to believe in.

It's also full of good jokes.

Gavin embodied many of the contradictions of his generation. He was a patriot who loathed racism, a lad who loved women, a loafer who worked extraordinarily hard, a clubber who couldn't dance, a man with very high moral standards who nonetheless broke the law regularly. From *Teletubbies* to the pixilated pin-up Lara Croft, he always picked up on trends first. But he also joined the Territorial Army, and wrote warmly about it. He was a mass of contradictions, and this struck a chord with readers who felt similarly.

Gavin wrote about anything from El Salvador to computer games in the same voice. He talked about clubs and music in his political pieces. He talked about politics in his fashion and football pieces. This was deliberate: both of us felt strongly that these things cannot be separated, that they feed into one another. We talked endlessly, passionately, about the best way to communicate difficult information – really to communicate it, in a way that would be understood and make a difference. I don't know if I've ever solved that problem myself, but I think Gavin came close at times.

In 1993, Gavin and Tim Leighton-Boyce, his editor at *RaD*, launched a new magazine called *Phat*, aimed at teenage boys. In Britain at that time there were very few magazines aimed at men, and none at all aimed at boys. *Phat* pitched itself as 'for hoodlums, by hoodlums'. It featured a mixture of skate culture, product reviews and listings, but also absurd lists, and a 'lust list' made up mainly of computer-game babes and manga-cartoon characters. Its début issue also tackled – somewhat crudely – the subject of guns, and led the *Sunday Telegraph* to cry, 'Would you want your teenager to read this?', before the issue had even hit the shops. Distribution proved difficult, and the magazine folded after three issues. It had, however, attracted the attention of a former *NME* writer called James Brown, who cites it as an influence on the magazine he subsequently launched, with rather more success: *Loaded*.

Gavin, meanwhile, moved on to the small independent publishing company Zone, for whom he launched and edited the official *Manchester United* magazine (a huge success that was quickly selling more copies a month than *The Face*), and then, in the summer of 1995, the official *England* magazine.

'We have to do something of a PR job with the England fan's image,' he wrote in a pre-launch proposal. 'We have to take on notions of nationhood and patriotism, displaying all the positive things about our country and team. The magazine is set up to forge a new identity for English football and will be actively combating racism and hooliganism. We hope to prove a positive force in the game and beyond.'

For some editors, this would mean dry, righteous articles about race and violence; for Gavin, it meant lively features on London's Asian football league, dressing up Les Ferdinand, offering pin-ups of English Roses from Kathy Burke to Mrs Merton and Lily Savage, and celebrating all that is great about England: Vimto, marmalade, Marmite, The Beatles, the cuppa, curries and jacket potatoes.

He also worked as a consultant for the *Guardian*, for BBC Radio, especially Radio 4's *Loose Ends*, and on a host of other projects. However, there is no doubt about the work he was most proud of. Many of the reportage stories you will read here he funded himself. The company which owned *The Face* at that time rarely spent money, and the most I recall him ever being paid in expenses for a trip was an advance of £500 – and I'm fairly sure that was deducted from his final fee. He persisted in writing them nonetheless, and in 1994, Gavin won an Amnesty Press Award for his article in *The Face* on the forgotten war in Angola. The award was presented by the veteran South African journalist Donald Wood, and that night the two of us were so proud we could scarcely speak.

Gavin worked for *City Limits*, the *Guardian*, the *Observer*, *Select*, *Elle*, *Big Issue*, *New Statesman*, *Arena*, *Arena Homme Plus* but, on the whole, *The Face* was the place he had room to stretch out, to write over 5,000 words rather than 500. He also cared about his work for the *Idler*, where he wrote more philosophical – spiritual, even – musings, about his life, his beliefs and his moods.

By 1997, the depression he wrote about so eloquently in his *Idler* columns seemed to be lifting. Gavin had signed a contract with Hodder to write his first novel, *Strings of Life*, a loosely autobiographical account of love, idealism and confusion set against the background of acid house and the club boom, the changes in football, the end of the Cold War and the places he had visited as a foreign reporter. In March he went to Beirut with his friend Miranda Sawyer to film a pilot for the *Rough Guide* travel series on BBC TV. And then there was the Labour victory – the first since any of us had been eligible to vote. We were all feeling optimistic that spring, and Gavin most of all. His last assignment was a travel piece for the *Independent*, on Iceland. He loved it there, but the feature never got written because he went away to Cornwall first.

There is a kind of glamour around those who die young, but there's nothing romantic about a death like Gavin's. It's messy, random, leaving so much unsaid and undone, and it blights the lives of the friends and family left behind. In his travels he had seen more of death than many people of his age, and there are many references to it in this book. But Gavin didn't want to die. He had plans. He was going to write about his latest love, a new children's TV show called *Teletubbies*. He was going to see U2 play in Sarajevo. He was going to Rome for the Italy–England match. He wanted children. An eccentric old age. A cure for male pattern-baldness. He packed more into thirty-one years than many do in far longer lives, but it wasn't anywhere near enough.

While preparing this book, I was given a note Gavin wrote to his girlfriend Heather Hodson after the death of her father. It seems appropriate to print it here. 'Someone once told me that you should wear grief like a medal,' he wrote. 'Pin grief to your chest and let it sit proudly in honour of your father. As the years go by it won't disappear, just sink beneath the skin to your heart. There it shall lie for ever. One day at a time.'

Gavin's death was a great loss. To his family, to his friends, to his readers. But the people who lost most don't even know it, because few of them had met him yet. They are ordinary people just like you and me, caught up in extraordinary circumstances. They are invisible, because few in the media notice them or find them interesting enough to tell their stories. People like Celo, who wore a shell suit, kept a pitbull, ran a nightclub and was fond of his cannabis plants – and was, for a while, a war hero in Sarajevo. Or Crazy Face, the young gang member struggling to broker peace and have fun in El Salvador. Or the gunmen in Somalia, high on khat and body-popping to the sound 'Rhythm is a Dancer' on the World

Introduction

Service. Perhaps the most fitting memorial we could offer to Gavin would be to try and see these people more often behind the headlines and the set pieces on the TV news, to try and put ourselves in their place if only for a moment, and see how it feels.

In 1996, Gavin joined the Territorial Army. This confused many of us, and he tended to make excuses. It was a way to get fit without the expense of a gym membership, he said. Then he told us that he just wanted to prove himself by gaining his beret. Then he was hanging on in order to go on jungle training in Belize, which he claimed was really a free beach holiday. In fact, he made a good soldier.

It wasn't until I was compiling this book, reading his work again and again and putting it into chronological order, that it really made sense. He joined the volunteer army because he liked the masculinity of it, the camaraderie. He did it because he liked handling guns. He did it because he was part of what he called the Airfix generation, boys who grew up seeing war as something distant and glorious, a playground game. But most of all, he did it because in his travels he'd met a lot of ordinary young people like himself, who had been forced to fight for what they believed in.

In Sarajevo, he met youths who were willing to lay down their lives to defend their richly cosmopolitan and multicultural city from hostile nationalists. Think, when you read the Sarajevo pieces in this book, whether you would do the same if your own home were under attack. The things Gavin saw forced him to consider these things, and I think he had already made up his mind. And if the time ever came for London, if Britain's curry houses and Chinese takeaways were to be closed and the dance music he loved silenced, he wanted to make sure he fought well.

9

Acknowledgements

It is customary, in books like these, to offer a list of thanks. Since Gavin can't, I'll do my best to do it for him. I was the editor of *The Face* when the pieces that form the large part of this book were written, but they also benefited from the patient attention of Richard Benson, Ekow Eshun and, most of all, Charles Gant. Tom Hodgkinson of the *Idler* was not only a fine editor who gave Gavin a regular column, but a close friend. James Freedman gave him a job at Zone, and everyone on the *England* and *Manchester United* magazines gave him love, support and a lot of laughs. Cynthia Rose offered Gavin his first entry into the mainstream media during her editorship of *City Limits*, and was responsible for introducing him to me, among others. Tim Leighton-Boyce encouraged his talent on *RaD* and showed enormous faith in that talent when they launched *Phat*. His close friend and regular photographer Zik Nelson travelled the world with him, came near death with him as they both sweated out diseases in an Angola hotel room, and gave his last $100 to fund the meal in Ethiopia detailed here in 'On the Piss in Addis'. Paul Lowe got him in and out of Sarajevo more than once, and Steve Blame would have funded Sarajevostock if only he'd been able to get in. Heather Hodson and Cathy Wilson also deserve special thanks.

I know he'd also have sent love and thanks to Fraser Hills, Miranda Sawyer, Becky Carroll, and to his editor at Hodder and now at Penguin, Simon Prosser. To these, for their support while compiling this collection, I'd like to add my own thanks. Gavin was a great collector of people and, inevitably, I will have missed many out. You know who you are, and you know how he felt. At some point I'm sure he probably screamed it loudly in your ear in the middle of a packed dancefloor.

Thanks to the care taken by Gavin's family and by his workmates at Zone in 1997, I had access to the hard disks of his home and office computers while compiling this book. Nothing was labelled very clearly, and so I read through rough drafts of articles we worked on together, letters to friends, invoices for work, joke faxes, proposals for new magazines, new TV series, lists of debts and money due – all of life's routine messiness exposed, and then left, unfinished. A sudden unexpected death offers no privacy, no chance to put affairs in order, no tidy endings. Not everything he wrote was on these disks, and there will inevitably be good things I didn't find to put in this collection; there are also one or two pieces obviously written for publication that I have included here without knowing if or when they ever did reach the page. If they *were* published, my apologies for not crediting the magazines concerned.

Some of the pieces collected here are not his best writing but are included because they said something about the decade Gavin was recording. Some I included just because the parties or events he was writing about were so absurd or unbelievable that it seemed worth putting them on record in a book. Other fine pieces were excluded because they seemed irrelevant to this theme, including fine interviews with P. J. Harvey and Keith Allen, and much of his work for the *Observer*.

Sifting through these disks, through copies of magazines and cuttings supplied by his family and friends, I tried my best to find the pieces I felt Gavin would be proud of and want to see collected in a book. But on the whole this is the work of a young writer, still finding his voice, finding what he believed in and wanted to say. It wasn't possible to print his best work here. He hadn't written that yet.

Sheryl Garratt, January 2000

1988

Follow your spirit; and, upon this charge
Cry God for Harry! England and Saint George!
                                    – Henry V

Here begins the descent. Here begin the terrors. Here begin the miracles. The summer of 88 was designated the second summer of love. The first large batches of Ecstasy were becoming available in the UK. Acid house was making its mark. New clubs and warehouse parties were emerging. Lives were changing.

At the European Football Championships in Germany, the hooliganism and rioting that occurred around the England matches led the *Sun* to describe it as 'World War 3'. On the eve of England's match against Holland in Düsseldorf, more than 2,000 German hooligans turned up at the central railway station and set upon the 50 or so England fans who happened to be at the station at the time. A battle of epic proportions took place as the England fans repelled successive German attacks until reinforcements arrived from the town centre. As CS gas filled the air, a youth climbed on top of a litter bin and recited the 'Cry God for Harry' speech from Shakespeare's *Henry V*. The Germans were then vanquished.

This is the tale of that youth. Of his return to London, where his world altered from one of football and violence, to the pharmaceutically induced love of the acid-house scene. A world of hedonistic escape from the problems of the real world. No matter how banal and superficial it appears, at the height of the Thatcher years, this is a scene that offered hope and optimism.

1989

As London acid-house parties are raided and shut down, rave events are organized in barns and fields off the M25. Events attract over 20,000 people to strange little villages in the home counties. The police are soon on the case and every Saturday night turns into cat-and-mouse games between organizers, ravers and police.

Our young man has the time of his life. His weekends are electric, filled with excitement and drugs. His weekdays are filled with anticipation of the weekend. He doesn't go to football any more, although he still watches it on television. He's stoned lying on his bed when the FA Cup semifinal between Liverpool and Nottingham Forest unfurls into the Hillsborough tragedy.

One night, returning from a club in Clink Street by London Bridge, nutted on Ecstasy, he stares in delight at the host of flashing lights that have covered the Thames. He sits skinning up, looking at all the boats coming to the riverside dock. Then he sees the bodies. The *Marchioness* has sunk, killing twenty-six.

1990

Acid house is dead. Tabloid hysteria and the subsequent police crackdown means few clubs can survive. The youth travels to Goa in India, where he divides his time between organizing acid-house beach parties and taking opium. He mixes with hippie acid casualties and scally smack-heads. Before madness can settle in too deep, he returns home. The lads he once knew as football hooligans are now the spliff-smoking vagabonds of the baggy scene.

Off to the World Cup in Italy, he spends the night before England's crucial semifinal with Germany under siege by Italian hooligans. As the campsite is surrounded and set alight, he puts on 808 State on the portable cassette player and they all have a little disco.

When the summer ends in the poll-tax riots, he throws a brick through the window of the Soho Brasserie.

From the proposal for Gavin's unwritten,
semi-autobiographical novel *Strings of Life*

Münster: England Wins the World Cup

The train jolted me from my crashed-out oblivion. My stomach spasmed. Bile filled my mouth . . . *sick*. 'Are you all right Gav?'

'Eh . . . huh?'

Oh, I was all right. Just about. Although I don't recommend the sparkling Blue Nun or the Ostend ferry. Not the two-litre bottle, anyway.

Where was I? What was I doing? Oh yes: it gradually came back to me. I was an Englishman abroad, grabbed by World Cup fever as well as a hazy hangover. Train tracks were trundling, Belgium was turning into Germany, and I was Münster-bound. Münster's Monster Titus World Cup – an arena for the world's top skate gladiators. An all-pro affair that was destined to deliver. As I arrived, my mind was filled with questions. *Who'll rip? Who'll surprise? Who'll cock up?*

Big Vern, my snap-happy accomplice, had his own questions. Where are we going to stay? Do you know where we're going? You can't only have £3.50?

I was not perturbed. This was an all-professional event, and I was going to act all professional. I led my doubter straight to the hall, obtained my press pass, got out my trusty pad and Biro and – fell asleep, slumbering in a back room while the day's events passed me by. I did, however, wake in time to watch [American champion] Chris Miller in the ramp prelims. Watching Miller skate elated me, yet I was saddened. Questions filled my head. *Why can't I skate like Chris Miller? Why can't I skate like Keith Chegwin, come to that?*

Life's cruel. I was a packet of Bovril crisps cast on a banquet table spread with ambrosia. Not only was I crap at skating, I was a crap spectator as well, having missed nearly all the day's events. But hey, this was only Saturday – anybody worth while would get through to tomorrow's finals.

That night, any idea of accommodation faded as pounds turned to Deutschmarks, Deutschmarks turned to lager, head turned to drunken cloud. Münster at night: skaters took over, sirens flashed. I found myself in Club Odeon, dancing like a fool. There were some nice girls about: exchanged glances caused stirrings in my groin, but I was wearing *Lager pour Homme*, the worst cologne if you're on the pull, and those girls just didn't want to know me. *Why couldn't I pull? Why had the really nice one who'd talked to me left with someone else? Why couldn't the Germans pour a decent pint of lager? And why was I standing on a table singing Pogues numbers?*

I was so drunk it was getting psychedelic. I proceeded to try and steal a bike to get home on. After eight attempts and only half a bell to show for it, I realized I wasn't capable of stealing a bike and, besides, I didn't have a home to ride it to. *Why didn't I have a place to stay?*

Oh shit! I took the last refuge of the drunken wanker: nationalism. The English marched to town *en masse* (well, a group of about five stumbled about). We sang every terrace song we knew – and many more we didn't. Lager-lout shouts mingled with Krauts. But would push come to shove with our EEC comrades? Was it Cowabunga time? English Mutant Lager Arseholes were on the prowl.

I plodded past a bar. 'Where ya from, lads?' a fellow Englishman questioned, rising from his alfresco bar seat. 'London,' I replied, more than willing to converse with what was obviously a proud member of the Queen's Army, lonely in a foreign land, eagerly awaiting news from home.

'I hate effin' Londoners, you southern bastard!' His arms made ready for the war he'd always trained for. Oh God! Xenophobia can be fun to flirt with, but when the real thing stares you in the face and looks like it wants to annihilate you, that's another thing. He wanted war, I wanted bed. I made my excuses and left, hurrying back to the hall in search of sleep.

I woke early, or maybe it was too late. I was shivering, half naked, face down on a dirty gym floor, my nostrils thick with the dusty grime of school-assembly memories. Time for a work-out. *Who am I? Where am I? Why am I?* I picked my way over the bodies of sleeping skaters, up some stairs to a piece of carpet. Tempted by this luxury, I laid down my head and slept again.

I was finally raised from the dead and, after an intake of caffeine, prepared for the afternoon's events. The finals delivered. What a sight, what a treat. Then suddenly the crowd were on the pitch, and it was all over. Bod Boyle had won. Gazza, eat your heart out: Eng-er-land had won the World Cup!

That evening a mayhem hit Münster which was worthy of any England away victory. McDonald's had to be closed after a food-fight evolved into a plant-fight and ended up as a chair-and-fist fight. Some local Nazi skins beat up on a black skater, then promptly felt the wrath of the hundreds of skaters downtown at the time. They chased and dealt with the skins, then held an impromptu 'Nazis out!' rally, which involved smashing shop windows, that sort of thing. Good stuff.

I made my way once more to the trendy Club Odeon for the post-comp knees-up. I was getting tired and emotional again, and the dreaded questions were returning. *Why don't I have somewhere to stay tonight? Why am I so crap at skating? Why are all the girls giving me the blank again?*

But then Bod put his arm around me and told me he loved me (in a manly, back-slapping kind of way, of course – no tongues). Well, at least somebody did! And he was a *winner*, who knew what he was talking about. With renewed confidence, me and [Yorkshire skater] Snoz got chatting with a couple of girls who were not only good-looking and prepared to talk to us, but had a car and a hotel room! Before I knew it, I was in back-seat luxury being chauffeured around town. Snoz directed us to Münster skatepark where, at 3 a.m., to an admiring audience, I did the run of my life.

Everything just clicked. The line just appeared before me, and the style? I was *on* it. Minor problem: I'd forgotten my board, but I didn't let that dash my moment of glory. I wasn't crap at 3 a.m., I was my own skate hero, at one with the world: England had won the World Cup, I was skating like a top boy, I was being driven round town by two nice German girls, and later we would go back to their five-star pad and do the nasty till dawn. By 3 a.m. on a Monday morning after Münster, life was good.

Well, it was nice while it lasted. By 3.30 a.m. we'd been blown out, by 4 a.m. I was on my herbal uppers and ended up skating round the train station like a madman until dawn, whereupon I took the first freedom train out of town. As the train lurched out, the world was in motion once again. No time for questions now, just deep, dear sleep.

RaD, 1989

1991

Ecstasy is in mass circulation, and house music goes mainstream. New Age travellers reinvent the outdoor-rave scene and start to organize free events. The Gulf War offers the comfort of the Apocalypse, only to limit it to those of Iraqi or Kurd descent.

The young man starts having adventures, travelling the country and going to raves in the strangest of places . . .

Come Dancing – A Directory of Modern Moves

Get down. Get out. Get funky. It's time to move your body. This is the dance generation, and wallflowers are wilting everywhere. There was a time when you could go down the local hop, drink a few pints of Tennents Extra, eye up the spare, and the nearest you'd get to dancing was a quick fumble with a fifth-year when they played the smoocher. Now, if you get the chance, you dance. Everyone is doin' it. They're struttin' their funky stuff, they're swinging their pants, they're shakin' their good thang, they're, er . . . just what *are* they doing, exactly? Truth is, no one's sure.

It used to be easy. In the early years, you lindy-hopped, you jived, you jitterbugged. If you didn't know how to, you went down the local youth club and slavishly learned the moves. Then it got easier. There was the twist, the mashed potato, the locomotion: I mean, these dances had records spelling out just what was expected. Every moron can do the twist – it was the 'Agadoo' of its day. Disco had Travolta films to emulate, and if you couldn't suss the pogo, then you really *were* punk. Even breakdancing and body-popping came with their own W. H. Smith wall-charts. Now you just . . . do your own thing? *Please!*

Ideally, dancing should be like sex: something you just *do*. But a lot of people out there quite clearly shouldn't be doing their own thang. Their own thang is a source of great ridicule and embarrassment. We need clues. Whole nations are afflicted. Natural rhythm does not exist – Milli Vanilli proved this. It would be a great help to left-footed groovers everywhere if we at least had some names for new moves. So let's get up off the wall, ya'all. Don't be tame, don't be shy, come on girl, come on guy. And do the . . .

TECHNO PUNCH

This little baby has been around for quite a while, and is usually a male affair. You wait until the bassline kicks, then climb on to something. A podium or a stage will do, perhaps a tractor – improvise! Put your feet together and point your toes out. Shuffle feet in and out to the beat while swaying slightly. Now, with your leading hand, punch the air above your head in a Eubank fury. Ideally, you should be wearing round sunglasses, have a hood, and be shouting something meaning-ful like 'Yeah! Let's go!', 'Hardcore!' or – lest we forget – 'Mental!'

SPREAD YER LEGS

Favoured by skimpy-topped Deee-Lite dollies and post-Pan's People Top of the Poppers, this dance is supposedly 'horny' (although it's about as horny as a tube of Anusol as far as I'm concerned). Place your feet as wide apart as possible and squat your bot down a bit. Proceed to wave your arms back and forth then up and down in a seductive manner.

RIDING THE WHITE HORSE

As above, but lips must be pouting, groin bouncing, and arms stretched out as if riding Desert Orchid to his third Gold Cup win.

THE DIALLER

A real ted special, this. Click your feet in and out and bounce your legs. Stick your lips out as if giving a frenchie to a water buffalo. Bring your right arm out and make circles with your pointy finger as if you were 'dialling' a phone. Sort of crazy cat/annoying bastard sort of dance.

WASH THE WINDOWS

Another ted special. More appropriate for spacious outdoor venues. Skip on the spot in an almost 'Moonstompin'' manner. Imagine your hands are chamois leathers. Wash the windows on the right (use both hands), then the windows on the left. Every so often, hop around a bit. To do it properly, you need a shaggy bob if you're a bloke, and a Karen Carpenter cut if you're a girl. When cleaning windows, make sure you're wearing a Grandad Bloggs flannelette nightshirt.

HELLOING
A downmarket version of voguing. Strike a pose, there's nothing to it. At all.

THE BALEARIC SHUFFLE
A lot of people too cool for their own good are now championing this: Michiko- and Richmond-clad clubbers who stand just back from the dancefloor. They want to dance, but they don't want to risk ruffling their togs. Sway your body. Jig arms a bit. Nod head. Shuffle around. Stop. Repeat. Also known as the Milk Bar Mambo.

Credit where it's due. A couple of hot movers have really put the dance in indie dance. Here's to . . .

THE BEZ BARNEY
Get wasted. Stumble on stage with a well-known northern band. Move around like Bruno in a sixth round with Tyson. Shake a maraca. Wave a tambourine. Stumble off stage. Get wasted.

THE MOONCULT STRUT
Named after Barry Mooncult of Flowered Up. Get onstage with some Camden renegades. Strut around like a poorly chicken. Fall off stage. Insist the whole audience gets back onstage with you. If the bouncers complain, get your lead singer to deck them. All this should be accomplished in an all-in-one, size-six leotard.

THE PESTS' CONGA
One trend I thought had died out in '88 seems to be on the return. A dance for three or more – although you'll never see more than

five joining in. It occurs in the early hours when a few novices find each other and bond after one half too many. Wide-eyed 'friends' form a neck-chafing buddy chain and proceed to do an upright version of the 'Oops Up Side Your Head' dance. They smile and pester everyone to join in. Shake their hands and pass them some battery acid to rub on themselves. How's that for an all-over buzz?

If these tips aren't enough, being a wallflower isn't too bad. Some places still serve Tennents Extra. Some even finish on a smoocher (although don't dance with a fifth-year unless you want the police called). If you're really forced to dance, try to remember some of the Wombles' better steps. Keep them guessing, they might think you're at the thrust of the avant garde. I mean, there was a time when Martin Kemp was considered a bit of a mover.

The Face, September 1991

Euro-Rail: A Survivor's Guide

Fear not the march of cynicism, Europe still has its idealists. The only trouble is, they're not sure what platform they should be on. In 1990, 63,000 of them voyaged on the couchettes, carriages and corridors of the European train network. Their shared article of faith is a one-month ticket to ride: Inter-rail. The Inter-rail card is now a well-established budget holiday option for the Euro-traveller, although the manically penny-conscious can do the trains cheaper – a mate of mine once accompanied me to Yugoslavia on a £2.30 London Transport Capitalcard. But if an Athens police cell is not your idea of overnight accommodation, Inter-rail is your best bet.

Trains are as good as any other form of transport. They're moderately efficient, pretty fast, and you get to see things like the glorious Belgian countryside. The trains aren't the problem. It's the other Inter-railers. They come in many a waterproof package, but for every Peter Storm label, read 'handle with care'.

First, avoid carrying one of those giant hurricane-proof backpack things. Not only is it impossible to sit down on a train with one, they're a beacon for the Inter-Rail Backpacker Fellowship. A backpack says, 'Hi, I'm here! Come and talk to me, I'm one of you!' But you're *not* one of them. They are idealists, they believe that the trains of Europe are full of nice, interesting, young people who wish to communicate with them. More to the point, they believe that *they* are nice, interesting, young people.

You've only just got off the Ostend ferry, when the Packers have cornered you on the 24-hour train to Venice. 'Inter-railing?' they'll ask nicely. 'Yes,' you'll say. Wrong. Welcome to *Question Time*, sponsored by Milletts. 'Where do you live? What do you do? Where are you going? What groups do you like?' You're trapped. Next thing, they want to know where you're staying. 'Got a hotel? How about sharing?' Within half an hour, they've forced you to give them your home address and a virginity option on your first-born. The Inter-rail rollercoaster has started. You can't stop it, you can't steer it, and it's too late to run.

Inter-railing is an international affair, and many fellow travellers are just Happy Wanderers. Decked out in badly fitting stone-wash, they'll be eager to practise their cool-guy English. They speak it excellently, it's just a shame they never have anything to say except, 'You like rock music, yeah?' They will then bung their Walkman headphones on you and play Bon Jovi's latest offering. Escape as soon as possible, because the next thing they go for is a political conversation. This consists of a half-hour or more of bland truisms followed by crap, Kilroy-Silk-style comments along the lines of 'They're all as bad as each other.' Share a smile, have a go at the Swiss, then leave. You'll now understand that the lack of cultural understanding English soccer fans used to show abroad has less to do with fashion or social conditions than the fact that they travelled by train.

The worst people you'll ever encounter are Travellers. They look kind of cool in a studenty way, and they talk hip enough. 'I'm just a traveller,' they'll say. In fact, they are creatures from couchette hell. A traveller is just a tourist who's downed a whole bottle of smugness. I don't care whether you're going to India, Istanbul or Islington Green – unless you're Marco Polo, you're not a bloody traveller.

What travellers mean is that they somehow have a better understanding and appreciation of the countries they visit. Look, no country likes tourists (especially young, bratty ones), but I understand and appreciate that they like tourist cash. Especially the poorer countries, which travellers seem to prefer. Yet the one thing travellers *won't* give is cash. They blab on about how much you're getting ripped off, and how they managed to live like a king in Budapest for 45p a day. Just because they've got a *Rough Guide to*

Ljubljana tucked in their shorts, they feel qualified to tell you how you should be enjoying the rest of your holiday, insisting you avoid all those nasty, touristy places. After sharing a carriage with these types, you'll want nothing more than to swig back five bottles of ouzo, spend six hours in a Disco of Death, then have a ruck with the locals.

As soon as you meet a traveller, show them your Millwall tattoos and be extra-friendly. They'll soon sod off. If you haven't got Millwall tattoos, then get some – it'll be far less painful in the end. You can also seek refuge in the toilets, although when passing through tunnels, the gush of air from the bowl can be distracting.

The fail-safe thing to do is choose your company carefully. A litre bottle of Czech vodka is an ideal buddy, perhaps topped up with some local toxic lager for longer journeys. Drink it down and anaesthetize yourself to the train terrors. Soon you'll be clickety-clacketing along on a happy holiday express. By the time disillusionment sets in again, you'll hopefully have reached your destination.

Hassles aside, Inter-rail is a worthwhile tourist caper. I may have shocking flashbacks of sangria-soaked Aussies who called me 'soft cock' for not helping them throw their mate out of the window, but I've also got the memory of travelling through Turkey with a young Palestinian who gave me more insight into real life in the Middle East than *Newsnight* ever could. Besides, I recommend it on the simple grounds that anything that makes you warm to the chilly indifference of British Rail is worth every penny.

The Face, August 1991

Whatever Happened to the Likely Lads?

'I like punk. I like Sham. I got nicked down West Ham.'
'Police Car', by the Cockney Rejects

As a young lad, I went to football. I wasn't alone. These days, I sometimes reflect. Switching channels at random, as I flick between Arsenal's European match and a documentary on joyriders, the sound of the telly is drowned by the Danny Rampling mix pouring out of my digital hi-fi system. Arsenal score, a car does a 180° turn, and a petrol bomb goes off. What is our civilization coming to? I didn't fight in two World Cups for the likes of them!

In my shoe-bin in the corner, a pair of kangaroo-skin Diodora Golds lie next to a muddy pair of purple Kickers which I swear are my brother's. Tucked in a drawer sits a Stanley knife and a godawful smiley bandanna. Both of these criminal items are there because over the last ten years I have seen fit to purchase them as fashion accessories. I wasn't alone. Times change, we change with them. Here we go.

Embarrassing as it now seems, ten years ago it was still a viable option for a fifteen-year-old boy to shave his head, tattoo his neck, lose his brains, and dive head first into 'Oi!' This was just one of the groupings in a rainbow of youth cults. In 1981 a likely lad could be anything he wanted: soul boy, skinhead, mod, punk, rockabilly, psychobilly, Crasstafarian. The list was endless. If you were really desperate, you could become a new romantic. If you were beyond medical help, there were always Numanoids.

You name it, you could be it. Just flick to the back of the *NME* and send off for an identity from those classy classifieds: Sta-Prest, zoot suits, bondage trousers or baggies. It wasn't that easy, though. A simple trip to the seaside could get you beaten up by any number of people. These were exciting and innovative times, when you'd sell your self-respect for some Indian ink and a bottle of peroxide.

In the ten years that followed, there have really only been two British youth cults: soccer casual and acid house. One of them is all but dead, and the other has been looking very ill recently, but the changes that have occurred in a lot of people's lives are a direct result of these movements. The trip from hooliganism to Ecstasy was a strange one.

Casual started in 1981 and ended in 1988. During that time, thousands of young men dressed up in designer gear and travelled around the country trying to cut it up. Please note: when I say it started in 1981, I'm referring to the actual name 'casual'. I am not going to enter into any suspect North v. South debate on who started what and when. Suffice to say that these guys were racing around, dressed to the gills, and feeling very vicious. Then along comes 1988 and they all start listening to house music, taking vast quantities of drugs, wearing bandannas and dancing with each other. In the space of ten years we went from glue, snakebite and a ruck at the Rainbow, through to Armani, Tacchini and Elland Road, and then on to dry ice, a few K of turbo sound, and another of those tablets please, mate. Today memories of all are beginning to fade. You see, now . . . well, everyone just sits around and gets stoned.

The transformation of Stanley-wielding hooligans into loved-up ravers is an easy picture to paint. But the reasons people became or stopped being hooligans can't all be explained in terms of pharmaceuticals. The casual movement of the Eighties was the culmination of many things. Working-class kids in flash clothes were nothing new; neither was soccer violence. Apart from a brief rest in the Fifties, violence of one sort or another has been around since the game started. It actually peaked at the turn of the century and in the late Seventies.

All the casual thing did was give a unifying look to the herbert element of soccer fans. This look then became the norm for young lads who may have previously fallen into any of the soul-boy, mod, skin or punk-type categories. So bowling around in a Fila Bj top and fighting in your local firm became the 'thing to do'. All soccer clubs had a hooligan element – the casual uniform meant anyone could join in.

It came naturally. Most of the lads of the early Eighties had been brought up on Richard Allen's *Skinhead*, *Suedehead* and *Boot Boys* books. They'd thumbed through *Tottenham Boys We Are Here* in the back of biology class. They were given the legacy of soccer violence in stories for playground consumption. Harry the Dog, who appeared in *Panorama*'s infamous 1978 Millwall documentary, may have indeed (as Spurs fans used to sing) been a poodle. But his battles were heroic in young minds. The rivalry between Spurs and Arsenal was a legend no Greeks or Romans could match.

The first casual gangs were brought up on this. They were not of the 'good piss-up, good punch-up' boot-boy variety. They looked up to the local villains on the manor. The original London look was that of the pickpocket or wide-boy: Farrah slacks, crocodile shoes and a Burberry jacket. European matches brought in the more continental sportswear look. Each firm had a different style. The *News of the World* even gave a rather bad club-by-club guide to firms. I think Leeds were attributed with the deerstalker. Some of us down south were very put out by that at the time – a jealousy that now fades into disbelief.

North and west London casuals developed their own flash attire. Many of these young dressers used to meet up in the West End at the Lyceum Ballroom, where fights would break out between the Ladbroke Grove (QPR/Chelsea) boys and the north London (mainly Arsenal) lads. When these young rascals met again at football, the old grizzlers took notice. Arsenal's appearance at Fulham Broadway decked head-to-toe in Fila trackers caused mirth in many an older Chelsea fan, garbed as he was in army greens. Younger minds, however, felt a grudging respect and went out shopping. Similar incidents were happening throughout the country. Far be it from me to say which contenders looked the best, although north London does appear to have had the best thieves.

Here were some new gangs with old traditions and some decent clothes. Everyone became soccer casuals and a lot of silliness occurred. Why casual came about is quite complex. Why it continued is easy: it was fun. And for most, this didn't mean the violence. For those stuck in boring jobs or still at school, casual was a great escape. They enjoyed hanging around in the big gang, dressing up in smart clothes, travelling to different parts of the country, and running to – and from – people like themselves. They enjoyed the characters, the top boys, the tales. They enjoyed a different brand name every month, a new word each Saturday, and a different posture each minute. There were stories to be told, adventures to be had. In another time, they would have been pirates.

Very few people actually enjoyed the violence itself. They enjoyed its atmosphere, its sense of power, the uneasy excitement violence creates. Most of the really violent types never wore decent trainers. For those without the muscle, it was possible to get by on a lot of front, friends in the right places, and knowing the score. Casual was about turning up on a Saturday in your new Armani jumper, some Ball jeans (red label, little side-pocket), and your first Timberlands – looking, and feeling, the business. It was about 'running Leeds at King's Cross, and not being able to sleep for three days because of the high', as one Chelsea chappie put it. Why did they do it? They did it for the buzz.

By 1988, the buzz had faded. Soccer was in a sorry state and so was hooliganism. There are various reasons why it fell flat. Heysel was one of them. Heysel was a disaster. It made a lot of people feel very sick, and some pained by guilt. The fight between Liverpool and Juventus fans at the start of the European Cup final at the Belgian stadium was no more brutal than other terrace battles, yet the panic it created caused hundreds to get crushed, a wall to collapse, and forty-one people to die. The Government and the police went into overdrive. Things became very difficult – this was no longer easy kicks. And while Heysel didn't kill hooliganism, it did herald a political shift in tackling the problem. Most of the Government's reactions did little to prevent trouble and a lot to annoy the normal football fan. The only positive results were the formation of supporters' associations and the proliferation of fanzines which tackled both the Government ignorance of football and the hooligans. These provided a starting block for the rebuilding of the game.

Population shifts saw a million fewer teenage boys by 1988 than there were in the late Seventies. The fodder for youth culture peaked in 1981 and has declined ever since. In the early Eighties most youngsters left school at sixteen. Most didn't really give a shit what they ended up doing. By the end of the decade, you could not sign on at sixteen. The choice was to stay on at school, find work, or go on one of the multitude of training schemes. You wanted money, you wanted a job, practically everything you did at school was vocationally bent. A career became something to fight for.

The traditional local communities that football clubs drew on for support had also changed. When you knew everyone in your street and went to school with everyone on your block, you became territorially minded. Soccer gangs were often a locally based hard-core, swelled by ranks of commuters. Some of the more notorious firms came not from the bigger football clubs, but from tight local communities. Only thirty West Ham fans could run half the country because they knew what they were doing, and they knew each other. But the privatization of council houses and the speculative property markets changed the social structure of many cities. London boys moved north into Essex, south into Kent, and west into places like Slough. You can't put an advert on the telly if you want to form a gang: they had to evolve at a local level. So by 1988, attitudes, places and people had all changed.

Then along came that smiling matey acid house, and the boys found a new buzz. But in any case the soccer casual and violence thing was already over. It stopped because people were fed up with it. Some were too old, some were just bored, and others realized the damage they were doing to soccer. Also the stakes had got higher. Knives had become commonplace, and a good biffing was now a good gassing and the loss of several pints of blood. You could do a firm one week, only to find them waiting for revenge at 8.30 a.m. at Euston the following Saturday. Firms began to know each other not just by sight, but by name, address and telephone number. The police got to know everyone and arrested *en masse* – the need to be 'seen to be doing something' led to many a fit-up. It wasn't fun any more, it was just sick.

Acid house was a nice little rescue ship that came along when HMS *Casual* sunk. Before, there were only two sorts of nightclubs: the ones where you dressed up in smart clothes, got down, and got incredibly drunk to whatever local radio jock happened to be playing; or the trendy clubs which you were never allowed into. The dawning of rare-groove and warehouse parties attracted a lot of chaps with a more urban-soul-boy/jazz-funk background. They started to attend clubs with good music, good draw and no violence. Some north London boys even started to get DJ slots at places like Soho's ultra-hip Wag club. When the doors of the club scene broke open completely in the '88 'summer of feeling nice', the remaining bulk of hoolies romped in. Happy to swap their designer-thug image for the most positive identity of acid house, many a sworn enemy was to be seen OD-ing together at Spectrum and Clink Street. Raving was proving far more fun than a wet away-day to Newcastle could ever be. A comfortable full stop was placed on casual.

So all the lads became loved up? No, this wasn't a cure for violence. Nasty pieces of work remain nasty, no matter how jovial they seem. It just meant that the fashion had changed. The 'thing to do' was to go out and get on one, not meet at Finsbury Park at 11 a.m. People conformed to happiness and peace as much as they conformed to hatred and violence. The guys who did enjoy the violence in the first place weren't changed. Some did mellow out a bit, became bouncers, that sort of thing. A few with good organiz-ational skills started their own small businesses. For some this meant a chain of gardening services, for others drug-dealing and club-door intimidation. The ICF (Inter-City Firm) became a kind of East End IRA without the politics. Some now run their own raves, others own clubs. The Government must be well pleased with the entrepren-eurial society it sprouted.

There are a few nutters who still go to have a whackabout at Saturday soccer. I guess they can't break the habit. All that the last few years have meant to them is that they're drugged up to the eyeballs with dope, charlie and E. Many of Millwall's minor away-game incidents have been caused by some old die-hards with a couple of Doves inside them. Ecstasy will not prevent you from fighting: it will, however, help you enjoy it more when you do. A couple of faces have taken one trip too many and killed themselves. Unable to come to terms with things, one prominent Eastender put a bullet through his head.

Meanwhile, the England team still attracts a few of the country's criminally unstable. They were occasionally in evidence at the 1990 World Cup. The rise of soccer hooliganism on the Continent has meant that there are plenty of foreign bodies to have a biff with, if so desired. It takes more than drugs and dancing to cure hardened psychos: the medical profession has known this for years.

Raving *has* achieved something, though. The inheritance of soc-cer violence has been halted. Schoolboy story-tellers are replacing terrace battle with tales of manic all-nighters. They listen to Flowered Up, not the Cockney Rejects. Bad boys will never stop being bad boys. A need for power, excitement and profit will see to that. But now there are new heroes for them to emulate. They're still smartly dressed, but they DJ now and then, they get the squeeze in clubs that count, and they've got a pocket full of herbs and chemicals. Every now and then, they wash'n'go the pony-tail that lies flaccid from the back of their head. It's still a mug's game, but at least they don't want to kick the shit out of each other so much.

These aren't flower children. Just kids with a bit more of a clue.

Will it all kick off again? It's all too close to call at the moment. The appeal of violence won't die. Not unless machismo goes out of fashion. Who'd have thought that, fifteen years after mods and rockers first battled it out on Brighton beach, the next generation would do it all again? Fashions have a horrible habit of coming back – look at Kickers. But for those likely lads of 1981, the last ten years have been a remarkable education in life. When you've stood in the middle of a full-scale soccer riot, with everything going off around you; when you've stood rushing off your head in a packed field full of friends, dancing and watching the sun come up – that's when you begin to know how confused the line between love and hate is. It's all just a buzz.

Tracksuits, trainers and Inter-City trains. Now turntables, trips and techno. Skin up, someone, *please* skin up.

> *'How did it go last night?' 'Great, I sold about forty.' 'I was talking about the party.'*

'It's On', by Flowered Up

The Face, December 1991

1992

Rave culture fragments into a plethora of musical categories. The drug culture becomes endemic, binding the vast majority of young people.

Travelling to Berlin, the young man experiences the booming techno club scene that has taken root in the deserted Government buildings of what was once East Berlin. After seeing Graham Taylor's England team get humiliated in the European Championship, he finds himself preferring drugs to football. In fact, drugs to pretty much anything.

Towards the end of the summer, he takes up the chance to travel with a photographer friend to Somalia, at the height of the famine. The next six weeks change his life. As he witnesses death, war and famine at close hand, the naïvety of his youth erodes. Political certainties become confused.

Strange links become apparent as he sits stranded in no-man's land watching gunmen breakdance to the sounds of the club hit 'Rhythm is a Dancer' on the BBC's World Service. It occurs to him that the hedonism back home is not a cop-out, but a statement of intent for western civilization.

On the isle of Eigg in Scotland, he proposes to his girlfriend.

Berlin: Tekkno Prisoners

Keeping in touch with reality is always harder when you're away from home. In Berlin, it's near impossible. Situated in the middle of the recently defunct German Democratic Republic (East Germany, DDR), it is now at the heart of the new Europe. Berliners have always been a bit different to other Germans. Even before the Wall came tumbling down, West Berliners were never really West Germans and East Berliners were never really East Germans. They were just Berliners, and played host to French, British, American and Soviet armies, as well as most of the world's paranoia. But now the old Allied forces are departing and Berlin is the capital of a new Germany. While most welcome the changes, some worry that by becoming 'normal', just another capital city, Berlin will lose its edge.

'You should understand, things have always been hardcore here,' explains Johnnie Tresor, a deep-eyed young East Berliner who now earns a crust from the city's shady club circuit. 'Always the extremes.'

A brief dip into Berlin's past provides limitless examples. Spartacists, Dadaists, National Socialists: revolution and revulsion have always run rife. During the Cold War, the world's pressures centred on Berlin. Now the Wall is gone and the country reunited, but the pressure still remains. Anxiety is high. Uncertainty is rife. The place is buzzing with energy, but no one quite knows when the party will end, or whether it's a celebration or a wake.

Johnnie's girlfriend, Dani, explains the feelings of many East Germans. 'I still feel good about having fresh orange juice and cornflakes in the morning, but it wears off. The East German news was full of propaganda about the West, but we never used to believe it. Now I think some of those stories were perhaps true. Before, we used to have complete security; now, things are uncertain. My parents are just grateful that West Germany took us – a lot of people have lost spirit.'

When Franco died and the fascists fell from power in Spain, Madrid went into a creative overload. After years of repression, the artistic juices flowed freely, causing an outpouring of films, plays, music and clubs. I'd come to Berlin looking for similar signs after hearing rumours of a resurgence in its famed nightlife. Liza Minnelli had been a recurring theme in my developing years, and I'd asked Johnnie to take me clubbing in the vain hope of a sniff at the decadence the Kit Kat Club offered in *Cabaret*. But the Kit Kats have now been replaced by Smarties – white, pink and blue ones. Smartie people are happy people, they smile all the time. Like many cities around the world, Berlin has pumped itself high on a diet of drugs and dance music. But this isn't Detroit, London, Ibiza or Rimini. This is Berlin, and they're doing it their way, with sweet, blue, chewy, 'warm' Es and a 'speed without the comedown' – an amphetamine reportedly synthesized by the East German army.

We spend Friday night in Tresor. Held in the security vaults of a crumbling old building just inside East Berlin, this now-celebrated club is within 100 yards of the notorious 'Death Mile', where many a DDR defector copped it heading over the Wall for the bright lights of capitalism. In its shadows are the ministry buildings, where numerous Stasi-like activities took place, now mostly empty.

Before the Wall came down, Johnnie was a hooligan for a while at Dynamo Berlin. He listened to English DJs and played acid-house tapes. The only clubs then were politically correct, state-run youth clubs. When the Wall came down, he remembers, 'It was like a 72-hour rave.' Now, he's one of the city's new underground entrepreneurs, running parties, a record label and marketing his own Space beer. He started Tresor with other partners, or 'fish' as he insists on calling them. 'Fish are very important,' he says with a fake German intensity. I hadn't a clue what he was talking about, but gave him a knowing smile. I did a lot of those smiles in Berlin.

Tresor, like many of the city's clubs, isn't strictly legal. It pays rent to an unseen landlord but has no licence. The risk is minimal as, unlike the bothersome British bobby, the Berlin police don't seem to be worried about evening excesses. It was this tolerance that enabled Berlin to blossom briefly in the late Twenties into the liberal Bohemia recorded in Christopher Isherwood's novels. Then people stripped off, danced, abused drugs (cocaine, mainly), and indulged their sexual preferences under the eyes of a tolerant, often indulgent, police force. Germany is often seen from the outside as soaked in authoritarianism. But there is a rival liberal tradition, and it is this which is enabling the current Berlin club scene to emerge from a reborn city.

The first people I met in Tresor were British: fine, upstanding members of Her Majesty's Army, all set for a night's raving and loved up to the eyeballs with something you can't get from the NAAFI. These younger members of the city's resident Irish and Welsh regiments had forsaken the traditional squaddie entertainments of lager and fisticuffs for all-night raving, and once they realized I wasn't part of the Military Police, they proved interesting and friendly company.

Before the Wall came down, post-war etiquette meant clubs were obliged to let squaddies in. Afterwards, it took time for this mixed platoon of British Army ravers to gain acceptance – although they still have a reputation for excess, mainly in the gurning department. Back at camp, they say they have to put up with harassment from the Military Police and officers, and the often-violent derision of 'pissheads'. There are regular checks of the barracks, and one of their number was caught recently with drugs and will be discharged shortly. Gaunt-faced and a bit paranoid, his biggest worry is what to tell his mother.

But though most will stay in the Army, all know their days in Berlin are numbered – their job is obsolete. 'It's got to be the best posting for raving!' one young private chirps. 'If only we could transport this back home.' I ask him if the army knows what they get up to at night. 'They know, but they don't understand. They show you this film of a guy smoking this big fat joint, then he goes off and steals a tank! They should show it to the pissheads!' They come to Tresor to listen to their favourite DJ, Tanith. The squaddies like it hardcore.

Tanith has built up a following on the scene playing a form of hardcore techno that Berliners call tekkno: a sound, like its spelling, that is subtly different. Unlike the Belgians, in Berlin they keep it simple, drawing heavily on early Detroit techno, which itself drew on the German instigators Kraftwerk. Now, I have a problem with most techno – I think it's crap. A few tracks now and then excite, but mostly it makes me want to take drugs: Nurofen, Anadin, that sort of thing. In Berlin, though, the music seems strangely appropriate.

During its punk years, Berlin gave birth to industrial bands like Einstürzende Neubauten. Now, during the dance boom, it is hooked on tekkno. Tanith plays some brutal stuff, a lot of it his own creation. 'I like it hardcore,' he says with deep sincerity. 'Very hardcore!' He's not messing about. Hard metallic sounds, minimal keyboards, and techno thumping. *Bish bish*, *bosh bosh* (or should that be *Bosch Bosch*?). He's not concerned, and neither are the clubbers. They dance all night to an increasingly scary playlist.

Last year Tanith and Johnnie were involved in a club called Tekknozid. Which, roughly translated, means 'techno suicide'. It was a room filled with 50 strobes and continuous smoke machines. They knew it wouldn't last long, but that was kind of the point. Tekknozid. 'You know, I think we liked techno before we heard it,' says Johnnie. 'There's always been techno in the street. Cars travelling 30 centimetres from each other.' I give him another of my smiles.

After a night at Tresor, some of the squaddies invite me to go on to Walfisch, a club which opens from 6 a.m. to 8 p.m. on weekends when other clubs are giving it a rest. As dawn was breaking and giving me a rosy glow, this seemed like a good idea and I followed them on to the S-Bahn. I didn't realize at the time I was actually departing on a magical mystery tour with five tripping squaddies. I don't know whether they genuinely didn't know the way, or were in such a confused state that they couldn't find it. Perhaps they just liked travelling on Tube trains. Anyway, about sixteen station changes and a whole morning later, we arrived. By this time my enthusiasm had severely wilted, and I decided to head for my hotel, getting hopelessly lost again on the way and ending up with just three hours' kip before Saturday night reared its smiling head.

Off I went to Quartiers, a large, legal club venue in West Berlin's Potsdamerstrasse. When people say a club has a 'mixed crowd', they usually mean the wrong mix. But Berlin's clubbers seem to intermingle with each other quite happily. Here, a high-fashion crowd, various ravey types, the odd ex-Deutsche hooligan in New Balance trainers, post-apocalypse punks and representatives of the city's large lesbian and gay population moved to the bizarre sounds of Formicula 4. A group of DJs improvising over the rhythms with synths and drum machines, they produced a pleasing mix of techno, psychedelic snippets, and old Chicago acid that they labelled 'new acid'. There were no vocals, of course. Vocals require soul, and this is not a thing Germans are famous for. Mind you, the Berliners I met seemed to defy most of the national stereotype. Tinged with insanity, they were neither dictatorial nor humourless. Shiny, happy people, in fact.

There are some wankers out there, though. I saw a few neo-Nazis downtown. Occasionally they attack the immigrant street traders who make a living selling old Soviet memorabilia and freshly sprayed pieces of rock which they insist are remains of the Wall. The younger members of the large Turkish community form gangs and fight back, going to the Nazi hang-outs, which are mainly in East Berlin. Reportedly, some of the Soviet army gave the Turks their rifles when they left. For West Berlin's ethnic minorities, the Wall coming down has meant nothing but trouble.

Returning to Tresor in the early hours of the morning, I bobbed around to the housey sounds in the upstairs bar, then went down to the vaults for Tanith's tekkno. Like many of the crowd, he was garbed head to toe in camouflage gear, a cross between late punk and Public Enemy. It's a look unique to Berlin clubs, and they're proud of their innovation. It suits the discipline of the music well, and works to help diffuse the city's military connotations.

At 8 a.m., I was confronted by the crazed face of my unstable accomplice Thomas, who had spent the night picking up various people he wished to photograph, as well as a six-foot wooden replica bottle of the Fish crew's Space beer. As the bottle couldn't fit in anybody's car, I got given the task of carting the thing to the Reichstag. With the club's bouncer giving me a hand, I took the quickest route – along the Death Mile, down the route of the old Wall.

The evenings had taken their toll, and I was in a confused state. It was about $-67°$ on a Sunday morning, and I was crossing the Death Mile with a bouncer and a giant bottle of beer. Bits of the Wall crunched under my feet. 'Look out for the mines,' a voice shouted. Mines? Surely not. Paranoia took hold. I trod carefully until I reached the Brandenburg Gate.

After the photo session, I grabbed a cab with Johnnie and finally went to Walfisch, which turned out to be the Berlin clubbers' casualty unit. People come to die here and dance the dance of the dead. Void of daylight, it is situated above an underground station, which is actually only a couple of stops from Tresor. This tekkno womb holds its babies secure from the harsh light of Sunday until evening falls, when they all trot off to the Tea Dance at Quartiers. Christiane F. would look like Naomi Campbell compared to most of these unlikely-looking bods. I stayed and stared at strange faces in the darkness until 4 p.m., when I realized I had a plane to catch.

At the airport, Thomas and I drank coffee and tried to speak. A man came and took my photo. Shortly after, he produced a keyring with my photo in it. It was ten Deutschmarks – exactly the sum I had left. I paid the man and looked at the photo. I was bloodshot, wrecked, wide-eyed, but smiling. Berlin had *bish-boshed* me into tekknozid. There's a time and a place for everything. Berlin is the place, but I'm not sure what time it is any more. Time for bed, I guess.

The Face, February 1992

Generation X

Quit your job. You are not a target market. The times they are a changin'. Yuppie was yesterday. Now is the generation that lives, loves and wanders. Come join the poverty jet-set, the generation without a name: Generation X. I'm talking about my generation, or rather Douglas Coupland is in his first novelette, *Generation X*.

The book documents the 'nameless' and 'forgotten' twenty something generation and is being touted as a signpost for the decade. Although it's probably best to read it before you change your life, as all it may signpost is another batch of second-rate lifestyle articles. More of a manuscript-script than a masterpiece, the book comes with its own Nineties dictionary, e.g., 'Mid-twenties Breakdown: a period of mental collapse occurring in one's twenties, often caused by an inability to function outside of school or structured environments, coupled with a realization of one's essential aloneness in the world. Often marks induction into the ritual of pharmaceutical usage.'

The book tries to exist away from the markers in its margins, yet can't seem to live up to the chapter-heading promises. What little story there is centres around a small, clapped-out condo in Palm Springs where three friends have drifted from jobs or lives they despised. Having given up hope of a career, they have doubts about the future and support themselves by working in 'low-pay, low-prestige, low-benefit jobs in the service industry', or 'McJobs'. They sit staring into the sun and telling each other stories which reveal their fears, anxieties, and search for faith.

Sitting as we are on the end of the millennium, there is bound to be a lot of reflective soul-searching. But by confining yourself to pinning tags on your own, closely observed generation, the picture distorts. There is no longer a generation gap. The old rules are gone now. What we're seeing is not a gulf between old yuppies and young Xers, but an ideological rift developing between people of all ages. Age no longer breeds a commitment to conformity. From fifteen to fifty, there are those whose beliefs lie with 'the system', and those who lie outside it.

Generation X records, but doesn't understand. The line of fate is going wonky: birth, school, work, marriage, kids, career, retirement, death. The certainties of life are shifting. A job is no longer for life. You can have children in your forties. Marriage, if considered, is arrived at later in life – and there is always divorce. As a proportion of your salary, housing is more expensive than ever before. Travel, meanwhile, is at its cheapest. So some of us talk work, Macs and security. Others talk of drugs, Nintendo and India. The fabric of the West, for all its denim glory, has no binding philosophy, no consensus, no dreams of the future.

The twentysomethings of the X generation may be more predisposed to quitting a job and drifting. But they're still faced with looking for what they really want. *Generation X* is not about post-yuppiedom. It's a small, warped mirror reflecting one of the crises of our age. A Western crisis, faced by those with some cash, some consciousness, and some dodgy career options. The twentieth century fades behind us and history rollercoasters on. We stare at the sun. Blindly we are carried to the abyss of the twenty-first century without a philosophical airbag to spring out and cushion us on impact.

December 31, 1999. Enjoy the ride down, let the wind fly through your hair, go with the flow and wait for the big crash. I hope I die before I get old.

The Face, June 1992

Disco Europa

It's 5 a.m., the lights are tripping tedium. I strain to sip down the last of my 'two for the price of one' cocktails. I will not be drinking Blue Lagoons again. The joke has now worn thin. Slumped around my shoulder is a lad I mistakenly bonded with a couple of hours ago. He's from Sunderland, he wears a Sunderland shirt. His hair is short like Matt Goss's, his shorts are long like Matt Busby's. His drunkenness borders on the psychotic. Every so often he opens his mouth to sing along with a top tune. All that comes out is slobber, which drips on to my peeling red arms. If I hear 'Let's Talk About Sex' one more time, I'm going to top myself. Be scared, be very scared. Here terror reigns supreme. This is a holiday, this is a nightclub. Welcome to Babylon – welcome to Disco Europa.

Every year we troop off to the Med with dreams of sun-kissed days and blinding nights of musical mayhem. But for every far-flung nightclub that creates a storm back home, there are a thousand hell-holes waiting to suck you in. For every cool little Italia house track, there are stacks of local Jive Bunny remixes. For every uplifting second of 'Ritmo de la Noche', we must suffer a lifetime of 'Una Paloma Blanca'. The holiday disco is a fearsome puppy whose only master is Satan.

To enter these places is to set foot in a land of glitterballed lunacy. It matters not whether you're on the turquoise coasts of Turkey or in a secluded part of the Algarve, walk through the doors of a Disco Europa and you are in the same place, with the same people, listening to the same records, drinking the same Day-Glo drinks, feeling the same queasy mixture of extreme drunkenness and paranoia. The devil is at work. It may say Bananas or Mad House or Samantha's on the outside, but it's all Disco Europa on the inside.

Disco Europas sprang up to feed the night-life fantasies of the get-away-and-get-out-of-it tourist-class traveller. With their mirrored walls and chromed bars, they imitated the flash fantasy palaces of jet-set stomping grounds. Originally full of punters singing along to 'Y Viva Espana' and doing the conga around the dancefloor with a cuddly donkey under their arms, this was followed by the golden years of group dancing. Who can forget those Iberian nights of the early Eighties, when we all swayed our buttocks to 'The Birdie Song'? Heady times indeed. I'll never forget those far-off days when I'd go to a Magaluf dance-dive and be happy with a frenzied 'Agadoo' and a quick fumble with a northern lass.

But as European nations united, the Disco Europa went through some bad years of hard drinking and big brawling. To a soundtrack of Europop, various low-life would get pissed up, and then set about pummelling anybody who hadn't had the sense to crouch under a nearby pedalo. The Disco Europa became a mecca for every lager lout from Halifax to Heidelberg.

But no sooner had the last *policia* been bottled and the final till been robbed than a new threat emerged: the concrete playlist. This list was purchased by every Disco Europa DJ, along with a small box of records which they then played relentlessly. It contained the following: U2's 'New Year's Day', '*Grease* – The Soundtrack', Madonna's 'Holiday', Michael Jackson's 'Thriller', Bruce Springsteen's 'Born in the USA', Jive Bunny's 'Swing the Mood', Eurythmics' 'Sweet Dreams', Rod Stewart's 'Baby Jane', Bob Marley's 'No Woman, No Cry', Simple Minds' 'Don't You Forget About Me'.

Every Disco Europa then promptly played these tracks to death and beyond. I think there was an EEC directive on the matter. If you were lucky, 'No Woman, No Cry' wouldn't be accompanied by a circle-load of hugging Dutch student types; if you were unlucky, the *Grease* track would be the megamix, and some bod would bash your eye out when punching the sky during the '*Hey, Hey, Hey, Heyyy!*' part of 'Don't You Forget About Me'.

When house hit big time, Disco Europa wasn't far behind, pumping up that jam left, right and centre. With only a few mind-numbing local tunes to compete with, any half-competent DJ from Blighty could earn his widget in puff by taking a couple of *Where's The House?* compilations out to the Med for the summer. There's nothing like an evening spent jigging along with some bint from Bradford to some *real* bad *musica de la casa*.

This year, the plague of MTV Europe has finally claimed Disco Europa as a victim. The EEC playlist has been replaced by a satellite Top Ten. The worst thing about this current club nightmare is that some of the songs they're playing you might have actually *liked* at one stage. Call me Mr Mainstream if you want, but there was a time when I quite liked REM's 'Losing My Religion'. But after hearing it sung along to by a rent-a-Scouse in a Disco Europa, you find yourself not only losing your religion but any *raison d'être* for human existence at all.

It's going to be a long, hot summer in the inferno of Disco Europa. Highlights will include Right Said Fred's 'I'm Too Sexy', Michael Jackson's 'Black and White', Salt'n'Pepa's 'Let's Talk about Sex' and Simply Red's 'Something Got Me Started'. A true feast for those long, lethal nights. A few tips. Those of you missing 'Don't You Forget About Me' can punch the air during the *'Yes I!'* bit of 'Something Got Me Started'. The best chance for a good beer-and-belch snog will be to grab your intended during another ruined favourite of mine, 'Change' by Lisa Stansfield. Always be sure to take any drug available in vast quantities, even if you saw one of the friendly peasant folk of a nearby village refuse to give it to their pets. When in doubt, finish off two packets of Arret, swill a gallon of whatever godawful spirit the locals drink, and take a Walkman.

It's 6 a.m., the first rays of sun fire arrows into my eyes from the doorway. I've finished another two Blue Lagoons. The guy from Sunderland pukes on my back, then punches me in the mouth for laughing. 'Cockney bastard!' Smack! Another punch floors me. My life is ebbing away. 'Let's Talk About Sex' comes pumping through the speakers for the seventy-third time that evening. I give up the will to live, and rise towards the light. The Pearly Gates appear before me. St Peter smiles and looks down into his book. He speaks. 'Sorry, your name's not down, you're not coming in.'

I fall into blackness. It gets hotter, and then in the distance I hear the opening chords of 'Don't You Forget About Me'. You have been warned.

The Face, July 1992

Jeux Sans Frontières

The other night I woke in a panic, shell-shocked from the Gulf War. An unlikely scenario. I've never been to a desert and the nearest I've ever got to authentic military action is when Action Man introduced eagle eyes and gripping hands. But this wasn't to do with fearsome flashbacks from the great TV war. It was a high-tech nightmare caused by video-game addiction. Playing *Desert Storm* on my Sega console had not only eroded my morals, it had disturbed my beauty sleep.

I woke shouting, 'More fuel! I need more fuel!' having seen my helicopter burst into flames and plunge towards the desert. It was all so horrifyingly real. I was on level four, I'd rescued hostages, destroyed the nuclear reactor and was all set to finally put an end to the madman. But just at that crucial point, my fuel had run out and my entire crew and I had perished in a piece of computer sand that will be for ever Hackney. All very worrying, especially since the only sleep I lost in the real Gulf War was in staying up listening to late-night doomsday discussions on Channel 4.

We've spent our lives watching TV, staring at the box until everything from *Wogan* to war washes over us. Now, the recent boom in home computer games has meant that fool boys like me don't sit at home flicking the channels for blood, guts and gore: they re-create it by playing silly silicon war games. The TV set has become a point of entry to worlds of personal fantasy. Yet, unlike watching the TV show or video, your complete attention is required. Your mind must be more involved with the screen image – the very nature of the games demands response. So warped fantasies about being a big, bad soldier start to be taken for real in

49

some dark corner of my deluded male brain. And I wake up in the night, panic-stricken over a lack of fuel.

Given the possibilities that the current crop of consoles offer, it does seem a bit worrying that the whole deal is such a male-oriented affair. 'The truth is men like gadgets, they like to control their environment,' points out Dr Margaret Shotton, author of *Computer Addiction?*, and one of the few academics to have taken a serious look at video-game culture. 'They also have a lot of testosterone to discharge, always having to play cowboys or Indians or drive fast cars!' Or win the Gulf War.

The appeal of the games to young boys particularly may be that a lot of the games are about some little guy fighting and eventually conquering a large, evil monster. Many see these monsters as father figures which young boys, obsessed with dear old mum, want to take on and usurp. Although such intellectual theories may hold some water, they don't explain why teenage boys appear to be the only ones with the manual dexterity required to be a video-games ace. Perhaps the secret's in the wrist action – testosterone isn't the only thing that males have to discharge.

Despite the spread of home computers, a certain old pastime hasn't been killed off. In fact, if you think about it, computer games and masturbation go hand-in-hand. Across the country, thousands of teenage boys regularly retire to the privacy of their bedrooms for some much-needed adolescent relief. Sexual frustration needs more than one outlet, however, and interacting with the television is the only sort of intercourse you're going to get at that age. Shooting 'em up on screen and soiling your hanky may both be furtive exercises, but they do train your digits a whole lot better than cross-country runs and cold showers!

Like all things essentially adolescent (rock'n'roll, spots, the Gulf War), this is not a laughing matter. Console users take gaming *seriously*, and their brand loyalty is frightening. The Sega versus Nintendo battle puts to shame anything Millwall ever threw up against Leeds. In one corner we have Nintendo, as represented by a dodgy Italian plumber named Mario; in the other we have Sega, which has put its faith in a trendy blue hedgehog called Sonic. Flick through the pages of any of the glut of game magazines, and you'll find torrents of abuse flying between Mario and Sonic followers. Many channel their hatred into art and fill magazine galleries with hedgehogs kicking their trainer-clad feet into a blood-splattered plumber's head. The shock of the new is techno-brutalism, and the medium is the felt-tip.

The only real difference you can find between Sega and Nintendo users is penis size. Sega owners are bigger in the trouser department. But it's not really that much of a boast given that they also have bigger buttocks, breasts, and just about everything, really. Sega users, see, tend to be older, hence the extra inches.

But if brand loyalty can indicate age, the kind of game you play can say so much more. One that everybody seems to have played at some time is *Tetris*, the original cartridge in the hand-held Nintendo GameBoy. The game is about fitting blocks together so that they make a nice, tidy brick wall. While most people enjoy fiddling with this latter-day Rubik's cube, some take it to extremes. *Tetris* obsessives find themselves placing the objects in a room neatly together in their mind. They stare from train windows trying to get all the houses to fit into each other, and watch the anarchic autumn leaves fall with sheer disgust. *Tetris* players want order from chaos. The subtext of this game is severe anal retention. It's no coincidence that it originated in Moscow – this was the Communist old guard's parting shot, a subliminal message to Western youth. Retain! Keep the order! Fit neatly into the wall!

Another player best avoided is the racing-game enthusiast. After a couple of hours on *Outrun* or *Road Rush*, you'll see them whizzing through Kwiksave with a trolley, on a mission, or storming through red lights in a Fiat Panda. You can sometimes hear them on a busy street, brrruming and screeching away to themselves, negotiating their way through pedestrians. This sort of behaviour may be cute and quirky when Tom Hanks does it in a feel-good age-swap movie like *Big*, but in real life it's pathetic, regressive and very, very sad.

Keep an eye out for the sports-simulation freak, too – most have a strong competitive streak. The tell-tale signs are a complete humour transplant, temper tantrums and strong Nietzschean over-tones to all their actions. Crap footie games like *European Club Soccer* will be played in an atmosphere of strained silence, and any game won will be celebrated with fascistic glee.

Advanced role-playing games sound like more fun, although I soon discovered that they had far more to do with trainspotting than they did with handcuffs, celery and a Latex grope-suit. Role-playing games (or RPGs) are basically Dungeons and Dragons-type affairs where you live life as Twinkly the Hapless Goblin or Anthrax the Warrior Wart-Hog. They're ideal if you just want to lose it for a couple of hours, but try not to get hooked. Serious RP gamers tend to have no social life and can afford to spend the best part of a month mapping out Narnia-esque landscapes and jotting down all the clues and facts they can glean from meeting a variety of talking mushrooms and jovial trolls. The notional idea of these games is usually to 'find the missing emerald of Garnath' or 'free the land of Codthorpe from the evil knights of Knobtwat', etc. But the real purpose is to provide a healthy alternative for potential child-murderers and perverts. 'Yes, Tommy, you *do* have friends! There's Mumphkin the Leprechaun, Spazzle the Wizard, and all the twitchy rabbits of Colostomy Castle! So be a good boy, remove the masking tape from your hamster's mouth and zip up your little trousers.'

Be it nuking the world, winning at Brand's Hatch or wrestling with pixies, will all this fantasy turn you into a blob-shaped, brain-dead computer zombie? And will too many shoot-'em-ups eventu-ally lead to blindness? Well, apparently not. Margaret Shotton doesn't think so, anyway – and she's a doctor. 'Apart from increasing your manual dexterity and hand-to-eye co-ordination, video games speed up your neural pathways,' she claims. These are the links in your brain through which knowledge passes. If you speed these up, information can travel round faster, decisions and judgements could speed up, and it could lead to a higher IQ! Dr Shotton pours scorn on mothers who chastise their offspring for playing computer games. 'It's far healthier than watching TV. Few children remember anything more than the adverts. If your child was playing chess all day, you'd boast he was a genius!'

Games like *Krusty's Super Fun House* and some parts of the much-heralded *Sonic 2* promote the skills of lateral thinking. To be successful at such games, you need to explore and find new levels and different solutions, seeking high and low for new rewards and new ways forward. Learning that there is more than one answer to a problem is a valuable lesson. Those who don't indulge in the world of video games may be losing out in many more ways. It's a language that needs to be learned to communicate fully in years to come. Games are increasingly the starting blocks to full computer literacy.

Arriving home from a particularly hard night's clubbing, I lay on my bed and my eyes finally fell shut. Squealing mice seemed bedded in my ears, and green hoppity things abounded, but right smack in my mind's eye were two teams of digitized ice-hockey players fighting it out in front of a packed stadium. They were large-as-life recreations from the *EA Hockey* game I'd been playing all week. Despite my appeals to postpone the match, things kept bashing away in front of me.

The most worrying thing is not that life was imitating video game imitating life; that my perception of reality had been fatally flawed by subliminal computer messages; or even that my brain was becoming all-too transparent to any two-bob amateur psychiatrist who cared to take note. No, the really annoying thing was that my side ended up losing, 3–1.

The Face, December 1992

Somalia: Darkness Has a Disneyland

'Life's a piece of shit, when you think of it' –
Monty Python's Life of Brian

You are driving down the road when you see a family walking along in front of you. They look tired, so you decide to give them a lift. You pick them up and they sit happily in the back. With them is everything they own: assorted blackened pans, a yellow plastic bowl and a small bag of split peas. They're a normal family, they've walked for days, for miles, seeking relatives they think are still alive and food that is rumoured to be available. The father limps along because he's been shot in the leg, the mother bemoans the loss of their cattle to the looters. The five hungry children sit silently, brushing the flies from their faces, stroking their magical eyes at the aliens in the front seats. When the time comes to drop them, you slip them some cash. They depart waving and smiling, trudging onwards to their pathetic parallel universe. Your gunmen return to position on the roof-rack, you place your Walkman headphones back on, and as the Orb start playing, you drive on. A Toyota Landcruiser, a dusty road, a normal family and another bloody guilt trip down memory lane.

Darkness has a Disneyland. By miles of golden beaches, through lush river valleys, across wondrous plains, lies a fantasy world of plague, war, pestilence and famine. Want to ride through towns of dying children? Want to walk through the city of gunfire? Want to witness live snuff as the bodies drop in the camps of the starving? Cheap holidays in other people's misery; sweet Somalia. Come now, hear the thunder of hooves on ochre soil. The four horsemen ride!

Body and soul were calm when I first landed in Somalia's capital, Mogadishu. The hungover pilot had swooped, then dived kamikaze-like on to a runway covered in armed bushmen. In normal circumstances I would have been risking the Persil whiteness of my underwear, but a bizarre sense of humour and an overdose of travel-sickness pills had left me in a serene state of mind. This wasn't real, anyway – I had nothing to worry about. This was all too far gone, too trippy, too dreamlike. Too culture-shock clichéd. I was watching a movie or shooting a video. I was in Somalia, sweet Somalia. Here to see the sights and take in the horrors of a world gone crazy. A Third World *Westworld*; a post-apocalypse country; year zero. A Disneyland of Darkness. An ideal place to choose to live life in the abstract.

Somalia has the dubious merit of being the most screwed-up country in the world. Though 'country' is a misleading term. It suggests a place with a government, an army, borders, a basketball team, that sort of thing. But Somalia is just a fated area on the horn of Africa. A race of people and problems that sit in the continent's top-right-hand corner and spill from the west into Ethiopia, and from the south into Kenya. Somalis are a distinct ethnic race, a cross between Arabs and Africans. Tall, stunning-looking people with straight noses but ebony skin. All from the same tribe, with the same language, they have divided and subdivided into a network of clans.

It may be screwed now, but for centuries the clans lived a life of pastoral egalitarianism: a 'have camel, will travel' kind of deal. They drove their herds, sang poetry (Somalia had no written language until 1972) and fought with each other. Two sub-clans would fight over a watering hole. Then perhaps they'd join up and fight another clan over grazing rights. Spears were thrown, then the elders would get together under a tree: brothers would sort things out. Centuries of colonialism by the British, French and Italians did little to affect the Somali lifestyle. When the various colonial powers had raped what they could, they called it a day. In 1960, Somalia, as we know

55

it, was formed. Its flag was a white five-pointed star lost on a sky-blue background.

The five points on the star were there to represent the five traditional areas of the Somali race, but of those five areas, only the old British and Italian Somaliland were united. French Somalia became the ridiculously small country/port of Djibouti. The Ogaden in the west was nicked by Ethiopia years ago and remains in their hands despite a bloody Seventies war. And, to the south, the area that became dubbed the Northern Districts of Kenya is lost to that country despite being full of Somalis. So a potential five-stroke has only ever fired on two cylinders.

It didn't help when, after a military coup in 1969, the only democratic government in Africa was blasted out of office. The man to get Somalia's number-one job and lead his country down the road of half-baked dictatorial 'kill your comrades' communism was a certain Siyaad Barre. He misruled for twenty-odd years, plundering the national treasury for the benefit of his own clan, the infamous Marehan, and massacring all who were against him. Which, unfortunately, was practically everybody. He got away with it for so long by playing the old Cold War game. First he got big backing from the Russkies, then, when they went sour on him and backed Ethiopia during the Ogaden war, he snuggled up for Western favours. These were soon forthcoming and dollars poured in to prop him up. Pol Pot, Pinochet, Saddam the man, Siyaad Barre: the whole world loves a dictator. Your enemy's enemy is your bosom buddy.

Over the years, Siyaad played off clan against clan. With the use of a good squad called the Red Caps, he squashed rebellious rivals and, on occasion, fed them to the crocodiles. At a football match in Mogadishu towards the end of his reign, the crowd booed him. He ordered his troops to open fire. They killed thousands, but the boos weren't silenced for long. A revolution swept the country in a bloody frenzy.

Over the months that followed, Siyaad, the Marehan, and all the president's men were slowly driven south out of the country. Driven away in tanks, with them went all the wealth: all the dollars, the gold, the gifts. And as they retreated, they destroyed and they murdered. Some they didn't need to kill. Why waste bullets? Smash the wells, steal the livestock, and leave the land to starve. Siyaad did a thorough job, then retired. He is now rumoured to be living in Zimbabwe on a large cattle farm purchased with his ill-gotten gains. He left Somalia with nothing, save guns and disputes. Somalia rejoiced as one when Siyaad fell. A brief unity – for the corpse of Somalia has many militias.

Every clan has its men with guns and scores to settle. Disputes that used to be sorted out with spears are now fought with Kalashnikovs. The campaign to be the new president has been fought for the last two years, and there's enough weaponry there to keep the bandwagon rolling until well into the next century. Meanwhile, with no means of supporting itself, the nation starves. There are few jobs except that of the soldier. Food aid comes in, and if you've got a gun, you eat. Sweet Somalia, and I was standing calm at Mogadishu Airport convinced it wasn't real.

The airport, and the area around it, is controlled by the Hawayidi clan. They were bushmen, camel-herders; some had never even seen a town. Then, come the revolution, they did their bit to oust Siyaad and flocked into Mogadishu. Where others had departed, they moved in. With the president gone, the real fun started. Life in the bush is hard, whereas running an airport and playing with guns is a right laugh. Old fire engines lie derelict, joyridden to the point of destruction. Goats graze where the duty-free ought to be. The air-traffic-control tower has sheets over the windows – someone's sleeping there now, for Somalia is one big squat. Quick to learn the ways of the world, the bushmen are charging a $100 landing fee, assorted handling charges and various departure taxes. They've never had it so good. Cash from chaos. Fat chance of them going back to a life of long walks to watering holes.

Staying in Mogadishu, you'll hear gunfire all the time. I mean all the bloody time, non-stop: *rat-a-tat-tat*, *peoww*, *crack*, *bang*, *ddrrr*, *dush-dush*. Morning, noon and night, the ambient warfare continues. It's reassuring to know the city is currently harbouring a ceasefire. A stretch of no-man's land separates the city between north and south. To cross from one to the other, you have a choice of two frontline checkpoints, romantically named 'Banque' and 'Hotel Gulle'. In reality, they're home to a couple of dodgy barricades separated by 100 metres of bomb-blasted street. Old Cinzano signs remain pinned to Swiss-cheese walls. Travel north and they lead to the domain of the 'interim president', Ali Mahdi, and his loyal band of Abgaal fighters.

Before all these troubles, Mr Mahdi was a hotelier, a wealthy man who could sense the tide was turning. He backed the revolution with cash and became the self-styled 'interim president'. Since I was travelling with Tony Worthington, the Labour overseas development minister, I had the pleasure of meeting Mr Mahdi. Sad, so very sad, he sits – a small man behind a big important desk inside a shocking-pink palace. To his left is a plastic globe, to his right a small Somalian flag perched upright in what appears to be a pen holder. The white five-pointed star is barely visible, the sky-blue background has faded. And all around are 'ministers', soldiers, even an official photographer, who records with glee the meeting of such a grand man as Mr Mahdi with the humble servant of a distant court. Mr Mahdi is very pleasant, his ministers very courteous. Mr Worthington is fed flannel, but he takes it with the decorum such meetings demand.

Rumours seep from Mr Mahdi's palace. They say that he is backed by the Mafia, who once laundered money through Mogadishu big-time. The Italian connection is strong in town, although Mussolini's triumphant arches are now riddled with gunshot. Or is he being backed by the Americans? There's oil up north, and Conoco has been drilling for a piece of the action for some time. The firm wants a deal, and if it's deals you want, Mr Mahdi is your man. His eyes are sad, his thin moustache covers a quivering lip. He asks Mr Worthington, honoured and distinguished guest sir, for 15,000 UN troops. Mr Mahdi needs them, for without them he will surely die, blood splattered on shocking-pink walls. To the south of the city lies his nemesis: General Mohammed Farrah Aideed.

General Aideed's contribution to the revolution was blood, and lots of it. Aideed led the troops to victory and kept on leading them until only small pockets of Siyaad's Marehan militia, the Somalia National Front (SNF), were left in the country. He then turned his attention to Mr Mahdi, the pretender president. Aideed is Somalia's *numero uno* warlord supremo. He is also clinically insane, twice committed to Western hospitals. He reads poetry to visiting camera crews. A proud Somali who will bow to no one, he leads an alliance of clans and militias called the Somalia National Alliance (SNA). Aideed won't be happy until he's president; the country won't be happy if he is. And while these two fight it out, the people starve and children get shot by mistake.

In north Mogadishu, amid the sand-dunes that roll down to the azure of the Indian Ocean, lies the city's hospital. Converted from one of Siyaad's hurriedly built prisons, it stands like a fort of the French Foreign Legion, the Red Cross flag fluttering high. It's staffed mainly by a Somali medical team who work non-stop for no pay except food (indeed, the majority of aid workers are native Somali). Since the ceasefire, the firing hasn't ceased and the hospital is taking in more casualties than ever. The looting and shooting leads to hectic crossfire. A rifle fires its projectile over 3 kilometres. Bullets fall from the sky, and hard – deadly rain picking off the innocent, unsuspecting public.

One packed ward housed nothing but children shot by mistake. Kids like three-year-old Fallis Abdi: caught in the crossfire, her little leg punctured by a bullet, left never to walk again. They call these strays *yussif*. Two stories why: some say this is the sound the bullets make as they fall from the sky; others talk of a saint who stalks the streets invisibly, a sniper from heaven, punishing the people for their evil ways. Fallis will remember the name of Saint Yussif all her hobbling days.

*

The main source of casualties is the area in and around the port, where the ships dock to deliver cargoes of food aid sent to support the dying people. The organization Care has the unenviable job of running the port and distributing the food. The only economy worth talking about in the country is food. The new blood, the new gold, the new power is food aid. Care took on the logistical nightmare of unloading and distributing tonne upon tonne of aid, all the time walking a dangerous political tightrope. There are fourteen districts to Mogadishu, and all must get their due – 'cause if they don't, you're gonna get yours.

In the spirit of fairness, Care hires three different crews to help staff the port on consecutive days. Each crew consists of unpackers, loaders and 'technical assistants'. Technical assistance is big business in Mogadishu. Aid workers and the UN found it difficult to explain to the outside world that the only chance of going about their work was to hire gunmen as security, so the term 'technical assistant' appeared on many an expense sheet. Times are tough and the protection racket is booming.

Security ride the streets in 'technicals', strange *Mad Max* machines, cut-down jeeps with large *ack-ack* guns on the back. Customized hot-rod death machines, they often have a huge 35 mm cannon running down the centre, though if they ever fired one of these monsters, the whole kaboosh would immediately self-destruct. Some have even ripped off the missile system from MiG fighters: huge bloody great multi-rocket launchers, and the only way you can fire them is by hot-wiring to your battery. Vorsprung durch technical.

And who are these gunmen, these security guards, these 'technical assistants'? Just the local lads, the looters and shooters. A man's got to eat. Unless, of course, he opts for an amphetamine diet, which many of them do. Khat is one of the few drugs allowed under Islamic law. A leafy plant, you chew it and it gives a buzz similar to cocaine. Everywhere you go, wide-eyed people are chewing frantically with what looks like the best part of a privet hedge hanging from their mouth. Somalia's security lies in the hands of coked-up gunmen.

Khat isn't native to Somalia. It's grown in plantations in northern Kenya. But since the stuff is only potent if chewed within twenty-four hours of picking, planeloads of it are flown in fresh every day to satisfy the chewing habits of numerous insomniacs. Through war and famine, the only constant import is a narcotic. It's dangerous down the airport when the khat is flown in. Because of its limited lifespan, it must get to the market as quickly as possible; the price declines as the day goes on. So every time the khat dealers are held up at the airport or at any of the various barricades around town, they're losing money. When profits are at stake, life is cheap, and killing on khat is the top buzz in town.

As the day draws on, the security keep chewing, the trigger finger gets itchy, and tension rises. Down the port they load up the trucks and pen them in behind giant walls of metal containers. When the trucks are all full and up to a hundred prehistoric diesel monsters are revving up *en masse*, they'll make a gap in the protective barrier of containers, allowing the trucks to make a run for it to their various locations around town. Outside the port gates are a hundred grabbing hands and a score of hostile guns. I watched once as the convoy left. The gunfire rose from lift music to 160 bpm of thumping hardcore. Serious hardcore. Some local racketeers drove up to the departing trucks in their 'technicals', sprayed the area with all their macho juices, then 'diverted' seven trucks. The Care co-ordinators who were standing with me just smiled. 'No problem?' they mused ironically, mimicking the voices of their workers.

Then the gunfire got really loud and really close. A small local dispute had erupted in addition to the diversion already in progress. A group of gun-toting, maimed adults (many with severed limbs, some even in wheelchairs) and a bunch of ragged kids had been caught stealing. They often bunk into the port compound, steal what they can, then hop (or wheel) off home. This is usually tolerated, as these people are often friends or family of the security.

But today, the security decided to take a stand for justice. Guns were fired, and the motley crew of looters scarpered. One boy in an old Leeds number II shirt hid behind me, then bolted for freedom, leaving his stolen split peas behind him, shots ringing around his ears. 'Situation normal: all fucked up!' chirped Carl, a fiery-eyed Care port regular.

Day in, day out, Carl and the rest of the Care crew keep on keeping on. A few days later, three tanks drew up at the port gates and demanded the dues for a clan that felt it wasn't getting enough. You don't argue with tanks, so poor Carl and his crew had to hide in the hold of a ship while they waved goodbye to all their fuel supplies and 500 tonnes of food aid. Evidently things get even more frisky when a ship docks with any cargo that isn't the lowest of the low in the food commodity stakes. Recent well-meaning gifts of pasta and mini-hampers signalled a large upswing in the port casualties.

About 200 miles west of Mogadishu lies Baidoa, famine capital of Somalia and therefore top tourist spot for political fact-finders, press and policy-makers. I voyeured there on several occasions. When you think of famine, you imagine small stick creatures lying lost and alone on an arid landscape. Well, strike that.

Picture a town with streets lined with bombed-out villas and gaudily painted shops. Fill the streets with people and donkeys and a market with stalls stocked with fruits, meats, herbs and hashish. See restaurants where Nike-shirted gunmen lay AK47s on the table. And picture, behind every brick wall outside every house, thousands upon thousands starving. Camp upon camp of the lowest of humanity, and a graveyard with 200 new arrivals every day. Don't stumble on the moral implications of restaurants in famine zones – I dined at one. There are plenty of goods in Harrods in London, but the city's homeless still go wanting.

The first thing you notice in a camp is the sweet smell of human excrement. It fazes you, but you're not really there, and this isn't really happening. Then you hear the coughing. Everybody is coughing, great guttural slices echoing in bird-cage torsos. Thatched with discarded plastic, rags and cardboard, small dome-shaped thorn huts house skin-and-bone people. Eyes stare at you in hope. Mothers drag dying children and hang them up in front of you.

I found that particularly hard. They wanted food and medicine: all I had was a pen and notebook and the sense that I was somewhere else. Fine time to be trippy. I went through the journalistic motions, pen in hand, recording so many sad, sad stories about families who'd walked for days from villages looted and destroyed. Of lost brothers, sisters, mothers, fathers and children, so many children. And while I wrote, the kids that walk in the camp, the ones with the strength to play, made zip-guns from wood and coat-hanger wire.

Over the weeks, I travelled on through Somalia and northern Kenya feeling dazed, as if I was viewing life through television news. While I was there, I heard the United Nations talk of a solution, and watched while America 'took the lead'. I flew with the US Air Force and watched as they shipped a bit of aid to a few people in an area only slightly affected by the whole sorry story. But things are 'seen to be done' and the world's attention drifts elsewhere.

Aid is a strange, complex, often perverted affair. Free food to an area not at death's door, and you can bankrupt the local economy and condemn it to a future of reliance. Set out on a mission of mercy to a centre of despair, and you may give false hope to thousands who hear of your good work and flock in, flooding the area with just too many people, too many problems. All the aid organizations can do in such a minefield of ills is try the best they know at a price they can afford. There's no such thing as a free lunch. At best, consciences are cleared; at worst, colonial empires are rebuilt.

The second time I flew to Mogadishu, I had chronic diarrhoea. A common complaint in Somalia, though I at least had the reassuring knowledge that I wasn't shitting out my only meal of the week. I was travelling in a small five-seater plane with no lavatory. An hour from landing, I really had to go. I clenched, and I clenched, and I dug my nails into the armrests, and bit my lip, and I prepared a plastic bag in case the dam burst. I held on until landing, whereupon I sprinted past the gibbering bushmen and their stupid little guns and squatted just off the main runway. I was finally getting a sense of reality. Life is cheap, and a good crap's worth it!

It wasn't just my bowels that rocketed me back to reality. Towards the end of my visit, it became apparent that Somalia had become big news. Press packed themselves into the safe house of the UN compound. They draped camera cables ten feet out of the gates, past an entrepreneurial souvenir-seller, to the foot of some makeshift thorn huts. Thus live pieces-to-camera from ravaged sweet Somalia could be done with an authentic background, yet all within spitting distance of sanctuary. What a circus, and what naughty boys and girls. Trolleys look too new in the hospital? Make them put the old ones back! Missed a burial? We'll get them to dig up the corpse and do it all again for prime time! You can get somebody shot for $6 in that city. I should have spent a grand.

Things get real when people you've talked to, people you've photographed, people with whom you've shared some brief bond of human contact and returned to see again, don't get better – only worse. Families visited start dwindling in numbers, friendly fathers become corpses, and sons stare with soulless eyes. You give your peanuts, you give your Jaffa Cakes, and you pass your last flapjack. Your rucksack now empty, you find ways to pass cash without causing a commotion.

At one point, I found myself helping distribute high-protein food biscuits in an emergency Care feeding centre. As instructed, I gave two biscuits each to the hungry hordes. They sat in line after line, carpeting the ground with their feeble bodies, hands pointing skyward in desperate anticipation. A grabbing sea of hands, and me treading carefully as every step I took seemed to plant my great Adidas-clad foot on someone's brittle bones. I definitely did more harm than good. Men stole food from the mouths of children. I hit one or two. Firm slap on skeletal face.

This was humankind at survival level and people pushed, shoved and cheated for that little edge that meant they'd live another day. Don't make judgements, don't think you'd stay noble. Stay noble, and you die.

On the last journey of my trip (the one to the big fat Red Cross Hercules that was going to fly us the hell out of there), we broke down. On a long road that stretched straight to the horizon in both directions, in the middle of the bush, in the heart of bandit country, the front axle went. While the driver got out his tool kit, our technical assistants took up 'anti-ambush' positions either side of the road. Sitting on the road with my photographer friend, I tuned my radio into the World Service. It was then that my brief sense of reality departed once again.

The World Service has a programme that explains the lyrics of pop songs to an African audience. Today it was 'Rhythm is a Dancer'. I kid you not. '*Rhythm is a dancer!*' spoke the Beeb in Beebspeak. '*And how serious is it? Well let's listen.*' The music thumps onwards. '*Yes! It's very serious. In fact, it's as serious as cancer!*'

After more explanations, they played the track fully, and I finally entered the twilight zone. The gunmen protecting us (gun*boys*, actually) stuck their heads out of the bushes. Big smiles came on their faces and they started to body-pop. Guns in hand, grins on face, jacking warehouse-style. I got up off the road and swung my funky hips. Sweet, surreal Somalia. And how serious is it? It's as serious as cancer!

Now here's the deal. I'm not a doctor. I'm not an aid worker. I'm a journalist. The only excuse for seeing such sights is to tell the world. But the truth is, the world already knows. We know the horrors that are out there, we know of hunger, pain and misery. We know of Auschwitz, of Nagasaki, of Pol Pot, of Bosnia, and now Somalia. Yet we hide from it, and pain remains a jilted lover or a pranged car.

We know right and wrong. We have no excuses. We have the luxury to love and care. It is wrong that people starve and fear the bullet of a predator's gun. We *must* give a shit. In the dark Disneyland of Somalia, Mickey Mouse militias are creating the hell of fear and famine. We as nations, as united nations, have the power to enforce right from wrong. We must give our power, give our gold, give our blood, give a shit.

You see, it's all still going on. Every day, every minute of our civilized lives, the apocalypse is continuing. And unless the powers-that-be jolt from being 'seen to do something' to actually *doing* something, we may all end up sleepwalking through the gates of hell.

I'll get down off the cross now: they need it for firewood.

The Face, November 1992

1993

Rave is institutionalized. It is no longer a youth culture, more an entertainment system like a video-recorder, a computer game or the Lottery. The charts are dominated by dance music. Cocaine starts to become commonplace in clubs.

The madness begins. Four-day drugs binges in Tenerife. Months of excess with a wedding and a honeymoon in the Amazon somewhere in the middle of it. Life blurs, relationships fall apart.

The young man journeys to Sarajevo and finds himself in the heart of a major European war, in a town like his own, among young people like himself. The nightclub is still open, though.

He is now avoiding the fact that his wife says she no longer loves him and has started spending a worrying amount of time with his best friend. He runs away, snorting cocaine in castles in Portugal and dropping acid in EuroDisney. He feels suicidal.

To shape up his act – or hopefully get killed – he goes to cover the war in Angola. Back home for the holidays, he splits up with his wife on finding that she is sleeping with his best friend. It's Christmas Eve, and he hears the news from a wrecked E-head in a bar.

Wonderland UK

In a Wonderland they lie
Dreaming as the days go by,
Dreaming as the summers die:

Ever drifting down the stream
Lingering in the golden gleam –
Life, what is it but a dream?
　　　　　　　　– Lewis Carroll

Curiouser and curiouser. Another year on and the dancing isn't over. A few summers ago, most of us thought the explosion of drugs and dance music which formed that four-letter word 'rave' would wither and die like so many youth cults before. Usually such things shoot up like a rocket from a milk bottle, sprinkle the sky with starlight glory, then quickly fall to earth in a burned-out shell of their former selves. But something funny has happened with house music and the drug culture it spawned. Instead of burning out it has spread out, sprinkling its pixie dust across our country. Whether it's Sunday-afternoon football or shopping in Dixon's, the music is there, harmlessly thumping along. And drugs have taken their place alongside the TV, video and satellite as part of our entertainment system. Youth culture is now public domain.

We are seeing a future where drug use becomes endemic and youths never grow up. The horrible truth is, we are living in a country where the only real prospect many people have is to retreat into wonderland. After twelve years of Conservative government, our society has become disparate, cocooned and cold. One of the few communities that remains today consists of the networks built up around clubs and drugs. However flawed and fake they may be, they exist, and provide one of the few support systems some people have. While trying to live in a world of constant hedonism may be an admirable enough goal, you have to ask where it will all end up. When is it time to stop? There must be more to life than a new Stone Island jacket and a cocaine habit. How shabby it all seems.

There was a time when youth had no culture. When youth slaved for pennies in dark mills, their way forward a roof over their head, enough to eat and a fair day's work for a fair day's pay. With this dream in their hearts, they trudged onwards. And every inch they moved forward, every battle they won, moved us that much closer to these: our glorious days of triumph.

From the Fifties onwards, the young people of this country have benefited from the changes in society which gave us a bit of cash and some leisure time. This small but significant empowerment gave us the lot: Teddy boys, Cliff Richard, mods, purple hearts, *Rubber Soul*, Slade, skinheads, Captain Sensible, Seditionaries, New Romantics, Wham!, casuals, and house music all night long. Forty years of youth culture all hinge around the fact that the social struggle of those who went before us gained us our status as creative consumers. Sitting in your bedroom listening to Nirvana or lying face down on a nightclub floor thinking you're a goldfish may not seem like one of the great triumphs of the working classes, but it is. The only way to enjoy such delights before was to break into the cliques of Bohemia.

Drugs and dance music are nothing new – only the sheer scale of those who are indulging is novel. Warehouse parties were around in the 1920s. Marek Kohn's book *Dope Girls: The Birth of the British Drug Underground* offers an excellent account of the moral panic which led to the criminalization of drugs. (They haven't always been illegal. You could once get cocaine at Harrods and opium from the chemist's, while squares impregnated with both were advertised as ideal gifts for the boys at the front.) After the Great War a combination of jazz, cocaine and female emancipation led to a booming London nightlife. According to a *Daily Express* report of the time, there were parties in 'unlit buildings in foreboding neighbourhoods. Costing £2 entry and filled with young dancing girls who were under-dressed, perpetually seized with hysterical laughter, and ogling foolishly'. Sound familiar? How about 'gum being chewed to stop involuntary teeth-grinding'?

Gurning flappers aside, the moral outcry of the time was due to the horrible idea that young white English roses, who obviously knew no better, were being fed drugs by 'gentlemen of colour' after a bit of deflowering. This was the fear that led to the criminalization of drugs in 1916 and later to campaigns in the press against 'dance dens and drugs'. The concern then, as now, was not borne of any deep-rooted worries for the health of individuals but from panic about the erosion of a prejudiced, conservative order. Despite such moral forces, this century saw pop music and recreational drugs slowly drift away from Bohemia and into the mainstream. Beatniks, mods and hippies were all propagandists for this winning mixture. Yet it has taken until now for there to be universal acceptance of such excesses as the norm.

What has occurred as a result is a certain loss of innocence. Primary schools hold junior discos, twelve-year-olds skin joints; life's little joys now come ever earlier. Job prospects are bleak and decent housing eludes most of us – as does the responsibility of adulthood. For mods in the Sixties, there came a time when they sold the Lambretta, got married, had kids and saved for a dream house in the suburbs. Even with hippies, when the acid got too much the drop-outs dropped in again, nursing their broken dreams of love and peace. Now there are no such full stops, no obvious end to youthful glory days. With the sham of Eighties enterprise culture lying bankrupt all around, the sons and daughters who grew up in those suburban dream houses will not give up Tennents and Ecstasy for the promise of lower mortgage rates and the hope of shares in privatized utilities. That simply isn't progress.

The Government, on the other hand, is having a hard time coping with the monster they've created. Its response is confused. It recently had celebs like Anneka Rice, Cliff Richard and Michael Caine instructing youth to 'Get the message' in European Drug Prevention Week. At a media seminar I attended in a plush London hotel, there was a lot of glib talk about the 'menace' and the 'threat', but little about reality or responsibility. Princess Di gave her now-famous 'hug your kids off heroin' speech, but between French mime groups and a Dutch theatre combo demonstrating their incomprehensible approaches to the anti-drug campaign, it was left to *Crimewatch*'s Nick Ross to give the only coherent comment of the day. When asked whether the media are responsible in reporting drugs, he said, 'No! We give them an antiseptic treatment, a PR job for the Government. The truth is, many people take drugs for pleasure and excitement and very, very, very few end up addicts. But you won't let us say that.'

Cheers all round for stating the obvious. Given the way things are drifting, you would hope the Government would realize and prepare a coherent plan for the future. Yet it still persists with a moral crusade to protect its prejudiced, conservative order. The lack of real concern is exposed by the failure to fund addiction clinics.

Smack and crack use is on the increase, and this is a real problem. But there's not a lot you can do about it when some see the grotesque spectacle of addiction as preferable to their normal life. All you can do is tell the truth about drugs and hope that others believe you. Groups like Manchester's Lifeline show the way forward. They accept that people are going to use drugs, so they show them how to indulge as safely as possible. And by telling the truth about cannabis and Ecstasy, they gain the confidence of drug-users and are believed when they talk of the real dangers of smack and crack. Yet they still can't change the bleak prospects that lead many to chase smack: you may have to nick a few VCRs a day, but at least you've got your dreams. Meanwhile, for many, the only realistic way to get a weekend out and some spare cash is to flog substances to willing, wild-eyed customers.

It appears that the only full stops to a life of dulled decadence is one rock too many, or a stay at Her Majesty's Pleasure. The Ecstasy may have faded and attitudes jaded, but no one leaves the Wonderland tea party for long. We have nothing to replace it, as our dreams are as hazy as our future. We are the first generation since the war who can't envisage doing any better than our parents. The alternatives of the real world are out of reach, the sums of modern living leave us permanently in the red, and the future holds no certainties. What could be better than a gramme up your nose, Andy Weatherall at the Drum Club and the knowledge that you're not going to make a complete idiot of yourself? Not a lot in John Major's classless, jobless, thankless, hopeless heaven. Time to get the mirror out.

In *Alice through the Looking Glass*, there comes a point when Alice meets the Red Queen, who's busy running. She's not going anywhere, she's just running on the spot. Alice asks why, and the Queen explains she has to run so hard just to keep where she is. Yoof culture is a bit like the Red Queen – it has to have constant momentum. We have to keep on struggling to protect what little we've got. The dreams of others – good dreams, the worthy dreams of our forefathers – allow us, like Alice, to fall down a rabbit hole and glimpse a Wonderland, an escape of fashion, of music, of Cheshire-cat smiles. For forty years, we painted the roses whatever colour we liked. None of us want to wake from the dream, but to stay there we have to keep running, and no one's even walking at the moment. So paint the roses red and let the greenfly feast.

The momentum has been lost and we're lying on our back retreating, too dazed to realize our fate. A hundred years ago a chap called Karl Marx quipped that religion was the opium of the people, the sedative that kept us content with our lot in life. Well, Christianity and Marxism are now dying, but if we were to wake just a little from our dream world, we might see the new sedative. Youth culture is now the opium of the people. And with the sweetness of smack, we chase it all in.

The lines are drawn and paranoia is rampant. On one side, the forces of conservatism protect their power through fear, scared of any real change. On the other, a large part of the nation clings to the anaesthetic of pot and pop. But we haven't gone this far just to mong out. We're all addicted. We can't give it up because there's nothing better to replace it. We need new visions, new dreams, and a new England. One free from the shabbiness of a grey Government. An economy where you don't need to be flogging Es to have a bit of cash for the weekend. Education which inspires people to greater things than pints, puff and pay packets. And a roof over our heads, enough to eat, and a fair day's work for a fair day's pay for the residents of this and every other country in this beautiful planet earth. Naïve? I hope so. Regain our innocence, and ours is the world.

The Face, January 1993

The Phat Manifesto

Welcome to the first edition of *Phat* magazine, the journal for the young gentleman of the hooligan persuasion. Despite what you may have read elsewhere, we are not yobs. We spit on ignorance, pour scorn on oppression and do the right thing when and where we can. This mag is about getting a life and having a laugh all the way into the next century: our century.

We humbly promise:

- That all articles will be ill researched, badly written and of no interest except to a couple of members of the editorial staff and their close friends
- Spelling and grammar will be experimental to the point of incomprehensibility
- We will change our morality according to who shouts the loudest
- Our photos will be blurred, out of focus and completely irrelevant to any text they claim to illustrate
- We will sing the praises of any star/film/trainer, only to slag them/it off the next month
- The layout will always make things unreadable and will be inspired by any other magazine that takes our fancy
- Interviewees will be selected on the basis of cash bribes received
- We will always make snide comments about people who can't defend themselves
- Anybody who has enough cash to sue us will be treated with kid gloves and grovelled to on every possible occasion
- We'll live in the fast lane but always make sure we have the bus fare home

- Anybody spending their hard-earned cash on advertising will find we lavish fawning praise upon their products
- From now on, standards start slipping . . .

Our mission is clear. *Phat* magazine is for hoodlums, by hoodlums. Together we'll take publishing into the twenty-first century by sinking it to depths previously unimaginable. Seven years, four months, sixteen days and counting. Read us and weep.

Editorial for the launch issue of *Phat* magazine, August 1993

Sarajevo: I Will Survive

SLAV SOAP — THE EVERYDAY STORY OF THE BALKAN FAMILY (UPDATE)

The Balkan family had always argued, but when Grandad Tito died, phew! What a stink! The family just couldn't get on. They squabbled so much over the inheritance that divorce was imminent. The first to leave the nest was sly little Slovenia, who packed her bags and went off to become a country in her own right – she couldn't stand all the arguing. This left Mr Croatia and Mrs Serbia fighting tooth and nail for what was left. Meanwhile, their son, Bosnia, decided he wasn't going to be part of a custody battle and joined the greater family of nations. Although the courts said Bosnia had legally ditched his parents, they never provided the police when Mother Serbia started surgically removing his limbs. What a mess! What a family! Tune into the news daily for the latest Slav Soap update. But in the mean time welcome to episode 42: *Sarajevo Tales*.

TALE OF THE CENTURY

On a bridge over the river Miljacka in the city of Sarajevo, one bullet from a gun: the starting pistol of the twentieth century. The Austrian overlord of Bosnia, Archduke Ferdinand, slumps dead in the back of his car. His country is mighty miffed. It blames Serbia for the assassination, and so starts the sequence of events that led to the 'war to end all wars'. One bullet sent the first of 10 million victims of the First World War to his death.

Now the century unfolds before us and history tells of world wars, cold wars, oil wars and cod wars. Of empires lost and fortunes gained. Of fascists, communists and the Rolling Stones. Here in Sarajevo, at the end of a century, the loop of history completes.

Once more unto the bridge, my friends. Not one bullet but many bullets. Not one pistol but many pistols, and thousands slumped dead. The war to end all wars continues.

Sod this for a game of soldiers.

DOG TAILS

Wherever you walk in Sarajevo, there's always the risk that someone is watching you, fixing his sights and about to pull the trigger. For Sarajevo lies in a valley, and the hills and mountains that surround it belong to the Chetniks and their snipers. It's like a hot dog. The sausage is the city of Sarajevo, the bread roll the Chetniks. The ketchup is spilling everywhere. The day I arrived, the Chetniks had just captured the last piece of roll: Mount Igman. The fall of Igman was big news and a lead story to the press who inhabit the yellow plastic corpse of the Holiday Inn. To the locals, it was a bolt of sheer terror. The only remaining route into the city had been severed, the strangulation of Sarajevo was complete. Bit of a choker, really.

Six quid for a packet of ciggies, no electricity or water and not a piece of fresh fruit to be seen: *c'est la guerre*. The local radio station gives out new recipes every week: nettle soup, cornflower cutlets, that kind of deal. But despite such meagre diets, they still find food for their dogs. More's the pity – the dogs I could have done without. Everyone seemed to keep a mean-looking dog: pit bulls, Dobermanns, Pyrenean Mountain wolf-like creatures. Every citizen seemed to be the proud owner of a canine death-machine. The horror of the shelling and gunfire was nothing compared to the absolute fear one felt when opening a door to a hungry Rottweiler. The dogs of war are mean-looking brutes, matched only by the city's drivers.

With snipers firing at cars, the highway code gets thrown out the window of your smashed-up Yugo. Vehicles hurtle along, screaming around corners and bumping up kerbs. Some days more people are killed by road accidents than the war. When you're sniped at, the natural reaction is to duck, which is a bit of a pain if your head's beneath the steering-wheel and you're trying to steer the car. But, like the constant sound of gunfire and the smashing of glass in windows, it's strange what soon passes as normality.

The people round town have put up with things for nearly a year and a half. They queue for water, they sit in sheltered cafés and they try to talk of other things, like music, sport – and anything but the war. But days, weeks and years of living dangerously have taken their toll. Psychologically, they've all suffered the same as a Vietnam vet. They share a nervousness, their eyes occasionally darting sideways when you talk to them. In the back of their minds shells are exploding, and what hope they have is darkened by the cynical antics of the United Nations. All that's left for them is a love of life and will to survive as civilized human beings.

Communication with the outside world is vital to what was one of Europe's most cosmopolitan cities. Susan Sontag was there, putting on *Waiting for Godot* with local actors. A young guy named Bill Carter was linking up live to U2 concerts, sending satellite images of Sarajevo people to the audiences. From the safe confines of a liberal viewpoint, it's easy to snipe at their efforts as exploitative. The reality, however, is that they are there, day in day out, doing something a little different for an appreciative people. No one slagged Glenn Miller for coming to London during the Blitz. My only criticism of cultural exchange is the fact that when generators occasionally restore the magic of electricity to idle television sets, the only channels you can get are Sky One and Sky News. The solace found in *Star Trek* is far outweighed by the sadness one experiences seeing a pink-power-dressed Stepford wife recite lead news stories on the opening of Buckingham Palace to the public. These people deserve better.

THE SOLDIER'S STORY

Before the war, Serji was an art student at the Sarajevo Academy. When he's not fighting on the front line for the beleaguered Bosnian army, he's working in his studio. The war has changed Serji's art:

he now makes his sculptures from shrapnel. When he was young, he used to listen to Deep Purple in his bedroom. Now the bedroom lies in tatters, hit by a shell. It's hard to face the fact that the war is here, in the house of his youth.

He fights three days at a time and is allowed sixteen bullets. Serji is not optimistic about his future, for he fights on Mount Zuc, where less than half of those stationed there come back alive. He's haunted by the things he's seen: friends mown down; dogs with arms in their mouths; the corpses of sliced comrades. He thinks Vietnam must have been a picnic for American soldiers. Their odds of survival were considerably better than his.

Sarajevo is a multi-ethnic city, one of the few places where the madness of nationalism has not taken grip. Serji is proud of this. He has Serb, Croat and Muslim in his family and refuses to be pigeon-holed. Sometimes when he fights, there are as many Serbs on his side as there are on the other. He doesn't hate Serbs, only Chetniks (Serbian nationalists). His grandfather was one of Tito's partisans, who fought against the Croat fascists, the Axis powers and the Chetniks. During the struggles of the Second World War, the Chetniks slashed Grandad's throat while he slept. Serji thinks the Nazis are winning again. When he comes back from the fighting, he puts on his Walkman and listens to the Pixies and Sonic Youth. It helps him return to humanity.

THE LANGUAGE OF FOOLS

A lot of this war's problems are caused by bad language. 'Ethnic cleansing' has calmly entered our vocabulary and sanitized genocide. Like Persil or Radion, it washes whiter and removes the stains of blood from the hands of criminals. If only the Nazis had called the holocaust 'Multi-Action Jewgon', the world could have slept on in innocence. How troublesome for us all that towns are laid siege, then their citizens culled. How much nicer it is that the language fools us. The 'Bosnian Muslims' is another handy term. No one refers to 'Church of England Londoners', just because the C of E is the largest religious group in town. Yet Sarajevo is constantly 'Muslim'. (In fact, for Muslim, read, 'Not one of us.')

These people know more of *Monty Python, Only Fools and Horses* and *'Allo 'Allo* than they do of Ayatollahs, Korans and fundamentalism. A few hundred years of Turkish invasions may have given many the tag of Mohammed, but like most of the West, the only tag they find important is the one on their trainers.

Pity the poor Serbs, too, for words damn them also. 'The Serbs' are doing this, 'the Serbs' are doing that. Not all Germans were Nazis, and not all Serbs are nationalists. Pity the poor men and woman suffocating under their slobbish leader's paranoid war-lust. And please mind your language.

SARAJEVO GHETTO SPECTACLE

War is an uncreative act. You don't have to be a potential Picasso to bomb the hell out of a town, or to sniper civilians as they try to bury the dead. Living in Sarajevo, you can find death on any street. The war encircles them, gnawing away at their sanity. But as mortars fall, the struggle for normality continues. An arts group, Obala, puts on shows and exhibitions. It had a good venue in town, a lovely piece of architecture which unfortunately took a direct hit from Chetnik artillery. The shell of the building provides an excellent short-cut to avoid a corner prone to sniping. The building had never been so popular. So Miro, Obala's chief, had the neat idea of sticking an exhibition in its crumbling ruins. While the citizens of Sarajevo dodged the bullets, art came to the masses.

Obala is currently exhibiting some pieces sent in from New York. They're not very good, but that's not the point. In the middle of Sarajevo there's an art exhibition, and one of mankind's nobler traits has triumphed over its worst. The thing about noble things is that they can be very dull, but it's not all oils and abstracts – they also show films. This week it's *Do the Right Thing*.

Kurt is part of Obala; he works in the conceptual world of multimedia. He's coming to terms with the war, reading a lot of

Nietzsche, that sort of thing. He'd just finished a video called *Sarajevo Ghetto Spectacle*, in which news footage is spliced together to a David Bryne soundtrack and the Hollywood sign appears on the city's hills. 'CNN is all part of Hollywood, and Sarajevo part of the spectacle,' he muses. The war drags on all around with no glitz to be found.

PORTRAIT OF A WAR HERO

Čelo (pronounced Chelo) lives on one of the nicer-looking estates in Sarajevo. He sits in his shell suit, stroking his American pit bull, on a beige-vinyl sofa in a suburban-looking living room. I ponder whether this is Peckham rather than Sarajevo. All around, his firm of friends drink Johnnie Walker, play cards and occasionally pick up the guns that are lying around the place. On the mantelpiece are several soccer trophies which Čelo picked up playing for Sarajevo. The lads talk about footie a lot. Čelo is the top boy on his estate. A 'businessman' *and* a war hero.

Before the war, Čelo was in and out of jail. He claims to have shared a cell with the so-called 'leader of the Bosnian Serbs', Dr Radovan Karadžić (he's the strange-looking geezer with the Don King hairdo you see all the time on the news). Although the only inside information I was able to glean from Čelo's grinning face was that the Balkan psychiatrist-turned-psychotic had 'smelly feet'. No Pulitzer prizes here, I'm afraid.

When war broke out, Čelo organized the local lads into a defence militia 6,000-strong. He led from the front and soon became a local hero. As the Bosnians became better organized, the government and the army found the likes of Čelo too much of a rogue element. He lost his position to the men with stripes on their arms. In this strangely familiar sitting room, Čelo is asked whether he had become cynical of the government, and what he'd want from a political settlement. A boring question to a man who has lived a little. He ponders, looks up to the ceiling and gives a knowing smile. 'What I'd really like is to smoke some grass.'

In the window-boxes and gardens of Sarajevo, people have dug a small escape network: the cannabis plant flourishes. Alcohol is expensive and hard to come by. Those not turned on by the local cocktail of aftershave and orange juice seek their solace in home-grown weed. The only problem is a lack of rolling papers. Čelo's mates sit there hollowing out cigarettes, then filling them up again with grass. (As you picture this scene, do not weep into your magazine, but put your hand in your pocket and find a simple twelve pence for the newly formed 'Rizlas for Bosnia' campaign.)

Čelo reckons the best dope in town was to be found at the BB. Entirely coincidentally, this is a nightclub owned by Čelo. It rocked and raved into the small hours for nearly the whole war, but recently he had to close it down – the soldiers on the front weren't too happy with it. There may have been other reasons for the closure, but pressure from Muslim fundamentalists wasn't among them. Čelo is very secular. He could happily live in Peckham. 'I have no God but vice,' he states. I liked Čelo.

THE BLACK CROSS OF DESTINY

In days of peace in 1984, the eternal flame burned for the winter Olympiad. Dobrinja was the Olympic village, a place for nations to meet and compete. This suburb on the edge of Sarajevo is now a front-line battleground – surrounded on all sides, and saved from extinction only by a thin corridor and a lot of balls. It runs its own affairs. Food is cooked and distributed communally, all spare land is farmed and the rubbish is burned in pits.

In some old store rooms, they have built a hospital. The Palestinian doctor, Hajir, is not short of patients; he and his nurse have had not a single day of rest for the sixteen months of the siege. They struggle on, taking shrapnel from arms, bullets from chests, and limbs from children. The town's defenders make *Dad's Army* look like the SAS. Teenagers fight in Levi's jeans and CND T-shirts. Hearts in mouths, trainers on feet, they fight back. They kill not for land or religion, but for the survival of their suburb. They play a good tune on the guitar, too.

Jesus is seventeen and the bass player in the Dobrinja hardcore band, the Black Cross of Destiny. He struggles to play while standing on his crutches (a sniper's bullet got him in the leg). The band is made up of Muslim Croats and Serbs, but Jesus will tell you that it isn't interesting or important. Why should anybody want to know?

As there's no electricity, the band have to play on acoustic instruments. It's a bit hard for these Sex Pistols fans to thrash it out with no amps, but they sing of others' dreams: of the evils of nationalism; of death so near; and lives so wasted. While the drum thuds and the guitar twangs, they break into 'Knockin' on Heaven's Door'. It barely covers the sound of the nearby gunfire, yet out pops an old crow from the flats. 'Can't you boys stop making such a racket!' she says. Rock'n'roll, eh?

LEAVING THE TWENTIETH CENTURY

Towards the middle of this century, the Nazis took Jews, gypsies, gays and other 'undesirables' into shower-rooms. As they pumped in the gas, they played Wagner. Now the opera of death returns. The gas seeps in slower, and a merry dance continues to the straining vocals of Geneva, Brussels and New York. In the morgue in Sarajevo hospital lie the mutilated bodies of young soldiers who've given their life fighting for what they hold dear. The blackened corpses stink, as they've lain for days on the hills. They couldn't be brought back down earlier because the bastards kept firing. They die with their boots, shoes and trainers on, but they do not take them to the grave: the next soldier needs them. So their muddy, bloodied shoes are piled in the corner of the morgue. Some will inevitably return. The hospitals overfill daily with bloody victim after bloody victim. For every child in the news headlines, there are hundreds waiting to be evacuated, tied up by the bureaucracy of the United Nations: the world's DHSS.

Take a look at the UN flag, and you'll see it pictures the world from above the North Pole. They see the world in a different way, hovering above, slightly removed. They are an army of bureaucrats and traffic wardens – fine as individuals, fatal as a group. They live in their fenced-off buildings in a paranoid world where their only chance to meet the locals is through the slit window of an armoured personnel-carrier. While the UN on the ground spend their time saving face, not people, that nice Dr Owen sits around a table in Geneva and draws lines on maps, appeasing aggressors. His eyes tell you that his soul knows this is not the road to peace.

This is not a smart war; missiles don't fly through doors to exact locations. This is combat from the Dark Ages. Towns are besieged and shelled into annihilation. People defend street-to-street and house-to-house, and the whole sickening, stomach-churning conflict slashes its way forward. Trained soldiers fight civilians for the ruins of towns, and thousands upon thousands of refugees seek nothing but a future without death.

These places may have strange-sounding names, but they're not far away. The echoes of gunfire in history tell us that the virus of war knows no boundaries. The virus was there eighty years ago when our young men got slaughtered in the mud. It was there fifty years ago when bombs turned streets to ashes and homes into graves. Penguins in the South Atlantic know of war; so do the oil-soaked cormorants of the Gulf. Imagine war not in the abstract of rented videos or TV news, but as a real, living thing, relevant to your life. What would you fight and die for?

For years, our powers-that-be fought a Cold War against a hidden enemy. Hurrah! Hurrah! We won. Now we have something tangible to fight – a throat-slashing, library-burning, mosque-dozing, child-killing, land-grabbing, flag-waving nationalism! The people of Sarajevo are fighting and dying for a multi-ethnic culture. They are protecting their way of life and *our* way of life. As this century closes, ask, deep down, what all the bullets have been for. Think no longer of hypocrisy, of empires and grand ideals, but only of the good things this world can offer us. The fight is one for tolerance, good music, a nice drink, a decent smoke, the freedom to hang around in bars, to complain about the government, the chance to purchase a tracksuit of distinction, to see Manchester United win the European Cup, to watch bad MTV and play Nintendo.

It's complicated, it's a bitch, it can screw up badly, but when we hear the ghost of history calling and the strains of Wagner drowning out Sonic Youth, we must stop switching channels and fight the fools who fight for flags. Click.

The Face, September 1993

Sack the Manager!

Notes on the England football team's failure to qualify for the 1994 World Cup

Despite what they say, football is not a funny game. I mean, until last month the only claims to fame Norway had were suicide, alcoholism and an unhealthy interest in killing whales. As I watched England's glorious eleven get outplayed to such a degree that the losing 2–0 score-line was flattery, I was somehow void of any sense of humour. Scotland losing 5–0 to Portugal: now *that* was funny. But unfortunately I failed to see the joke in the fact that FIFA now rank us somewhere below the Pitcairn Islands, and the only chance we have of going to America next year is if San Marino beat Holland 45–nil.

I took an eager interest in the press calling for Graham Taylor's head. Personally, I'll stand for nothing less than a public stoning and his testicles pierced on Wembley's twin towers, but for some reason they can't even get him to resign. I mean, he'll escape with his life! What more does the fool want? Oh, I forgot, he's such a 'nice' man. He's so *normal* and he's had to put up with so much stick recently. My heart bleeds. He makes my country the laughing stock of the world, and he gets to keep his job. A bit like John Major, really. In fact a *lot* like John Major: I sense conspiracy.

Consider the facts. Both men were picked because they were non-controversial. Both men have made tactical errors that have made our country a laughing stock. Both of their teams lack imagination and flair. I'm sure I could go on, but if there is a conspiracy there I'm afraid it's wider than two boring men and some crap results. The 'English disease' is not a few bastard sons of Albion

smashing up bars abroad. It's on our doorsteps in plague proportions: complete managerial malaise. In sport and politics, creativ-
ity and flair are being replaced by the equivalent of the long-ball
game. Just kick it up the pitch and win at all cost. I suppose in that
respect the government is more like Arsenal than England.

Arsenal FC/the Tory Party: grind your opponents down, beat
them into submission, keep flair players on the back benches and
close all avenues of attack. Kick it up the field and give your
supporters the silver that keeps them happy. I suppose, in Arsenal's
defence, I have to say, at least they've got some black faces in their
squad, and they didn't arm the Khmer Rouge, but then again the
Government has never arrived at the Commons in shirts that look
like cat sick, so I guess they're even.

Quiz time. Why is Graham Taylor England manager? Why did
the nation that gave the world the Beatles give Europe Sonia? Why
are all our best architects working abroad? Why does the BBC pay
Noel Edmonds 10 million quid? Why is Mike Gatting in the England
cricket squad? How come some drunk suicidal Viking mammal-
murderers can piss on us at football, and why do we still have
thousands of our citizens homeless yet acres of empty office space?
Answers please to: E. I. Adiyo, We're-Out-the-Cup, Repossessed
House, Third World, UK. The most creative answers will be rejected
out of hand.

The Big Issue, June 1993

Sweaty Bollocks and Sterile Frolics

Something isn't stirring down below. In the deep recesses of gentlemen's underwear, a problem is occurring which could mark the end of the human race. I don't know how you go about counting sperm, but those who do have some pretty shocking news. Western men are currently producing half what they were fifty years ago. The number of those little tadpole things that journey on your average reproductive trip is now getting very low. So low, in fact, that if the trend continues, life's maiden voyage could soon have no passengers. By the year 2030, we could all be sterile.

The reason for this potential embryonic disaster is unclear. Scientists have come up with a number of reasons for this ongoing spermocide. One theory is that certain pollutants can mimic the action of the female hormone oestrogen, so 'feminizing' males – human and animal alike – and also raising the levels of disorders such as testicular and prostate cancer by interfering with masculine development in the womb and early life. Other scientists fear that low-level radiation may be taking its toll and point to speculative surveys on birth rates around nuclear-power plants.

But while the problem of pollutants is yet to be given wide coverage, and radioactive groins might pop up in the next century, we have a number of more suburban sperm assassins to deal with. The most talked about is tight jeans. You see, there was a time when a gentleman's tackle hung freely beneath a loincloth, tunic or baggy trouser. A combination of genital-hugging Y-fronts and tight shrink-to-fit jeans has shackled male equipment as never before. The boxer-short revolution of the Eighties may have arrived not a moment too soon. A swinging sperm is a happy sperm. The muscle-bound fitness freaks who currently parade in tight-fitting Lycra may actually be destroying the very manhood they wish to proclaim.

Unfortunately, they can't seek any solace down the pub. Alcohol is renowned for its withering effect on nights of passion. 'Brewer's droop' is a medical condition which has been recognized since the early days of civilization. Plato himself is believed to have had a couple of embarrassing moments with young nubiles and too much grape. However, the level of consumption today would have put even the most prominent Greek orgy-goer to shame. The testicles are not keen drinkers. As boozer begets boozer, the plums of life wilt into prunedom and so the sperm count dwindles.

Even for those non-drinking men who wear saggy briefs, the news is little better. Few men deny themselves the pleasure of a hot bath. We forget that hot running water is a recent visitor to most homes. Now that even the great unwashed can afford to bath at a reasonable temperature, we find that we have to spare a thought for our spunky friends. Apparently, gonads are just not meant to be lightly boiled for a quarter of an hour and then scrubbed with a loofah. The family jewels are precious things and are best kept at just below room temperature. Lobster-pink privates do not contribute to a productive love life.

Nature is dealing man a cruel blow. While a future without tight jeans and Y-fronts is hardly that bleak, the omission of alcohol and hot baths strikes at the very heart of our pleasures. The choice is one of bubble bath, beer and burgundy or cold showers, cots and crying kids. To many this would appear no choice at all. In reality, science could probably cook up test-tube *kinder* from even the lowliest of sperm. But the thought that we could be one of the last generations is actually quite fun.

At least that way we will all get a big retirement home. There won't even be young yobs around to mug us and laugh at our dress sense. Drop your pension plans immediately, and invest in Radox and Guinness.

Observer, 5 December 1993

Mickey Mouse – My Part in His Downfall

European idealism isn't exactly thick on the ground among British youth. I think most of us are scarred at an early age when we are sent off by the school on dubious 'cultural exchanges'. This usually involves staying in some boring suburb of Calais with a dodgy pen-pal who smokes all your Gauloises and sells you a sub-standard flick-knife for twice the going rate. By the end of the week any vision of Pan-Europeanism is lost when you puke up your third bottle of grenadine and vodka and are reliably informed you have disgraced both your school and your country. So fair play to Nicky Holloway for arranging the Dance Europe Weekender, where the youth of Europe could meet on relatively equal terms.

The weekender was an ambitious affair originally set to take place within the EuroDisney complex. An unreasonable insistence by the Disney organization that any party closed at 12, led the event to move ten miles down the road. Three thousand people from all around Europe made their way by car, coach and plane to see some of the best DJs and acts the Euro-dance scene has to offer, with the largest contingent arriving on the Friday evening on coaches from across the UK.

Friday did not start as planned. After spending a week decorating the three adjoining marquees, the organizers were visited by the French constabulary, fire officers and the local council official just as the event was about to open. These delightful people announced that the place was a fire hazard and the decorations had to come down, even though everything would have passed UK safety standards. Down came the clouds, the canvases and a very passable replica of the Berlin Wall. Officialdom arrived *en masse* again at 11.30, to swan around and check anything slightly creative had been crushed. These were tense times all around. Inside, the organizers were praying to whatever god they had that the chief of police would just sign the papers and sod off. Outside, it was pissing down on to the thousands of people who were waiting to get in and getting rightly narked.

But it seemed to kick all night when things finally went ahead. High-life from Paris mixed happily with low-life from Liverpool, and as moody Stone Island Scousers flirted with the French-model set, D-Ream brought the house down with their late-night set.

On Saturday we set off to the land of the mouse with the big ears. EuroDisney has been described, among other things, as 'a cultural Chernobyl' and 'corporate America's Vietnam'. And make no mistake, the place is a nightmare. But in the right frame of mind, this sort of bad dream can be a real laugh. You have to see it through the non-cynical eyes of a child, as an adventure.

For us, the *Alice in Wonderland* Maze was the top attraction. Its biggest plus point was you didn't have to queue for it, and you queue for *everything* at EuroDisney, including the urinals. The maze takes you on a surreal Lewis Carroll trip. Round and round you go, this way, that way, up, down – curiouser and curiouser it gets. You meet the giant hookah-smoking caterpillar on his mushroom and the grinning Cheshire cat with his spinning flowery eyes. It's all top fantasy action that should appeal to even the moodiest of club types. When you finally make your way out, it really does seem like it was all a dream.

Which is more than can be said of *Captain Eo*, which proved disturbingly real. A state-of-the-art 3D cinema movie starring every child's favourite star, Michael Jackson, this intergalactic eco-movie certainly had me convinced. Perhaps I was still under the weather from the night before, but I was *on* that spaceship! I ducked the meteorites and lasered the baddies, and if it wasn't for me, my close buddy, the mutant elephant-like Snorky, would have copped it from a cyberman. I like to think, in my own small way, that this great planet Earth now has something to thank me for.

Enthusiasm for EuroDisney was dampened by torrential rain all day, but Saturday night was something special. The sweet combination of Paul Oakenfold, M-People, Peter Tong and Inner City lifted spirits and got even the most knackered legs dancing. When Mr Holloway got on the mic to thank everybody in the early hours of Sunday morning, the crowd's enthusiastic reception was proof that the lad done well. Next year they're planning an event in the Vatican: book now to avoid disappointment.

The Face, November 1993

Men of the Nineties

I. NOUVEAU SOCCER MAN

On a Sunday afternoon you'll find Nouveau Soccer Man in front of the telly. He'll be watching the Italian Soccer on Channel 4, commenting knowledgeably on Sampadoria's away record. These thirtysomething creatures have ditched football's image of fighting, thuggery and lager in favour of a world of artistry, grace and, er, lager. To them, soccer's golden era was the late Sixties/early Seventies: they talk non-stop of Charlie George and Chopper Harris. In their wardrobe is a selection of vintage and foreign soccer shirts, and on their bookshelf is a copy of their bible, Nick Hornby's *Fever Pitch*. The way to this man's heart is in finding him a complete set of 72/73 Paninni soccer stickers and an original copy of 'Chirpy-Chirpy Cheep-Cheep' by Peter Osgood. A word of warning, though: don't try and be polite with Nouveau Soccer Man and ask him what his favourite match ever was, or who should be in the England squad. You could be in for a very long evening.

2. MAC MAN

Mac Man isn't, as some might believe, a latter-day version of a raincoated flasher. Yet he is, in some ways, just as frightening to meet. Mac Man owns a Macintosh computer. This will come up in conversation probably way before you find out his name, where he lives, or what he does. He has an Apple Mac and Apple Mac has him, submerged in a pixilated world of digital double-talk. His mood swings vary depending on how many clever little screen-saver programmes he's got, or what nasty little viruses he's picked up. And like an old radio ham or CB enthusiast, he'll bore you rigid with tales of how he's linked up with the meteorological department in Tokyo or a Siberian computer-chess club. Don't make the mistake of telling him you know nothing about computers – he'll only explain.

3. MENU MASTER MAN

This guy loves to cook. Italian, Chinese, Indian – Menu Master Man delivers prime cuisine to your eager lips. No chance of a Marmite sarnie round his house. It's out with the ciabatta bread, on with a thin layer of wild-mountain-elk's cheese. A quick whip under the grill, a flurry of herbs from his window-box, and before you know it you'll be snacking on some top-heavy creation, most of which ends up on the carpet or your nose. Menu Master Man is never happier than when he's got his chopper out. There he is, slicing away his baby spinach and ruching his red peppers. If all this flash gets to you, simply swap his virgin olive oil for a pound of lard and see him cry into his Albanian goulash.

4. FEMI-MAN

Is it possible to be a male feminist? Well, Femi-Man thinks so. He among all men seems to know the ways of woman. He shares their injustice, he sympathizes with their lot in life, and he feels, in a very real way, their monthly pain. His motives, however, are a bit questionable. Why is it he never seems to have a steady partner? Why is it he complains so vigorously about everything from Vinnie Jones to Wonderbra ads? With his Oxfam cardie and his little round specs, he may seem harmless, but isn't he just as predatory as other males? Probe a Femi-Man and you might just find a lounge lizard in a different skin. All these overtures to the opposite sex may well be another nasty little ploy to enter the pants of females. Don't ever dare to question his motives, though. At best he'll engage you in a four-hour debate on the rights of humankind, at worst you'll push him into another expensive course of therapy.

5. NINETIES BEATNIK

What do you do when you're a white, middle-class man with a good education and a promising career? Of course, you become a Nineties Beatnik and try and convince the world you're actually a black, working-class bongo-player from Brixton. It all starts when you notice that a friend, who probably works in the City, is growing a goatee beard and throwing words like 'man' and 'vibe' into any conversation. Before you know it, he's swapped his Paul Smith suit for a parka, has named his first child Shrub, and is telling you to 'loosen up' every time you meet him. He'll insist on a rambunctious display of cannabis-smoking every time you go around to his house, and will embarrass you thoroughly down your local by turning up in a series of preposterous hats. Don't worry too much, though. Give it five years, and the Nineties Beatnik will transform himself into Suburban Man and willingly pay large cash sums for all your old photos of him.

6. BITTER MAN

He's sad, he's depressed, he's had a little too much to drink and he's just put the Buzzcocks on the CD jukebox. He's *Bitter Man*! Bitter Man is bitter about life. Once a young stag around town, he now finds himself with two kids, a mortgage and a job he hates. He seeks comfort in immersing himself in popular culture, only to find further disillusionment when he realizes that he has absolutely nothing in common with today's youth. The songs don't have good lyrics. It's all on CDs. Whatever happened to rebellion? Bitter Man is an old punk rocker in *Q* clothing. His life is a series of drink sessions and musical nostalgia trips. Sad but true, as life goes on, his bitterness will grow. His children will look on dolefully when he tells tales of when he first saw the Sex Pistols, just as he looked on dolefully when his father told him about rationing and the Blitz. Yet Bitter Man has a purpose, for as long as he shrugs, sneers and moans, there will always be an England.

7. QUALITY OF LIFE MAN

During the Eighties Quality of Life Man was actually Entrepreneur Man, busily working his heart out for the fruits of the Thatcher revolution. He set up his own business, bought his own house and got the Sierra Cosworth of his dreams. But now he's had a sort of spiritual awakening. Did all his shares and profits bring him happiness? Did his sweat and tears improve his soul? Alas, they did not. Now he's finally realized that there's more to life than sales forecasts and fax machines. Unfortunately, the first ones to suffer are the children, as their fool of a father insists on spending quality time with them, telling his unfortunate offspring how wonderful walks in the country are and how they should do more things as a family. The tell-tale sign of a Quality of Life Man is a sudden interest in a new hobby. Books on painting, photography and wine-making may start to crop up everywhere, and you might notice him sifting through the Fair Isle sweaters at M&S. Things can get very scary when he starts talking of yoga and meditation, but keep your calm and hope it passes. Because it's all about quality of life, isn't it?

8. IRON MAN

Iron man is in his thirties and forties. A worm who's turned after years of oppression. He's seen the light. He has no truck with feminism. He thinks the world's gone mad and women are taking over. With the fire-and-brimstone zeal of a Baptist preacher, he'll reduce the entire female race to a selection of sluts, dykes, demons and whores. He'll slap you on the back, buy you a pint and call you 'mate'. He never used to do that, but that was before his wife left him. In fact, he never used to talk about rugby or football, but now he's constantly eager to bond away with talk of Will Carling or Ryan Giggs. He's a man's man, an Iron Man, a lone voice of sanity in a deranged, male-hating world. He's tough, he's strong, he speaks his mind. Give him four pints and he'll burst out crying and say he'd do anything if she just came back.

Publisher unknown

Make Love, Not War

In Belfast there's a children's song that goes to the tune of 'Tom Hart'. It's sung in the playgrounds and youth clubs, and it goes: *'When I was young and had no sense, I bought a flute for fifty pence, the only tune it could play, was fuck the Queen and the UDA!'* You alter the last line to *'the Pope and the IRA'*, depending on which school you go to. They like a good sing-song in Northern Ireland. From an early age you hear the drums and you learn the tunes. You sing of the sash or Bobby Sands and you burn bonfires or bang dustbin lids. Hatred starts young in Ulster.

Young people are always desperate for an identity. In Northern Ireland you're lucky enough to have one already prepared for you. It's hard for anyone growing up on the mainland to comprehend the turmoil of 'the Troubles'. Why do they do it? we ask. But the nearest most of us got to juvenile indoctrination was a spell in the Cubs. In Ulster you get a religion, marches, songs and even football teams all decided for you. You get an enemy and some hate figures, and if you're either naïve, vengeful or just plain violent, you get a gun to kill with. Most people I know behaved abominably on the simple presentation of a prefect badge.

Considering what the people of Ulster are born into, it's actually surprising there's not more trouble going. Perhaps politicians should take this on board a bit and start to think the unthinkable: there is no solution to the problems of Northern Ireland. This may not be as pessimistic as it sounds. Under the present circumstances, things are not going to change. As soon as people understand this, then perhaps then we can start to work out how to develop a situation where some sort of solution *is* possible.

We forget these people have very good reasons for hating each other. You pick up a lot of grudges in 600 years of fighting. You can't realistically turn around to orphans and widows and tell them to forgive and forget. The truth is, people don't *have* to like each other. The Scots still hate the English after all these years together. Yet they have somehow managed to reduce this hatred into a highly ritualized state whereby nobody gets killed any more. That the UVF and the IRA should spit each other's name is without question – what we want them to do is end the murder and heartache and save revenge for the rugby field.

Perhaps someone should tell the Unionists that we're all in the EEC now. The reality is that it makes little difference whether Dublin or London governs them – it's Brussels where the power lies. Perhaps someone should tell the Provos that their only real chance of a united Ireland is not in the bloody mess of 'the long war', but in the fact that if the present birth rate continues the Catholic population will soon be larger than the Protestant. It lies in teaching children not to *'fuck the Queen and the UDA'*, but each other. Sing of making love, not war, and your day will come.

The Big Issue, November 1993

Angola: Claret Thick Shake on a Ripped Cherry Pie

> 'Too many cocks prolong the night'
> – African proverb

Two cocks roam the village at night. They peck at each other and fight. They both want to be the top cock in the village. They fight so long that neither of them heralds the break of dawn with their crow. It remains dark, the cocks continue to fight. Dawn never comes. Too many cocks prolong the night.

You can always tell when a pop group is going under. The first clue is when they start to talk about wanting to be treated as *serious* artists. This is usually followed by a period of inter-band bitching and a prospective solo project from the lead singer. Sooner or later you notice that they've started to cancel gigs. Then the music papers will start to report on legal wrangles. A single will barely dent the top forty, the fans will stop screaming, then it's over, bust-up time. There's still money to be made, though. The merchandising heads where they don't know the news or just don't care. Perhaps they've never heard of them.

On arriving in Angola, I noticed several things. There was the heat, the smell, and the poverty. There were people everywhere buying, selling, trying to earn a living. There were soldiers without legs and kids without a home. You had burnt-out tanks on the roundabouts and cheesy music in the bars. But the thing I noticed most, the one thing that stuck in my head in the first few days, wasn't any of these. It was the fact that every second person seemed to be wearing a New Kids on the Block T-shirt. Poor old Africa, still paying for our mistakes.

> 'The two things they ask you first in Angola are, do you believe in God, and do you like Phil Collins?'
>
> Chris Simpson, BBC World Service

Saturday night in Luanda, the capital of war-stricken, famine-stricken Angola. There's a cool breeze which occasionally wafts something nasty your way. It carries the sound of the local kids' chants. Ancient tribal songs? Alluring folk melodies? Nah! *Teenage Mutant Ninja Turtles* is showing at the funfair. A carpet of eager little faces peer upwards to the giant video-projection screen. It's the only real attraction in a fair which resembles a Canvey Island gypsy site. There's a small dirt circuit around which you can ride a bicycle, there's a slide, a few table-football games and some spartan-looking refreshment stands. The movie is definitely the highlight. Every time a hero-in-a-half-shell gets in a fight, the kids punch their arms in the air chanting, 'Go Ninja! Go Ninja! Go Ninja!' At the back of the crowd, a pair of policemen swig from bottles of Super-Bock beer. They're smiling and joining in with the children's chant, 'Go Ninja! Go Ninja!' They love it, Ninja is *their* nickname.

With their black-leather jackets, twenty-four-hour sunglasses, Tardis-blue fatigues and twenty-hole boots, the Ninjas are top dudes on the streets of Angola. The Ninjas were formed when it was thought there might be peace. When the Soviets crumbled and South Africa liberalized, Angola stopped being a struggle between the Western-backed 'freedom fighters' of UNITA and Marxist ideologues of the MPLA government, and things started to change. There were to be elections, and both sides agreed to demobilize. Either cynically or sensibly, the government put many of its top MPLA troops into a special police force, 'the Ninjas'.

In October 1992, UN-monitored elections were held. José Eduardo dos Santos, the MPLA top cock, vied for votes with UNITA's top cock Jonas Savimbi. Santos called on the services of a Brazilian advertising agency. It groomed the man, promised a peaceful future and flooded the towns with 'I—MPLA' baseball hats and T-shirts. Savimbi, on the other hand, gave public slogans of 'New trousers in September' and private threats of war if he didn't win. He didn't win. There was war!

Bitter in defeat, the UNITA forces quickly mobilized, seizing vast areas of the country. This time it was for real. No Russians, no Cubans, no CIA or South Africans, precious little politics at all, just a whole lot of blood. They hated each other, they'd fought for years, they were different tribes and the gloves were off. In the capital, Luanda, the government was nervous. With the aid of the Ninjas, it armed its civilian supporters. In the days and weeks that followed, UNITA and the Ovimbudu tribe were driven from the city. That is, the ones that weren't beaten, butchered or burnt were driven from the city. Some say the Ninjas saved Luanda, others that they ended any hope of détente.

In the year that followed, the country resorted once again to its familiar pattern of civil war. The United Nations declared it the 'biggest war in the world'. A bloody stalemate was eventually arrived at, with UNITA holding the bulk of the country and its enormous mineral wealth while the government controlled Luanda and other large cities. Neither side could expect to make progress from these positions without a great deal more slaughter. Meanwhile, the bulk of the Angolan population carried on, eking out a living, in what passes as normality. There's a ceasefire now but it's a hard life: even the Ninjas earn only £9 a month. An orange juice in a Luanda hotel costs £4. A New Kids on the Block T-shirt is £2.

In Luanda, the war is an animal in the bush. It lives 100 miles away, it scares the children, abducts the young men and fills the hospital with casualties. With selective eyesight you can still see Luanda as the homely colonial town it once was. A few grandiose Portuguese buildings line one side of the palm-strewn bay. On the other a spit of sand, known as the Island, juts out to the Atlantic Ocean.

The Island is where Luanda's beach life is concentrated. It's like a cross between Miami and Moss-side. Bars, clubs and restaurants line the seafront where bikini-clad lovelies mingle with the hippo figures of the town's expat businessmen. With the sun in your eyes and a couple of gin and tonics down your neck, it's easy to erase the war. But even here, on the Island, the makeshift homes of the country's dispossessed fill every space that isn't occupied by sun-beds and volleyball nets. The years of war have taken the city's population from 40,000 to over 1.5 million. Space on the beach is at a premium.

At the Island's far end sits the pristine building of Barracuda Club. Every weekend it fills with the city's élite: Lebanese traders, Portuguese mafiosi, South African mercenaries, UN officials and other neo-colonialists. For all its problems, Angola is still a desirable destination for entrepreneurs. The place has natural resources that are the envy of most African nations: oil, diamonds, decent farmland and several large coffee-plantations. Half the problem in the Angolan war is that these men are not fighting over scraps. Jonas Savimbi and UNITA make an estimated $500 million from diamonds each year. With only his army to look after, Savimbi is a wealthy man. Even the government with its schools, roads and refugees to maintain still finds a bit of spare cash for new Audis to be imported for its ministers.

Angola is a story of waste. Money, years and lives all thrown away. When the fascists fell in Portugal in 1975, their colonial states broke free, and those who'd been struggling for independence in Angola now struggled among themselves. With the aid of the Cubans and sympathetic African countries, the Communist MPLA took power. Backed by South African troops and large wads of CIA cash, the southern-based UNITA battled for the top spot. For years Savimbi was the darling of the Western right wing. Along with the Contras in Nicaragua and Renamo in Mozambique, these 'freedom fighters' were praised and courted by the Commie-bashers. Ronnie Reagan and Lady Thatcher regularly shook the tin for them. I mean, all they wanted was free and fair elections.

The *Daily Telegraph* used to run full-page adverts in support of UNITA. Conservative students spent time fund-raising on its behalf. Where are these people now? Now the elections they fought for have come and gone. Where is Jonas Savimbi, the hero of democracy? He's in the bush somewhere counting the cash. His old supporters here now tell us how *misguided* aid is. Too true. If their chums hadn't put their hands in their pockets in the first place, how many lives could have been saved?

The citizens of Angola see little of their country's riches. The economy has gone haywire. On every Luandan street corner, gangs of female money-changers wave fat wads of 'kwanzas' in the air. With annual inflation running at over 1,200 per cent, the exchange rate changes significantly in a few days. Off the main Kinaxiyi Square, in the shadow of the huge plinth with an old tank on it that passes as a civic sculpture, Rita Armando and Albertina Juade make a living as currency-dealers. The ladies check all dollars carefully. Due to extensive forgeries, newer-dated notes receive a better rate than old ones, and anything marked 1988 is a complete no-no. The going rate is now 100,000 Kwz to the dollar. In this former socialist republic, everyone really *is* a millionaire.

Luanda is not really a pretty place. With the exception of possibly Sheffield, few large cities in the world can match its dreary, decaying architecture. Luckily, on Saturday, and most of Sunday, the focus of the town shifts to its edges. On the distant reaches of Luanda Bay, a mother of a market stretches as far as the eye. Half a million people gather to buy, sell, barter and steal. It's like a flattened department store – you can walk through areas the size of a football pitch all devoted solely to the sale of soap, charcoal or garlic. Among the crumbling soil of ochre cliffs, the social strata stretch before you. At the top end, among the fridges and television sets, hard currency changes hands between shell-suited ragga-style wideboys.

At the other, young boys sell plastic bags made from rice sacks. The youngest, who have nothing, offer to sing love songs for pennies.

The smart time to go to the market is in the morning while the police are still *compos mentis*. By afternoon, drink and dope take their toll and 'indiscipline' breaks out. You often hear indiscipline as the day wears on. Even though the war is miles away, gunfire is far from uncommon. Alcohol and firearms don't really mix. They say if you have a gun you must be prepared to use it. And if you've had six bottles of Super-Bock and a boring day, you most certainly are.

Many of the city's wounded end up at the Josina Machel Hospital. With its crumbling, overcrowded wards and lack of basic medicines, victims find little comfort there. In scenes of Crimean squalor, nurses make the best of it. One of the most common operations is the amputation of limbs.

There are *a lot* of landmines in Angola. Estimates range from one to nine million, the only concrete statistic being that the vast majority of victims are civilian. Kids out playing, women collecting firewood, all take that one wrong step that lands them here in hell. The lucky ones lose half a leg and have relatives locally. Those less fortunate find themselves with bloodied stubs where their legs were and nobody to feed or look after them.

It is not uncommon for individuals to discharge themselves from the hospital to go in search of food. Hands drag their legless torsos across the floor and out of the door, slow-motion runaways desperate for a future. A new hospital was built with aid money from Europe. Though well-stocked at the time, it has yet to open. Aid officials claim the government insisted that large sums had to be paid for its upkeep. Meanwhile, more casualties arrive on transport planes. They have escaped from the besieged cities of the inland. For them the Josina Machel may be unsanitary and under-resourced, but at least it ain't being shelled.

Menongue lies in the south-east of the country. This sleepy sprawl of villas and huts is typical of Angola's beleaguered towns and cities: cut off by the war, isolated for months, opened up only by the war's temporary stalemate. Aid flights have now been arriving sporadically for the last few months. There are still cases of severe malnutrition and, despite a nominal ceasefire, young soldiers regularly return from the front riddled with bullets and shrapnel. Some of them are really young, press-ganged from the city and sent straight to the front.

When you pass your local McDonald's, look at the young lads who hang out there. Imagine the police pulling up, sticking all of them in a van at gunpoint, then sending them off to fight and die. I'd pass these boy soldiers all the time, they'd smile and pose with their weapons: fifteen-year-old kids forced to play soldiers for real, by commanders younger than I am, in a war older than us all. In Menongue, there was a boy called Malues. He had recently arrived from the front, having been shot twice and hit by a mortar. I couldn't work out just how long he had left – each groan and twitch seemed like his last. His face was blown apart, but somehow blood glued his whole body together, like a claret thick shake on a ripped cherry pie.

It's not just the boys who get old before their time. Maria Mbango should be enjoying life as a young mother. Instead she nurses her malnourished baby in an intensive-feeding centre. Her husband and most of her family are dead but 'things are better now', she says, knowing her child now has some chance of survival. 'When the fighting was fierce we had to hide in holes in the ground. We were afraid of being hit by bullets or bombs. All we could eat was insects.' It's hard comprehending what people like Maria have gone through. There were a few sad souls in Blighty who thought the world had ended when the Smiths broke up.

There are still few dependable resources in Menongue. Aid organizations work together in the town. Their programmes do their best to feed the hungry and treat the sick, but the shadow of the war means all effort could be wasted if the shelling starts, the planes stop and the war drips onwards. The flights to towns like Menongue are always on the dodgy side. They have to be negotiated with the commanders on the ground and any resumption of fighting, no matter how trivial, means their immediate suspension. Unauthorized aid planes have been shot at by both sides. In one notorious incident, a plane was holed by a ground-to-air missile. The Russian pilot miraculously managed to land the plane safely in the bush. On leaving it, he and two crew mates were blown up by a landmine.

Recently, the organization Care has set up a project in the town with part-funding from the British Overseas Development Organization. The aid is to form a series of local-run feeding centres and health posts throughout the town. Aid workers will tell you that the Angolans are the most industrious people they've worked with. It can't be a bad job. Preventing wide-scale famine must be quite rewarding.

The irony is that world donations for Angola have reached only half of what the UN appealed for. Governments apparently want more stick legs and bloated bellies before they see fit to dish out. Without further donations, they surely will. News from areas of war and famine inevitably focuses on the extremes. You can't tug the heart strings on prime time with pictures of *half*-starving kids. In Angola the extremes exist, yet they are at the top of a vast population who are being held tenuously from the brink.

Angola. Day 17. A Luanda guest-house. I'm trying to put the pieces together. I woke this evening after a solid thirty hours of sleep. I was smothered in vomit and had crapped myself. I took my Italia '90 'No Alla Violenza' T-shirt from my bag and mopped up the mess. Zed (the photographer who accompanied me) lies shivering in the bed opposite me. His face is cut, one of his teeth is missing, blood is dripping from his mouth. He has malaria and is delirious. He keeps blacking out in the bathroom, letting his body smash on to the porcelain. I was shot at by a policeman last night. Except it wasn't last night, it was the night before. This place sucks.

By the end of my trip I was tired, ill and edgy. A whining white boy with a ticket home. I hated the stupid bloody war and the stupid bloody people who caused it. And yet, for a people so brutalized, everyone seemed unnervingly tolerant of moaning scum such as I. They talked seldom of war. Some still had a reassuring optimism about the future. To get a life, I visited the naval dock in Luanda Bay where the ship *Mediterranean Sea* is moored. It contains a bar, restaurant and disco as well as the 200-berth Westminster Hotel. The locals nickname it 'The Love Boat' on account of various extramarital bonking sessions that supposedly go on there.

The Love Boat was brought to Luanda by Greek shipping tycoon Georges Doussopoules. 'The government asked me to bring it here during the elections. There weren't enough good hotels in town so I brought this ship out to house the UN monitors and officials. Pik Botha stayed here!' explains the smiling Georges, now the country's honorary Greek consul. The ship is his act of faith. 'When the war started people said I should set sail, but I stayed. I like it here, I like the people.'

For all its problems, there's still fun to be had in Angola. The on-deck Saturday-night disco is the top event in town for those with the money. Those without the cash to boogie at the Love Boat go to the downtown sleaze bars and dance to Phil Collins. Those who stay at home hope the electricity stays on long enough to watch the TV. If a recent shock-horror newspaper survey is to be believed, videos are busy corrupting their nation, too. 'Over 96 per cent of videos rented are pornographic,' screamed the Sunday edition of *Journal d'Angola* in an article that would put the *Sunday Sport* to shame. Those citizens who aren't tuned to depravity will usually be engrossed in their other national pastime: basketball.

In Angola basketball is *the* popular sport. Hoops are everywhere, youngsters sport shirts with the Chicago Bulls logo, and to be tall is to be treasured. The national side have been African champions on two occasions, and when they beat Kenya last November the celebrations lasted all night. In the Barcelona Olympics they were pitted against – and outplayed by – the multimillion-dollar American 'dream team'.

Bitter-sweet Angola. Makes you sad, makes you sick. Along with their basketball team, they'd love the opportunity to compete with the world on an equal footing. And the sad truth is, they probably could. If the war ends, if the country survives, they can win. If only the two cocks could sort it out, peace and prosperity could dawn. Slam-dunk.

The Face, March 1994

1994

House music is dead, but the beat pumps on oblivious. 'Drugs are just the biscuits on every table,' says new Britpop star Brett Anderson of Suede.

The wife leaves for Mexico with the best friend. After bingeing on drugs, alcohol and casual sex, our young man sets off to El Salvador for the elections. In a refugee camp for those who fled the civil war, he sets up a rave.

Later in the year, he puts on a concert in Sarajevo using local bands. The city is completely under siege, but he manages to get out.

He attends festivals of excess: Berlin's Love Parade, Glastonbury, the riot against the Criminal Justice Bill in Hyde Park.

He flirts with suicide again, and ends up being treated in hospital.

Kurt Copped Out and It Means Nothing

(Notes on the April 1994 suicide of Nirvana's Kurt Cobain)

The first time, the coma in Roma, we all got jollied up. 'Will this mean anything if he pops it?' we thought. And, after three months to think about it, we all decided yes. Second time lucky.

Perhaps if I lived in the States, I could understand it more. They do things by generations there: Baby Boomers, Blanks, Generation Xers, blah, blah. Bye-bye Brett Easton Ellis, hello Douglas Coupland, 'the voice of his generation', with another magazine article parading as a book. Hello Slacker Kurt, 'the sound of a generation'. Oh, sorry, boom-boom, bye-bye. Like, everyone is really sad. Frances Bean, that's sad. But less sad than England's exit from the World Cup.

As it's officially dead now, ask yourself what grunge has ever done for you. I mean, apart from the odd good gig, a nice rock-band soap opera and one classic album?

Kurt was good at being a rock star, but he'd had enough lessons. *Nevermind* was great in a kind of Killing Joke/Police type-of-way. But then they went and decided they wanted to be all 'experimental'. They were scared. They'd had a huge, successful album, and shat themselves because they didn't think they could follow it up. Hence we were left with *In Utero*, which, like Kurt's suicide, was one big cop-out.

If Kurt 'nice guy/loving father/good personal friend' Cobain's death means anything, it's lost on me. A sad, messy suicide – let's hope it buries another bozo generation as blank as the one before.

The Idler, April–May 1994

El Salvador: The Story of a Gun

'When history cannot be written with a pen, it must be written with a gun' – Farabundo Martí, 1932

This is the story of a gun. A sleek, sexy Colt AR-15, the standard United States service weapon in the Sixties. When the GIs were fighting in Vietnam, they were pulling the trigger of this baby. Out in the jungles, with napalm in their nostrils and Agent Orange in their nervous system, the forces of democracy sent Charlie to his grave. Yet Rambo just wasn't tough enough and Charlie fought back. Soon the Vietcong were in Saigon and, as the flocks of US helicopters fled, guns got left behind. Ho Chi Minh had new hardware.

A few of these guns made their way to the killing fields of Cambodia, but most stayed with Vietnam's new regime. This fledgling Commie country was not planning any more wars, so it shipped its spoils to brothers-in-arms. The PLO in southern Lebanon received a new toy to shoot Israelis with. Now, the Israelis are not known for their tolerance when it comes to being shot at. They wanted teeth for teeth, eyes for eyes, and the best part of Lebanon as a 'security zone'. In 1982 Israel invaded and captured southern Lebanon, driving the PLO into boom-town Beirut and seizing a large part of its weaponry. As the Israelis already had lots of nice guns, they left the Colt AR-15 assault rifles in store. There they lay redundant until somebody Stateside had a 'neat' idea.

Ronald Reagan did not like Commies. Commies under Reagan were broadly defined: the Women's Institute, Bruce Springsteen, the Pope, that sort of thing. When some college students and farmers decided that they didn't like a corrupt, murderous dictator ruling their country, they did not count on becoming an ex-film star's leading bad guys. But the Sandinista revolution in Nicaragua was treated as virtual declaration of war on American foreign policy. 'Not in my back yard,' said Reagan, somehow forgetting they didn't actually own Central America. Well, not *legally*, anyway. So the Reagan administration sent the CIA and the military in to Honduras to supply and train a Contra army to restore Nicaragua to, er, 'peace and democracy'. Right.

But things got tough for Reagan's mission. The American Congress didn't like the idea of an unofficial war being declared. The Contras had a nasty habit of blowing up school buses, decapitating farmers and raping nuns. Things started to get even more embarrassing when the US was found guilty by the United Nations of violating a sovereign nation by mining its ports. Without the backing of Congress, the Reagan administration had to think of more surreptitious ways of arming their fighters. It was about this time that Colonel Oliver North had the 'neat' idea of funding the Contras by selling arms to Iran.

With wads of dodgy Iranian cash to spend on untraceable weapons, the CIA got in touch with its friends in the Israeli Mossad. Colt AR-15s were dusted down and sent to Southern Honduras. There they were used by the Contras to shoot the Sandinistas – and anything else that moved. Yet, despite the scale of their backing, the Contras were not the most motivated guerrilla force in the world. Many were captured, and whole battalions simply defected. Some Contras had neat ideas of their own. They'd get tooled up in Southern Honduras, then flog their weapons to the FMLN guerrillas in neighbouring El Salvador.

In El Salvador the guerrilla armies of the FMLN (Frenté Farabundo Martí para la Liberacion Nacional) were fighting one of the world's most brutal military regimes. They needed arms and, keen to make a buck, the Contras obliged. Colt AR-15s became a standard service rifle amongst the left-wing guerrillas of the FMLN.

As the years wore on it became clear to El Salvador's military and government that they could not defeat the guerrillas. Despite funding by the United States worth $1,000 a year to each and every Salvadorian. Despite having its army officers trained at West Point. Despite its death squads and their regime of murderous terror. Despite complete air superiority. Despite all of this, they just couldn't win. They sued for peace, and agreement was reached. This year they held elections.

As El Salvador now moves in to peace, the guns have a new purpose. To raise funds for their election campaign, the cheeky FMLN sold mounted wall-plaques. Upon them a rifle, the Colt AR-15. A gun with a story of Cold War tensions, imperialist struggles, revolutions and counter-revolutions, deceit, deals and above all death. The story of a gun, the story of El Salvador!

It's a funny place, El Salvador. You're always in sight of a volcano. You can be frolicking in a pine forest, smooching on a sandy beach or sweating in the heart of the city, but always the pert nipple of a volcano lies somewhere on the horizon. The size of Wales with a population of 5.6 million and a history as turbulent as its landscape, El Salvador is a country of extremes. Bang in the heart of Central America, it's where the wealth and affluence of the first world meets the third world head-on. I took a trip there to be an observer at the country's first all-party elections. As it turned out, lava flowed.

Sitting in the Wendy's on San Salvador's Bulevar los Héroes, supping on a Frostie, tucking in to a Big Bacon Classic, you could happily convince yourself you were in a suburb in California. Skaters zoom by, rich kids snog and drink beer in the back of pick-ups, baseball-hatted bozos flick fries at each other. Nirvana blares from car stereos. You can even hang out in one of the biggest malls in Latin America. It's not a bad life – assuming, that is, you can afford it. El Salvador is owned by about 200 families, and 95 per cent of the land is in their hands. This is actually an improvement on the old oligarchy, which consisted of only fourteen families who were descendants of the Spanish conquistadors.

The conquistadors were an early version of the Chelsea Headhunters. They used swords instead of Stanley knives, ran the Mayan Indians out of town and slept with all the women who stayed. As a result of this post-conquest bonking binge, El Salvador has few indigenous people left. Over 90 per cent of Salvadoreans are a half-Indian/half-Spanish Mestizo crossover. The legacy of the conquistadors left centuries of extreme inequality. But, if you're supping on a shake at Wendy's, what do you care?

Venture a few miles downtown, and you're faced with shanty sprawls and squalor equal to that of Haiti or Calcutta. The poor outnumber the rich by over ninety to one. At best they live in the sort of buildings you might get housing the toilets in a one-star French campsite. At worst they live, and die, in the gutter. The country has one of the highest infant-mortality rates in the world, and nearly half its children suffer from malnutrition. For years the poor were controlled by a tried-and-tested method: when they got uppity, they were killed. In 1932 an uprising of peasants, led by the Central American communist Augustin Farabundo Martí, fought for land reforms. The result was a military crackdown which led to the massacre of 30,000 people. Martí faced the firing squad. Yet despite being the instigator of what must be one of the most unsuccessful revolutions in the world, years later his name was revived by the guerrillas of the FMLN, the Farabundo Martí National Liberation Front.

The FMLN was basically a coalition of five different guerrilla groups formed to fight for the poor, land, democracy, revenge, the right to wear a nice red bandanna and all the other things guerrilla groups fight for. They ranged politically from the shining path of Mao to the grey roads of Owenite social democracy. After struggling against repression in the Sixties and Seventies, they united in all-out war in 1980 when one priest too many copped it.

The cleric in question was Monsignor Oscar Romero, an initially conservative Catholic priest who became politicized by liberation theology, the murder of friends and the impoverished lot of his flock. He remembered that tactless bit in the Bible about it being easier for a camel to get through the eye of a needle than for a rich man to enter the gates of heaven. He preached that exploitative systems should be changed, and that God didn't intend the poor to go without hamburgers. It was a popular message that won him the Nobel Peace Prize and got him murdered by death squads. The man behind the killing was a crater-faced military chief called Roberto D'Aubuisson.

D'Aubuisson has another great claim to fame. He was the founder of the National Republican Alliance Party (Arena), a right-wing nationalist party that would make Norman Tebbit or Bob Dole look like Body Shop sales assistants. They were too right-wing even for the CIA, which spent the bulk of the Eighties not only fighting the guerrillas but also trying to ensure that Arena didn't get into power. Reagan and Bush preferred their installed puppet government of 'Christian Democrats', but in March 1989 Arena gained power. As a spokesman for the party told me, 'I think the CIA did us a favour. The people saw we were anti-Yankee *and* anti-communist. The only *true* Salvadorian party.'

Eight months after Arena gained power, the FMLN launched its biggest offensive. After nine years in the mountains, its forces moved into the Sheraton hotel and the rich suburbs of San Salvador. Arena did not like revolutionaries in their swimming pools, so peace talks were entered into. A range of issues were settled, land reforms were offered, a new civil police was to be set up to replace the hated Guardia Nacional, all-party elections were to be held, and a 'truth commission' was set up to investigate abuses of human rights and the activities of the death squads. On 16 January 1992, a peace accord was signed. Heady stuff, but, despite gains which would have been unthinkable years ago, things haven't gone exactly swimmingly since then.

When the results of the commission were published, hundreds

of military commanders, politicians, judges and other thugs were identified by name in connection with atrocities. Of the hundreds of murders and massacres which took place during the war, less than 5 per cent were attributed to the FMLN. The extermination of an entire village and over 1,000 inhabitants in El Mozate in 1981 and the murder of six Jesuit priests in a San Salvador University in 1989 were the work of the military's infamous Atacatl battalion. I visited El Mozate, where only a small silhouette marks the spot where the village once stood. I stopped by at the university where the priests had died, and saw pictures of their hideous slaughter. It was sickening, even more so when I learned that, to help the country's post-war 'healing process', six days after the Truth Commission's report was published, the governing Arena party declared a complete amnesty for all concerned. Many of the Atacatl battalion's murderous commanders now have cushy embassy jobs around the world. Arena: nice people to do business with.

The elections I witnessed this March were billed as 'the elections of the century'. For the first time, the FMLN was allowed to stand as a legal political party. But the new party did have some reservations about just how 'free and fair' the elections were going to be. And it wasn't just being picky. In the last year and a half, over twenty-six FMLN leaders have fallen victim to re-emerging death squads. The fear this created prevented a lot of civilian candidates from standing for election. There had also been big problems in registering people to vote. The cock-up and conspiracy theories appear to combine in El Salvador.

Thousands had not received their voting cards. Polling stations had been moved by 30 miles in some 'sensitive' areas. Wads of ballot papers had been turning up in mysterious places, and it was discovered they were being printed by a company owned by an obviously neutral former death-squad general. It had been 'decided' that those who reached the age of eighteen after October 1993 could not vote (the blind were excluded, too, for the bizarre reason that they couldn't be guaranteed a secret ballot). The FMLN's reservations were real. They turned out to be the chronicle of a farce foretold. Think of this in the context of the upcoming domestic council elections, and ponder your rights.

I spent polling day in San Miguel, a middling town in the country's east with housing that looked straight out of a *Thunderbirds* set. They'd sealed off the main high street and lined it with a couple of hundred school desks. Each desk was allocated a letter of the alphabet and a list of registered voters. To vote, you had to have a registered-voter card with your name on it. To get one of these, you had to provide a birth certificate and fill out several forms. Birth certificates were 'unavailable' to a lot of people. So, too, was form-filling: 30 per cent of the population are illiterate. Still, those who'd applied for voting cards and actually received them (over 600,000 did not) trundled up on polling day to find the right desk. This itself was quite an achievement in an overcrowded street full of coconut- and fizzy-drink sellers. Once you'd found your desk, the real fun began. You checked that your name was on the computer list taped to the wall, tree or donkey behind the voting table. Many found their names missing and walked their weary way home again. But if you were lucky enough to be at the right table *and* on the list, you then had the privilege of queuing up to three hours to vote.

Voting consisted of marking a ballot paper on a table about as private as the centre spot at Wembley, then placing your 'secret' vote into the safe confines of a brightly coloured cardboard box wrapped in masking tape. Arena deputies in sub-Texas cowboy garb moved through the crowds taking the odd photo of 'subversives' and giving all the welcoming appeal of the BNP at a bhangra night.

Ballot boxes were stuffed with extra ballot papers. Many papers were deliberately spoiled. The dead voted, as did Nicaraguan immigrants and several six-year-olds. It was hardly a huge surprise to all concerned, then, when Arena ended up victorious. Well, semi-victorious. Despite everything, they didn't even get the majority required to gain the presidency. A week later I attended a protest rally with the Frenté Youth (the FMLN juniors). Decked head to toe in red, they led a passionate attack on the Hotel El Presidente, where the votes were being counted. Well, they danced outside while the police stood dolefully by. The soundtrack was the tuneful rebel classic 'Two Ladies, One Road', the theme tune to a local soap opera about a truck driver with two wives. Why they were playing this wasn't clear, but their chant was: 'Elections of the Century? Ha! Ha! Ha!'

El Salvador is a young country – over 60 per cent of the population is under the age of twenty-five. The new civil police have an average age of twenty. Young people played a large part in the war. Many were conscripted into the military, and others joined the guerrillas. In the FMLN's 1989 offensive, the majority of its urban commandos were from the city's secondary schools. Some guerrillas were really young. The Frenté youth told me the story of Los Samuelitos, a brigade led by a thirteen-year-old called Samuel. Before his death he led several daring raids, including an attack on an airforce base which destroyed three jet fighters. At that age, vandalizing telephone boxes was the nearest anyone I knew got to attacking the power of the state.

The Frenté Youth are from a variety of backgrounds. Some were ex-combatants or urban commandos, others had lost parents or siblings to the death squads. The majority just wanted to help, and this seemed like a fun club. As political movements go, the Frenté Youth is pretty unique, a kind of *Double Deckers* gang with a few Kalashnikovs thrown in. They pushed a special youth platform for the election, getting each of the parties to support better vocational training, decent education, sports facilities and other youth-related issues. They also organized concerts, rallies and the painting of propaganda murals on every blank bit of wall available.

On top of the direct political activity, they even find time to do some social work with the city's huge gang population, acting as negotiators during feuds, putting on buses for trips to the beach and supplying the kit to set up soccer teams. Whether the last idea is a good one is debatable – El Salvador is one of that select group of nations who've actually gone to war over football. (It started in 1969 after a World Cup qualifying match with Honduras. Crowd trouble, spurred on by economic and immigration problems, led to the two countries kicking off for 100 hours of full-scale rucking with a war that left even Jimmy Hill speechless.)

Gangs have been big in El Salvador for quite a while now. They started as highschool gangs in the early Eighties, extended to neighbourhood gangs, and now are a fully fledged menace to society. You join by getting beaten up for thirteen seconds by the rest of the gang. If you struggle or scream, they give you another pummelling, and so on. This initiation gives you the right to wear a really long soulboy-type belt and get a dinky tattoo.

The big push into major-league gangsters came three years ago with the end of the war. Thousands of refugees returned from exile in Los Angeles, where they'd been hangin' with the homeboys for a few years. Most of the young bucks had received some sort of military training before they'd gone to sunny California and had quite a fearsome reputation, even by LA standards. There they'd joined either the Latino 18s, named after 18th Street, or the hardcore MSs – *Maras Salvaduchas*, Salvadorian Gang. Translated literally, *maras* means 'killer ants'. Returning to San Salvador with its extreme poverty, zero job opportunities and hordes of weapons, the LA gangsters shaped the city into minor war zone. Gangs either got affiliated to the MS or 18s. Raiders caps and Nikes were imported *en masse*.

The Salvadorian gangs remind you more of New York in the Fifties or Glasgow in the Sixties than modern LA. One whistle down a street and your fellow gang members will pop their heads round the corner, Wanderers-style. These are local gangs who are known by the whole street. They even profess to stop crime in their area. I guess that means crime by anyone *else* in their area. There are other differences to their LA brothers. These guys don't just have

Uzis – the war has left them AK-47s, AR-15s, mortars and the odd surface-to-air missile. Suffice to say they could probably invade Belgium without too many problems.

Talking to the gangs, it becomes apparent that the gang is *all* they've got. Even a blossoming career on the McDonald's litter patrol is not open to them. This is a country where kids sniff glue and smoke spliff, not because they're bored or because they're rebels, but because they're hungry. Many can't attend school because they have to work to feed their families. Welfare is virtually non-existent. When you ask what can be done to help, the answers are touching in the extreme. They dream of sports facilities, parks and youth clubs. They want to be living *The Wonder Years*, not *Boyz N the Hood*.

I was introduced to the gangs by a guy called Crazy Face. An ex-hoodlum turned gang go-between for the Frenté Youth, he looked a bit like a brown version of James Cagney in *Angels with Dirty Faces*. After hanging with the gangs for a while, I naïvely asked him if there were ever any drive-by shootings like in the States. 'Drive-by shootings? What do you mean? We're too poor to have cars. We have to do them from a bus!' he joked. At least, I thought he joked.

Apart from a couple of pretend gangs in the rich part of town and one from the area where the old Guardia Nacional lived, most gangs are left-leaning. The gangs are poor, and FMLN guerrillas fought for the poor, so the gangs say respect due. During the war, the death squads didn't actually endear themselves to the gangs by taking out a few members whenever there was any trouble. While you can't pretend any of them have real political savvy, many of them sport Che Guevara shirts or badges. Crazy Face saw Che as a kind of Latino Malcolm X. Except Che didn't just talk revolution, he fought and died for it.

The Salvadorian music scene is none too hot. The local music is like a cross between ska and your average Eurovision Song Contest entry. There was one really catchy tune. It was on the radio all the time. I kept humming it everywhere I went. It turned out to be the Arena rallying tune. '*El Salvador shall be the place where we bury the reds in their tomb!*' Oops! The nearest I got to dance-floor action was the third birthday party for the village of La Nueva Espranza, a dustbowl in a former cotton field settled by homeless refugees. There was nothing there but shacks and mud, but apparently this is one of the better ones. Most places still have tents. For their celebrations they had a Communion where they all sang Simon and Garfunkel's 'Sound of Silence'. Later they turned the altar into a sound system blaring out 2 Unlimited into the early hours. Every so often, the DJ would get on the mic to remind everyone to put their safety catches on.

Easter weekend, El Zonte surf beach (there's amazing surf in El Sal). A guy walks on the sand, leaving only three toe impressions. His name is Mario. He lost his other toes when a mortar exploded. There are cigarette burns and scars on his back, from when he was captured and tortured. He was a guerrilla in the FMLN. He told me about his brother, who was shot by the police and hanged on a tree. And his ninety-two-year-old grandfather, who complained and was also shot. 'I'm not worried about their deaths,' he says. 'They gave their lives for the people. If it takes another hundred years, the people will still win in the end, because we are not scared of death. I gave my toes for the people,' he chirps, without a trace of irony.

The concept of 'the people' was pretty alien to me. Thatcher told us that there was no such thing as society, no such thing as 'the people'. Only ever the individual, the single soul. Yet 'the people' of El Salvador taught me a lesson, giving me an insight in what being left-wing is really about. It's about empowerment of the people. It's about the right to vote, the right to a good education, to a job, decent health care and a nice shirt for the weekend. It's about hundreds of years of struggling, fighting and dying so the generations after have a better life. They're a very poetic lot, these Latinos. One young idealist told me, 'The future is ours. Because the future is in loving the oppressed, not hating the oppressor.'

On my last day in El Salvador, I was out painting murals with the Frenté Youth. 'People First' was the message we were taking to the streets. A guy went past and recognized me. He was going to the hospital – Crazy Face had been shot. I went along to see Crazy Face sitting in a squalid waiting room with a drip in his arm. He was covered with blood but smiling a cheeky smile. He'd been victim of a drive-by bussing. A rival gang had been trying to kill him for a long time. They would try again soon. Two of his mates weren't so lucky, and were fighting for their lives in intensive care.

Crazy Face was shot because he was poor and dumb by another poor dumb person. People don't have to be poor and dumb. Ideas of change can start right now. They start with small gestures. On a door at one of the FMLN's offices I visited was a tatty paper sign. Roughly translated it read, 'Our right to govern will be determined by how clean we keep our toilets'. Viva la Revolution.

The Face, May 1994

Berlin: Of Love and Lycra

I can now confirm that, No no, No no no no, No no no no, There's no limits. None at all, bar overdose. The acid/house/rave/techno scene has spanned the globe and snatched the souls of the world's reckless. It reaches every corner of what we call the West and happily entertains those in the developing world who are at economic liberty to indulge in such follies. Apolitical, agnostic and asexual, this particular brand of hedonism has taken modern computers and pharmaceuticals, then plonked them together with dances and beats as old as our species. And what a great success it's all been. Now it even has its own annual festival. The Berlin Love Parade draws huge crowds from all over Europe and beyond. It's a celebration of house music, of peace, love and tolerance. It's a coming-together of the world's youth in a spirit of, er, togetherness. It's also a damned good excuse to dance and take lots of drugs.

For years the town of Munich has paid host to regular beer festivals. People gather from this planet's furthest corners all to celebrate the old god alcohol. Now the city of Berlin has provided a rival session for the young. Here, in the first weekend in July, the Love Parade pays homage to the new idol ecstasy. At only six years old, it is a pretty young tradition. But with over 100,000 people in attendance this year, it's a calendar date that looks likely to have some longevity. This much fun doesn't disappear overnight.

The Love Parade was one of those six-in-the-morning ideas, an abstract concept set up by the city's camp club crowd. They just thought it would be a laugh to nut around town proclaiming their love for fellow human beings. Originally an odd mix of the Notting Hill Carnival and Gay Pride, it's developed rapidly into the march of the rave generation.

This year's event started at 4 p.m. on Saturday 1 July. This was a very reasonable time. Left-wing activists tend to do things at about 10 a.m., and eco-warriors think dawn raids are a good idea – trust clubbers to get things right. So I made my way to the Wittenburg Platz in the centre of what was – and I suppose still is – West Berlin.

At first I couldn't really work out what was meant to happen. All down the main highstreet and right into the Platz, everywhere was jam-packed with clubbers. They were cheering, whistling, pinching arses and indulging in manic water-pistol fights. It was all good fun, but I didn't really get it. Then, from the back of the Platz, the drums were heard. A faint beat drifted over the horizon and ignited the crowds into motion. Over a lake of bobbing heads and waving arms I saw the tip of the first articulated lorry. Smothered in dancers, sound system blaring, it entered the crowds and Pied Pipered the awaiting mass further into the city centre. It was the first of thirty floats put together by clubs, record shops and groups from abroad. They banged out the tracks and set every building thumping. The city hadn't taken such a pounding since the war.

A jolly mix of trannies, straights and gays then paraded their love around town. And what an attractive love it was. Tight Adidas outfits do something for our passions that fishnets provoked on previous generations. Oh, for a leggy blonde in Lycra now that summer's here! There is no crustie element on the scene in Germany, and things seem far more united than they could ever be here. Even your average Mr and Mrs Schmidt seemed happy enough to sit at one of the many pavement cafés, drink a beer and clap along to the throngs of dancing *jugend*. What police there were confined themselves to a few traffic duties.

After strutting down the *strasse* with the sun in my hair and sweat on my forehead, a strange thought occurred to me. Germany is actually a *really* nice country. Actually, knock me down with a *bockwurst*, but the Germans even have a sense of humour. You can't drop two Es and march down your main street dressed in a frock holding a large blow-up duck without seeing life's more mirthful side. I almost found myself becoming uncynical: dancing away a weekend has its purposes. As a result, I got to know the German people particularly close up by crawling around their gardens and fish ponds at seven o'clock Sunday morning. (Fair play to the *fräulein* who fished me out, incidentally. One at a time in the future.)

The parade was a kind of Poll Tax Riot in reverse. After the last sound system drove off into the sunset, everyone was left buzzed with excitement and heading off east to the city's numerous clubs, most of which were initially squatted when the Wall came down. Berlin has a plethora of dandy night-spots. E-works, the Bunker and the legendary Tresor all provide the headstrong with a far more banging soundtrack than you hear in the UK these days. Clubs all over town were jammed, but Tresor was particularly insane. I'm not used to grown men showing me their cuddly toys, and I'm not sure if I approve.

'Handbag' is not a genre that has reached Germany, and to be honest I don't really think it will catch on in a country where practically anything with lyrics is considered disco. Gabba and hardcore provide lads' music in a lot of the clubs, and the quest for a bit of piano proved an elusive one. But at the Tresor it's still techno, techno, techno. This sound is still the erratic heartbeat of the city that was once the centre of the Cold War world. Despite the thaw, Berlin remains unique. And for the young, the Love Parade still gives it the edge on a lot of Euro destinations. For all concerned it is a particularly mad, unusual, barmy, bonkers, bender of a weekend.

After a weekend of prime Berliner abuse, my *vorsprung* had lost its *durch technik*. I crawled into my hotel bed and took notes, trying to make sense of what had gone on. This unique event, this weird music, these happy-go-lucky people – this strange *nothingness*. In a bizarre attempt at drugged-up self-analysis, I took out a pen and preposterously started to look for meanings and concepts to explain what's happening to us all on planet party. It was tempting to write that we live in a world so remote, so fucked up, that pure hedonism is our only escape route. Or perhaps attempt to justify it all, not as submission, but as a strong force for empowerment, a push for a liberal agenda of equality, tolerance and freedom.

Trouble is, I'm not so sure of anything, certainty being what it is these days. I threw the pad to the floor, raided the mini-bar, skinned up and put on the TV. CNN is the only channel in English, so I sit and stare. It's *Larry King Live*. And guess who's on? Noel Edmonds is pushing Mr Blobby to the Yanks. 'I don't get it,' says Larry, understandably. 'All he says is "Blobby, Blobby, Blobby". How do you know what he's going on about?'

'It's obvious,' replies Noel. 'Mr Blobby is on a mission to save the world!'

Bingo! Inspiration. Follow me, if you will, away from Berlin and into our vaguely collective psyche. Blobby, Blobby, Blobby: techno, techno, techno. Read what you like into it. Can it save the world, or is it complete nonsense? All I know is that it leads our lives out of the mundane. The vacuous feeling of Monday mourn has little to do with what has gone before, and more to do with the future we face. With our souls on slide and our hopes dashed, maybe things *can* only get better, maybe there *is* no limit. Where will the Love Parade lead us?

The Face, August 1994

Ethiopia: On the Piss in Addis

The quest was simple. Alas, confusion reigned. I went looking for the Ark of the Covenant and got a golden fleecing. They say pot causes memory loss, but I'm not convinced. My recollections of Ethiopia are vivid and disturbing. The taste remains. Piss washes around my mouth swilling the shit caught in my teeth.

Just before landing in Addis I'd flicked through the Air Ethiopia in-flight magazine. I chanced upon an article entitled 'Ethiopia – seasons all year and sunshine aplenty!' Between the exhilarating passages on the delights of tourist Ethiopia, I chanced upon an amazing sentence: 'In the ancient city of Axum lies the famous church of St Mary of Zion, home of the Ark of the Covenant.' Hosanna in the highest!

Theologians, scholars and historians have spent centuries in search of this mythical container of the tablets of Moses. They had scoured biblical landscapes and spent lifetimes analysing ageing scripts. I had found the answer in business class of an Air Ethiopia jet, just opposite an advert for Paco Rabanne. Eat shit, Indiana.

I saw fit to make the Ark my quest. Well, I saw fit for about six hours. Then unfit for a couple of days. A combination of dysentery, lethargy and insanity saw to that. My original plan (go to Axum, find church, grab Ark, leg it) was fundamentally flawed: I didn't have enough money for the bus to Axum. I would have had. I am a man of means who can often afford to travel by bus. Why, on some occasions, I even travel by train. No, I was the victim of crime. An innocent abroad. A victim of Solomon's golden fleece.

Addis is a magical city tingling with a warm uncertainty. Apart from a brief fracas with Mussolini, Ethiopia is the only African country never to have been colonized. It understands culture in a

European sense. Its ancient orthodox churches mix with a toy-town architecture of Fifties kitsch buildings. The surrealism of Blackpool combined with the heritage of York. And, despite a socialist revolution and subsequent revisionist coup, one man still lives large in Addis. The four-foot-eight-inch frame of Haile Selassie towers over the city. In sculptures, shops and song: Jah lives!

Hotel Ethiopia reeked of underachievement. The decaying grunge of the past it never had was self-evident. My room gave me wonderful views of an Army depot. As dusk fell, vultures and eagles caught the air currents and circled around at window height. I called upon the room of my photographer friend Zik and we decided to venture into town.

On leaving the hotel two things became clear. Firstly, it was very dark. Secondly, we did not know where we were going. Most capitals give way to the aimless wander of the tourist. Unfortunately, Addis has few tourists and plenty of hawkers, blaggards and conmen. The aimless wanderer must appear to be neither wandering nor aimless. As we strove purposely to nowhere-in-particular, we were soon rumbled. Three guys resembling the Marx Brothers tailed us and soon were keen on conversation. 'Hello, my name is Solomon,' said Groucho. We grunted replies. Just enough to say we're not *really* rude, but we're not interested.

Like insurance salesman who've just found Jehovah, they started a gat-gun spiel. Where were we from? What were our names? Where were we going? What was our job? Did we like it here? Where were we going? What music did we like? Were we married? Where were we going? Did we have sisters? What religion were we? WHERE WERE WE GOING?

'Er, for coffee?' said Zik, with all the command and elegance of a tortured hamster. But *where* were we going for coffee? Before we knew it, we'd been herded into a restaurant. Our large ears and swinging tails had been obvious. We thought we'd been marching purposefully – unfortunately, it was the swagger of two fat donkeys.

The restaurant was basic. So basic, in fact, that it obviously doubled as someone's living room. After insisting on just a coffee, we buckled under pressure to try the local wine. I could have done with a drink, especially as it seemed to provide a temporary relief for my dysentery. A bottle of off-yellow liquid was placed on the table. This was 'honey' wine, a traditional Ethiopian beverage. After much research and deliberation, I have arrived at an unfortunate conclusion. I now believe I spent that evening ploughing through five bottles of what was probably a mixture of orange squash and urine. Apparently this con is quite common in these parts. Further folly occured after the second bottle. I said I was hungry and ordered the shit.

We dined on traditional Ethiopian fare. A large, circular tray was covered in chapatti-style bread. Upon this had been placed some of the finest turds from a selection of the country's indigenous species. While we dined Solomon (Groucho) told us his life story. He was an ex-soldier. He had been trained in Leningrad. He knew David Dimbleby. Like most of his countrymen, he thought Rastafarians were very strange indeed. Once, fighting in Eritrea, his unit was over-run and he and his comrades had to walk for fourteen days through rebel territory without food and water. He'd survived by slashing the throats of cattle and drinking their blood. This, I thought, was a positively mouth-watering prospect compared to the example of the country's cuisine I had been presented with.

As the evening rolled by, the highly spiced crap slipped down, washed by steaming golden nectar. Soon it was time for coffee. Nescafé was not on the menu. We endured the 'traditional coffee ceremony', an hour of suspect shenanigans performed by an attractive local maiden. Some vaguely erotic motions resulted in coffee beans being roasted on a fire of suffocating incense. The only rest from this tedium was the offer of some grass.

They have no Rizla in Addis, and make do by emptying cigarettes and sucking up pure grass into the remnants of the flaccid tube. Apparently this was the stuff the monks grew. Fair play to the monks. I soon realized why they'd based a whole religion around it. One spliff, and things went very uncertain. This was the most powerful substance ever to enter my innocent lungs. Within about two minutes, Zik was doing the coffee dance, then convulsing into uncontrolled hysterics. The crackle of popping brain cells could be heard for miles around. The world was not as it should be and we were both beginning to struggle for our sanity. It was clearly time for the bill.

I was just compos enough to work out we were being shafted. A hundred dollars to feast on urine and shit seemed a tad too much. It had been a fisting worthy of James Herriot. Delirium reigned, but how we roared. Every time we tried to get shirty and complain, fits of laughter would cascade from our pathetic mouths.

Solomon told us it was time for bed. We followed him, knowing this was the route to certain death. Dogs howled in the darkness. Vultures flapped above. Down back passages we stumbled. Our journey terminating where it began, Hotel Ethiopia. A donkey sanctuary for lightweight Jah warriors such as I.

Two days later, I returned home, without the Ark.

Publisher unknown, 1994

Sarajevo: Everybody's Happy Now, OK?

*Bang! Rat-a-tat-tat! Splat! It's all getting a bit tiring, isn't it?
I mean, this war business doesn't half drag on.*

NO FUTURE

The buildings are burnt out, the hospitals are overrun and the graveyards are full. But good ol', plucky ol' Sarajevo still survives. And it's starting to get very embarrassing. Like a dotty grandmother shoved in a hospice refusing to die, we praise her for her endurance, we visit and bring gifts, we even give a comforting ear to her ramblings. Yet, as the months go by, we secretly wish she'd hurry up and pop her clogs. Sarajevo, and what's left of Bosnia-Hercegovina, will soon be sent to surgery. The Chetniks (Serb nationalists) are about to cause another haemorrhage, the aid agencies will have to mop it up, then it's back out with the diplomatic scalpel for the final carve-up. The United Nations will announce the operation a success, but the patient will have died. It's all getting very messy, and very predictable, but we mustn't give up 'hope', eh?

NO HOPE

No, I know I shouldn't. But I'll dispense with the journalistic niceties up front. I've had enough. Hope? Bollocks to that. If the past is anything to go by, the future of Bosnia stinks of the foulest excrement. Hope is the big lie, just another commodity we currently trade around the world. Here's 500 tonnes of 'hope' for Rwanda, a lorryload of 'hope' for Somalia, and three Hercules full of 'hope' for Bosnia. Hope is what the media sells all the time. We hope things will get better, we really do, it would make life so much simpler. So we play a cruel joke on others, we tell them not to give up hope. I'm not going to play any more.

Bosnia has played wallflower too long. Every week we tell the girl we'll take her to the disco. Every week we stand her up. Your day will come for the flashing lights and stroboscopic glory, don't give up hope, we say. But sooner or later she's going to stop hoping and start hating. Hating the empty promises, the broken heart, the floods of tears and the lonely walk home. And then we'll have the gall to think she's getting uppity and ungrateful . . .

There can only be hope when there are solutions. And the solutions that are available are off the agenda. I'll say it up front, it's just not worth me going into the complexities of imperialism, appeasement, the arms industry, international human rights, the International Monetary Fund, the faceless men of power – because they're all off the agenda, and try as I might I don't understand them anyway. All I can work out is that hope is a con. There is no hope, because there are 'no solutions'.

Enough said. Let's rock'n'roll. There is no hope, but there is humour. Deep, deep cynicism and black, black humour. Welcome to Bosnia.

FUNNY OLD WORLD

As I return to Sarajevo I am heartened by the fact that a four-month ceasefire has, by Bosnian standards, held well. Only a couple of sniper deaths a day. The city is alive, its mortar-ridden troglodytes have been allowed out to see our friend the sun. Its warm glow falls upon a packed city centre filled with rambling cafés and busy shoppers. A couple of local Krishnas try to flog dodgy books on the Lord Vishnu, and a pizza-delivery service has already reopened. This, I think, is 'hopeful'. They've even started to tow cars away in the highstreet. Traffic wardens, Hare Krishna and pizza delivery: the pillars of civilization are being hoisted into place.

Revelling in this 'spirited city on the mend', I walk down the Old

Town with a friend. I'm jollied by this paradise regained, so she tells me a joke. There are these two Chetnik soldiers walking in the woods when they come across this Bosnian girl. Eager for sex, one of the Chetniks drags her off into some bushes. When he returns his friend asks, 'What did you do to her?' and the other soldier replies, 'Everything!'

'Did you get a blow-job?'

'No, of course not!'

'Why's that?'

'Because I had to fucking hack her head off first, didn't I!'

Ha ha ha. How foolish. Have no illusions, there's something deeply sick about Sarajevo.

STARING AT THE RUDE BOYS

Sarajevo is surrounded. It's a zoo, a prison, encircled by the mountains which played host to the 1984 Winter Olympics. The mountains are now controlled by the Chetniks, who man a front line which extends from the ski slopes down into the heart of the city. From this advantageous position they stare down. Up there they play cards, drink, moan about being misunderstood and rape the odd Bosnian girl. Sometimes they get bored though, and then they start shooting. Trams are currently a favourite target.

Now, as the ceasefire dissolves, the city of Sarajevo turns into a bizarre black comedy. In the empty shell of a 'war-torn capital', the citizens act out the vestiges of cosmopolitan normality. In the hills, the Chetnik soldiers daily open the doors in their 'advent of the apocalypse' calendars, hoping today will be the day when they can saddle up the four horses and ride into town again. In the mean time, they snipe. Everywhere you go in town you know you could be a target, the jackals' sights hovering over your head, ready to squeeze the trigger. So you all play your roles, act normal, smothering the fact that, at the very least, your subconscious is blasted by years of anguish and haunted by the snipers' sights. Every now and then you walk through town and glance back over, beyond the rusting barricades of the front line, to the blocks of flats flying the Serbian flag, and up to the hills whence cometh the hate. There you stand, staring at the rude boys.

STAIRWAY TO HEAVEN

Picturing yourself on a mountain staring at life below, it's strange to think what would cause you to pull a trigger and take out a kid playing football or a woman getting her shopping. But entering the mind of a sniper is a lot easier than you might think. At the end of the day, it's only a job. I think there's probably more to it than that, but that was the reason given by the nerve-stricken dickhead who explained it all to me. I didn't want it explaining. Anyone whose opening gambit for conversation is 'You know, I don't think there has been a decent band since Led Zeppelin. Nirvana were just copycats. What do you think?' should be avoided at all costs.

But this guy wants to get to know me. Or rather he wants to get to know my wallet and all the big bucks any visiting media man must have. He is a translator for the media. But the media isn't coming. The war is starting up again. The Chetniks have already fired on airplanes and closed down the airport, and they are now cutting off the roads. Few eager newspeople can get in or out. So he picks on me and gives me his spiel. He must have said it to a thousand out-of-towners before.

He used to be a sniper. It did his head in, playing God and all that. It's so easy to take a life. The trick, apparently, is to injure people in the knee. They fall to the ground and have to be rescued by others. This not only causes maximum disruption for your enemy, it also provides you with new targets and is easier on your conscience. But, at the end of the day, it's only a job. There you go. But this is from a man who wears a bright-yellow bomber jacket and thinks rock music ended with Jimmy Page.

VEIL MEET AGAIN

Anyway, I'm getting settled in a bit and I'm walking through the centre of this 'war-torn besieged city', stepping over the mortar blasts in the pavement and looking at the souvenir shops, like you do. When all of a sudden this girl I'm with, Elma, starts laughing. 'What you laughing at, Elma?' I say.

'See those girls over there?' she says. 'They're wearing veils!'

'What's so funny about that?' I ask, perplexed by her mirth. 'I mean, you're a Muslim, aren't you?'

'It's not that,' she says. 'You don't understand. They used to be the biggest slags around! I guess they think that if they wear the veil, everybody will think they're virgins again. Hilarious! I must go tell my sister.'

I have now grown to believe that the biggest fundamentalist threat coming out of Bosnia is not, as some would have you believe, from the imaginary extremist forces of an Iranian-backed, Koran-touting army, but from born-again virgins. That and the dark post-grunge sound of their thriving indie music scene.

SARAJEVO: MY PART IN ITS DOWNFALL

We had this idea. We were going to put on a concert, Sarajevostock. There were some good local bands and we were going to put on a concert and MTV were going to film it. It was going to be free and fun and . . . take years off my life. I thought it would be like one of those Cliff Richard movies where everyone runs around smiling and saves the youth club. But this is war, and the only thing people can believe in is the certainty of death and hard cash in your face. Setting up a concert with only a week to do it in is, at the best of times, a hard enough task, but trying to do it in a foreign country, at war, having only the minor previous experience of having been a stagehand in the school panto is a bit stressful, to say the least.

It proved an organizational nightmare. Not my organizational nightmare, thank God. That privilege I'd landed on one of the town's café-owning club promoters. He informed me he could get all the equipment, but it was going to cost. I naïvely thought this would be a matter of a few hundred quid slipped in the right hands but later realized the guy was fishing for about a grand. Not to worry, though – via satellite phone, I begged Steve Blame of MTV News, who was due to fly out in a week's time. He, in turn, begged the managing director for the money, and the gentleman was forthcoming. Well, it was promised, anyway.

I spent days running around town shouting, 'Hey, kids! There's going to be a concert!' I was even interviewed on the local radio and went out at indie prime-time proclaiming that this would be the best concert Sarajevo had seen in years. What a twat.

Meanwhile, back in the real world of guns and devilry, things were getting tricky. Top Chetnik and self-proclaimed leader of the Bosnian Serbs Radovan Karadžić had rejected the umpteenth peace proposals. As usual he'd told the rest of the world to get shafted, and opted yet again for the 'let's kill lots of people' option – the option nine out of ten jumped-up demagogues who express a preference say their people prefer. The airport was closed after it was decided that Hercules air carriers made much-needed target practice for short-sighted Chetnik snipers. This was followed by a twenty-four-hour shootathon on traffic travelling along the only road into Sarajevo. Effectively, the ceasefire was over.

It soon became apparent that nobody was going to get in or out. Least of all Steve Blame and MTV. The day before the concert was due, things were looking very bad indeed. Everyone wanted cash upfront as nobody trusted anybody and the black market is the only market. And a rather heavy one if you fuck around with it. As no one was getting in, my promised cash would not be arriving. If the concert didn't go ahead, I would be held personally responsible by the promoter, the bands, hordes of screaming indie kids and every shady figure in every shady doorway in town. And the fun thing about the whole set-up was – I couldn't even leave.

To my immense relief, at the eleventh hour, a winged saviour cropped up and lent me the money. That was a *big* lend, and one I'm eternally grateful for. However, on reflection, my public hanging might have done more for the town's morale than the musical mayhem that ensued the following night at the city's Obala arts venue. Still, one tries, doesn't one?

BOSNIAN CHESS

The night comes quickly in Sarajevo. The town is under a ten o'clock curfew. I defied it a few times – strange, drunken parties where journos mix with UN and local nobs. Where odd men hand you pieces of paper saying, 'Don't talk to him, he's a Bosnian spy.' Where people guess and double-guess, and double-think, and drink whisky like there's no tomorrow. Debate on foreign-policy flows. Policy schmolicy, because no one knows. Not even dear General Rose, commander-in-chief of the UN forces. It's all bollocks – Bosnian chess. The only certainties I can ever fathom are that the sins of your father come back to haunt you, the innocents always suffer most, and some people are *real* bastards. Especially Radovan Karadžić.

On the night before the concert, after an evening of Bosnian chess, I retired to my room with a bottle of Mostar red. A fine wine with the bouquet of a British Rail urinal and the punch of a Sauchiehall Street bouncer. In dearest Bosnia, oblivion is the only true 'safe area'. Despite my nightcap, sleep eluded me. There was only broken glass in my window, and about 500 metres away a fire-fight was going on in the much-disputed Jewish cemetery. Noisy business, war, and very inconsiderate to a stranded Londoner trying to get a good kip. Stress, tiredness and drunkenness are the holy trinity of foreign news reporting.

On the day of the concert, I wake after a good two hours' sleep to find no running water. I'm hung over, my nerves are shot, and I'm smelling foul. My crew turns up an hour and a half late; I get thrown out of the local alternative radio station who decided they wanted to be paid before I could interview them; a French UN guard steals my diary, notebooks, script and address book. The electricity has gone and Paul Lowe, my friend and photographer, is stuck in a lift in pitch-blackness with an army captain who is chain-smoking Gauloises. I'm not a happy man.

NEVER MIND THE BOLLOCKS, HERE'S SARAJEVO

The day proves to have its highlight, though. *Sikter* is Bosnian slang for 'fuck off'. It's also the name of one of the best bands this side of Tuzla. Sikter are the Sarajevo Sex Pistols. The aggression of Johnny Rotten with the funk of Boney M. Love it. And what a motley crew they are. Their lead singer Bure declares, 'Rock'n'roll is sinking. It's ill and we are the only ones who can save it.' I'm inclined to believe him. The drummer, Faris, tells me that the needle marks on his arm aren't real junkie marks but fakes so he can draft dodge. (On the morning before his most recent medical, he swallowed a few packets of analgesics and pricked his veins with a syringe. It worked, and he got three months' reprieve.) No such luck for Sergi Sobe, the lead guitarist, who has just come off the front line on the mountains. He was taken off early because he went a bit nuts. 'There were bugs, wolves and land-mines up there. I couldn't sleep. You go a bit crazy. It's very dangerous, you know?'

Like Iggy Pop, he's looking wired but a survivor. Surviving is what it's about. Anybody can be a hero, anybody can go under. To make it, you have to survive. 'Rock'n'roll keeps us insane like we were before the war,' pipes up Bure. And he's not trying to be clever. I ask what religion they are, knowing them to be multi-ethnic, but wanting them to chat about it. Faris replies enigmatically, 'Do you *know* who the messenger is?' Stars, every one of them.

SMELLS LIKE WHITE SPIRIT

The concert happened. It happened well. Everyone enjoyed themselves. There were strange grunge/punk bands with names like Lay Down Monkey, the Moron Brothers and SCH, and hundreds of deranged souls danced away to them in the dimly lit haze of the

Marquee *circa* 1978. Sikter went down a storm. Needless to say, my camera crew's batteries ran out on their wondrous encore, and I have only my addled memory to playback a quasi-spiritual Scotch-induced rock moment when they played a stunning version of 'Purple Rain' followed by a rapturous 'Pretty Vacant'. A guy broke his leg stage-diving. There'd been problems, there'd been setbacks but hey, it was worth it all just to see the smile on one kid's face as he puked up a bottle of what smelled like white spirit.

THE TEARS OF A CLOWN

After the concert, my only problem is getting out – something the citizens of Sarajevo can only dream about. All exits are officially closed. After certain reassurances, Paul Lowe thinks it safe enough to drive out across the mountains. We set off and are shortly passing the spectres of a blackened convoy. This is a British aid convoy that has been ripped to pieces by Chetnik gunmen. (Radovan Karadžić apologized about the incident. 'We thought they were civilians,' he explained. Good one, Rado.) Paul puts his foot down and we arrive safely in Croatia in time for G&Ts and bad nightclubs.

At seven in the morning I stumble to Split airport to catch my plane home. To my surprise, the entire British battalion are congregated on the balcony overlooking the runway. I join them, thinking someone special must be turning up. Perhaps it's Douglas Hurd, that mealy-mouthed Neville Chamberlain figure who promises our boys peace in our time, but knows of the true blackness he's dealing with. That jobsworth who shovels the manure of hope around and calls it a foreign policy. I debate whether to slap him, and wonder whether these men would beat me or bless me if I did.

A Hercules lands. Guards troop out in honour. The tail-gate comes down. I get ready to heckle, at the very least. A Union Jack is raised, but it reaches only half-mast. The army stiffens rank and salutes. Out comes the corpse of Philip Bottomley, an unsuspecting squaddie killed on Mount Igman in the convoy I'd passed the day before. There but for the grace of God and all that.

Emotion's a funny thing. You put up barriers in extreme situations. You hide behind adrenalin, front and humour. I did something at that point. I let the barriers slip. Reality's sniper found the mark and punctured my dulled heart: I cried. Poor Philip Bottomley, poor tens of thousands, poor hopeless Bosnia.

Two military policemen shed tears next to me. 'We should get the fuck out of here. Let them shoot it out, then come back and clear up the pieces,' said one.

'I dunno,' I said.

'No, we should get the bastards,' said the other.

'Yes,' I said, 'we should.'

And our tears they ran, down our cheeks on to the earth below, to where hope springs eternal.

The Face, October 1994

London: You've been Framed

(review of the V&A's Streetstyle exhibition)

When John Lennon was asked whether he was 'a mod or a rocker' by an inquiring newsman, he replied, 'I'm a mocker.' This witty retort was the response of a man desperate to avoid the crass labelling of the media, but these days the difference between a mod and a rocker is clear to even the most clueless of hacks. Today, you can look up that sort of thing in a museum. Quite literally with V&A's Streetstyle exhibition, which follows the world of youth culture from zoot suits to what it calls the 'supermarket of style'.

It used to be you had the cool and the fool. Now it's all signed, sealed and archived off. In the past year the 'death of youth culture' has become the favoured topic of old hippies with nice jobs on national newspapers who commission ageing punks to tell us that the creative juices of British youth have dried up. Nothing is important any more, things were better in the past, we've seen it all before, it's just not original, there's no agenda, blah, blah, blah, yackity-schmackity.

Of course, what the pundits lack is not so much an understanding of today's yoof, but a comprehension of their own history. There have been youth cults in this country for hundreds of years and, rest assured, there will be many more in the future. Today's nouveau casuals can trace their roots to the nineteenth century. 'Professional scuttlers' prided themselves on their Punchers caps, large buckled belts and the forerunner of flares, 'narrow-go-wides'. They even wore slimline brass-tipped clogs up north (true!). After the Second World War, immigration from the Commonwealth led Britain on its first faltering steps to a multi-ethnic culture. Our country's working-class youth benefited from a diversity of musical and stylistic inputs. Along with the emerging influence of black American music, these newly tagged 'teenagers' were blessed with relative independence, wealth and mobility. Youth cultures as we understand them today appeared.

Yet even then, at the supposed birth, the Teds were mimicking the flash and dash of the Edwardian gentleman. In the same way, years later Malcolm McLaren mimicked Teddy-boy style. Nothing is *new* new, it's all evolution. Today's youth cannot be condemned as less original than their forebears. They are more eclectic simply because there's a far greater supply of stuff in the attic to pilfer from.

The obnoxious thing about all this media coverage is that it has always favoured bohemian culture over that of the working classes. Why does Fifties rock'n'roll have a white face? Why are there hundreds of books and films about Sixties hippies and so few about mods and skinheads? The arbiters of youth culture are still largely white middle-class people with a taste for fancy.

The driving force of a movement like the New Romantics was to get photographed and appear in magazines. Ideal for gormless press types and pseudo-style gurus. Casual and hip hop – both of which appeared at roughly the same time – are still here, while Blitz kids are long dead. Yet somehow history tells us they are all of equal worth. Which is the real problem with the V&A show. It presents the history of style as a linear progression, collecting rather than analysing, and so opposing values remain unexamined and misunderstood. Like politics, youth cults form a spectrum of ideas with many grey areas in between, but there are clear groupings of bohemians and modernists at either end. And it's the bohemians who always seem to get the bootie.

The truth is that working-class boys and girls, and, God forbid, the darkies, just don't really get the breaks. If they do, they have to bend over and take it that their story will be told by middle-class, white voyeurs. Achievements will be confined to a few confused manuscripts and some strangely sanitized mannequins. In consolation you get credibility, suss and a far better social life. But when you hit forty, all you'll have is the memories. That, and a pile of bills. No one is going to pay *you* to moan. What pundits neglect to realize is that, for most people, youth culture is *all* they've got. Until that one gets solved, youth will have its fling and remain gifted but broke.

The Face, November 1994

The Glorious Void

Sometimes, when I'm on the Underground, I play a game called King of the Tube. The rules are pretty simple: you just get on, sit down, then stare at everybody. If, after about forty-five seconds, you have managed to out-stare everyone and make them feel uncomfortable, then you're King of the Tube. If, however, someone catches your eye with a strong pupil and forces you to immediately look at your shoes or study a Travelcard, then you've failed and are forced to spend the rest of the journey in a state of edginess.

Other times, when I'm on the Tube, there's no need to play games. I'll get on at Mile End, then suddenly realize it's Notting Hill and time to get off. Somehow time has passed, yet where did it go? Such voids in our lives are glorious moments. They eliminate Bethnal Green, Liverpool Street, Bank and beyond. They're impossible to re-create consciously. You can't just opt out – more's the pity. It would save me panicking all those torturous times about why everybody on the Tube is reading self-help books. No carriage is complete without some lost soul tucking into M. Scott Peck's *The Road Less Travelled*. This came to my attention when fortune dictated that I too was sad enough to read these bibles of the broken. There's a desperate camaraderie among the nation's depressed. The capital's casualties flash doleful eyes and half-smiles across the ageing rolling stock of London Regional Transport. Oh, to be in the void, where time accelerates!

I often wonder what my brain does in the void. Does it just switch off? Is this the natural state of the chicken-packer or check-out girl? Or, as I fear, is this God's time? Is this what mystics, gurus and unisex rectors call 'real being'? It's definitely a kind of infinity, a timeless state of oblivion that we could construe as heavenly. But time's a funny thing. It's getting faster.

When I was seven, a year was a huge, event-packed period. Birthdays took ages to arrive. Back then, a year was a seventh of my entire existence on this planet, so I judged time accordingly. Now, when that scale is altered to twenty-eighths, things travel faster. 'Christmas already?' my Gran used to say, in what I now understand to be a completely sane manner. When you reach ninety, the seasons really do fly by; a Christmas always catches you unawares. As memory erases, the whole of your past must become the void. You're not all there, you've lost it, and yet perhaps this really is what true happiness is all about. Then again . . .

Anyway, as the train chugs forward from Mile End to Notting Hill, it's not just my personal notion of time that's moving faster. The whole world is currently propelling itself into hyper-history. When you're at school and they explain about how old the world is, they show you a scale with a week on it. They tell you that there was a big bang on Monday, followed by lots of swirly gases till about Sunday morning. Sometime in the late afternoon Earth was formed, and at about quarter to midnight the primeval soup spunked out its first tadpole of a life-form. Five minutes before midnight, we had *Jurassic Park* happening for real, and at about five seconds to go, homo got erectus.

The point is that it's only in the last half an hour that things have started to happen, and if you take that week and supplant just human history into that scale, we are now entering the five-to-midnight Sunday scenario once again. The sum of human knowledge is set to increase *seven times* in the next fifteen years. According to the records, Crawley had a pretty steady population from the Domesday Book onwards. That is until the last forty years, when it went new-town loco. In the Eighties it grew twice as big as it had in the previous twenty years. A sixty-year-old resident of Crawley has seen more changes in their lifetime than all of the town's previous residents put together. And guess what? There's more to come, and we all live in Crawley!

It happened just then. The zone, the void just happened. I'm trying to remember it, but failing miserably. There was some shit about swirling gases and Crawley. I seem to remember it being really good, but documentation proves otherwise. I should try and forget it all. Then again, there *are* these moments, honest. There are these strange, lucid moments, when the void becomes a reality, and death develops into more than just a concept. When your body engages its tasks without effort and the soul lies still within. When you finish off a bottle of Scotch and sing 'The Sash' without ever having known the words.

To pass the time while waiting for the Tube one ponders on LRT's own measurement of time, movement and space. 'One Minute Ealing', it'll say. A minute will pass, another minute will pass, yet still 'One Minute Ealing'. Go to the end of the platform and look at yourself on the screens that the drivers use to ensure no one gets trapped in the doors. In some societies, they would run from the camera, for fear it steals the soul. Here in the West we have proven it does.

Jump. Bring on the void. Speed me my death. Life, time's fool. And time that takes survey of all the world must have a stop.

The Idler, July–August 1994

Down and Out in Heaven and Hell

It's all gone wrong again. Face down on my bed, my right arm under the pillow, I dream of finding a gun to comfort me. My finger squeezes an imaginary trigger. I snooze. As my mind turns to white alligators, mud, cobras and panic, I pull the sheets tightly around my neck. I want rope, I want the hangman's noose to lift me up from devilish nightmares and pull me to the land of the angels. Suicide fixations calm my consciousness, delivering me from this routine purgatory. I lie broken, in the cesspool of my solitude, feeling shit.

Bar the sound of a cheque on the doormat, or the priestly whispers of the last rites, few things can comfort the wretched morning soul. One tries to find solutions, one really does, one scrambles through the possibilities of abstinence, change of diet and/or therapy, yet one comes to the same sorry conclusion. At the point of Hell, the only solution that works is the final one. Death. In this deranged world, it holds a logic and clarity that few of the standard healings can supply. Cheap wine, Manchester United, a gramme, a pill, Alan Partridge, the Cross club, meditation, Graham Greene: what can heal greater than the purity of the ultimate escape? Yet still we love life, even in our rage, and so the sham of our existence continues.

I used to think there were reasons, excuses for feeling shit. You know, hangovers, come-downs, rejections, defeats. But I've come to think it's probably an inevitable consequence of our presence on this planet. Life's burden crushes you, full stop. All the rest is delusion, but oh, to be a member of the ranks of the lost.

It struck me when, on a recent Sunday, I rose with my usual tirade against the injustice of existence. My body ached, my stomach retched, the head it did hurt. I blamed drugs, I blamed alcohol, I blamed the whole sorry affair of the previous evening. Only then did it come to me: I'd actually spent the previous night at home, in utmost sobriety, watching *Match of the Day* and retiring to bed early. Hedonism was not to blame. It was the real world that had failed. I'd tangled my brain into blaming the escape, not the prison.

Hedonism works; real life lets you down. A simplistic assumption, I know, but it's hard to steer a sensible course when feeling shit. You see, as life goes on, hedonism appears to fail you also. While heading for higher highs, you experience lower lows, and sack it all for the safety of mundane depression. If death is not the answer, then life must be maintained at all costs. Grey day upon grey day. Yet if we are to sack our peccadilloes and prefer the everyday, we must realize that it's not the crutch of escapism that we are ditching, more the crutch of excuses for feeling shit. The cold realization that there are demons within that cannot be slayed by abstinence is the most frightening hurdle on the road to a life of smiles.

One man's amazing hallucination is another man's paranoid hell. So feeling shit has a lot more to do with interpretation than a rigid fatalism. How I want to rise above, to float in the clouds, staring at our world with the wisdom of a smiling sage. Why can't I be a member of *The Next Generation*, a calm Captain Picard, amazed that our planet once had famine and war? Why can't I search for final frontiers instead of roach butts? Why can't I bring myself to believe that, with careful planning, my intellectual processes might lead me anywhere but back to the sewer and feeling shit? Is the choice really between Prozac and death?

Life *can* work. Some days I feel happy. Sometimes it's when I remember what the emotion is, other times it's when I absent-mindedly forget the melancholy. Happiness is also triggered by places which stir memories of happiness. The fickleness of such happiness is illustrated by two small sections of road. One is outside the Centre for Tropical Diseases in Camden; the other by the Grove Road area of Bow, where the road goes under a railway bridge and a blue plaque marks the site of the first V1 flying bomb to land in

London. When I walk through these places, I get a *déjà vu* of the smile I, for whatever reason, first had when I passed by there. I remember the happiness, and so become happy. It is that simple.

Yet with these smiles comes a fear. A fear from an understanding. My feeling shit is wrapped up in my duvet and my pillow. My bed and the rise of the sun is the trigger to that feeling. So each new day is a dagger, the only escape the longest sleep. Yet, despite this realization, I spy a kind of hope. A soul that craves a desperate execution can find its happiness in the last supper, and so be released from its rut. The kiss on the forehead, the smell of the cypress box. A feeling of shittiness removed. An enema of such force that life's rich pageant erupts, quaking, from your innermost depths.

Ah, to let it all go. One day, my friends, one day.

The Idler, October–November 1994

1995

House music is what Brit-pop grew up on. Cocaine replaces E as the drug of a generation. Radicalism is spreading, yet coated in alienation and thus apathy.

The young man is dancing from Ibiza to South Africa, from Benidorm to Belgrade – waking up an adult from the pupae of his twenties, bitter but not broken.

Apathy in the UK

WHO GIVES A SHIT?

Who'd be a young person today, eh? Unemployment, AIDS, drugs, pollution, crime, Jeremy Beadle, Whigfield . . . In fact, let's not be so selfish. Who'd be *any* person today? While the old are freezing in their bungalows, the middle-aged are discovering their skills are redundant. Even those on the gravy train are looking down in the mouth. Who'd be a Tory MP now you can't even get a freebie from the Ritz or sexual favours from lobbying firms? Hey, let's face it, who'd be bloody Royalty these days? So, things are not so good in dear Britannia. But who gives a shit? Yet when you really think about it, when you talk in pubs, when you listen in club toilets, when you stare at the eyes of strangers in the street: definitely maybe all of us. Maybe we definitely don't know what to do about it, though.

IT'S A RUSH

To work out what to do about this mess, we have to understand it. And that's the problem. The world is changing very fast indeed. We live in what is known as hyper-history. Events that once took centuries now take years. New countries are created, new conflicts started, old ideologies and faiths are crumbling. Nothing seems certain or stable any more. More people died in a few months in Rwanda than there were British casualties in the Great War. The sum of human knowledge (i.e. everything the human race understands) will apparently grow *seven times* in the next fifteen years. Just keeping tabs on technological 'advances' could occupy every hour of your waking day. As we accelerate through yet another year packed with world-shattering events and inventions, we're bound to feel lost. Yet we're made to feel it's all *our* fault. As comedian Tony Hawkes put it, 'We've never had it so bad!'

POLITICAL BANKRUPTCY

It must have been nice to live in a time when you knew all the answers. When the theories of Marx – or even Hitler – excited you because you *knew* they were right and you knew the world would adapt to your vision, because you had the truth, the *answers*. How sad the broken promises of left and right look now that this century has played its hand. They still talk of vision, just about. John Major apparently lacks one. Tony Blair apparently has a marvellous one. There's some with European ones and some even with world ones. I just wish somebody would tell us what they *were*. You see, without knowing the visions, we're just left with the knowing. And the knowing tells us this is still a very bad world indeed.

KNOWING ME, KNOWING YOU

The feeling we all have of impotence, of helplessness, and the apathy that stems from it, comes from the knowing. We know because we see it every day in the papers and on TV. We know that babies starve in Africa, that entire villages are massacred in Bosnia, that children murder children in Liverpool, that muggers stab grannies in Peckham and people go missing in Colombia. We know that the evidence on global warming is now so overwhelming that we'll be bronzing ourselves in the Orkneys by the time we're forty; we know that it's bloody hard to get a job that pays enough to live on; we know that, statistically, we'll never win the Lottery. And that's that. We are left with a knowing, but not an *understanding*. We are never informed what to do about it all. And even our knowing is becoming increasingly distorted. Is a new book about the royal family *really* more important than a thousand dying from floods in Bangladesh? Is the massacre of over half the population of East Timor or the war in Angola unimportant, or is it just not on TV because it's hard to get good footage? We not only have to struggle to try and understand what we know, we have to try and understand whether what we know is worth anything. What most of us end up knowing is disillusionment, cynicism.

THE POLITICS OF DESPERATION

Roll up! Roll up! Welcome to the circus of the damned! Pop a pill, snort a line, take a trip on the acid roller-coaster, come to the mushroom kingdom, roll up Leb, roll up skunk – all the fun of the fair is available. Unfulfilled? Feeling empty? Tried religion? What, no God? Want politics? We've got politics! Anarchists, Lefties, Greens, New Agers, New Edgers, what do you want? The main parties have failed, so just pick from the jamboree bag of radical ideas. At least that way you can *feel* you're doing something positive. Hearts sank this year as Tony Blair formed his new model Labour Party. Political choice seemed to blur between the grey of John Major and the new pistachio-green of the mainstream Left. Radical politics, however, had something of a revival. Around 150,000 people attended an anti-racism festival in Clapham. The anti-road campaigners had some minor triumphs, and the fight against the Criminal Justice Bill politicized a generation. And yet . . .

FAKING A REVOLUTION

When the hippies sang or the punks snarled, or when we all waved our hands in the air, we felt empowered. It changed us, so we thought it could change the world. We grew up believing that you could change the world with a song or a T-shirt. We still genuinely believe it's important what pop idols say. But the real world doesn't give a toss – they lifted an eyebrow in the Sixties, but in the Nineties? Forget it. The Hyde Park demo against the Criminal Justice Bill was a glorious affair, but it didn't change a thing; it barely even made the news. Still, talking and faking a revolution is fun. Today, we storm the barricades not to bring down capitalism, but to get revenge. After all, riots are a good laugh. But even they get boring after a while.

BLAMING OURSELVES

Few actions seem to end in victory. Life is quite a burden. Luckily, this century has provided us with two great thinkers on the subject: Mr Freud and Mr Jung. We know our sadness, and we are told to look inwards. There we find people to blame: our mothers, our fathers, our first love. Never are we told that the problem might lie out there, right now, in Westminster, in the United Nations, in the smog, the neon lights and the black rain. From *Cosmopolitan* to *Richard & Judy*, it's organize your day correctly, take control of your money, satisfy your partner completely, dress to impress, lose weight, get fit . . . sort your life out, loser, because no one else will and it's all your fault! Gosh, no it's not. Thank you, Mr Therapist. I blame the parents.

FAMILY VALUES

Parents are where it's at. Now we are told that the heart of our country is in its family units. Cocooned, sterile, neo-liberal units of illusion. There's nothing wrong with Mum, Dad and the kids, but why must the weight of the world fall on their shoulders and everything else be seen as dysfunctional? We still have, or wish for, communities – the units from which nations are built. But those who should unite us isolate us further. The majority are now marginalized and ostracized. We should be courted, not divided and ruled. What do we get? Another *knowing*. The knowing that we don't fit in. Wouldn't it be nice to be living in a nation we loved as much as our dogs?

CLUB UK

So what do we do? More action, more riots, more opting out, more drugs? Or we could make sure that *we* become the mainstream, *we* redefine it with *our* rules and *our* values. It's happening already, we don't even need to try that hard. Here we live on Britannia's Isle. Floating safely off Europe, in a world we know to be beautiful but bad. We are young citizens of the United Kingdom. A nation we understand from history books and old movies. A land a hundred years from empire, fifty years from war, seventeen years from punk rock and four years since Thatcher. Yet although we live here, although we *are* here, still in our heads the Union Jack flies not for us. It waves for Royalty, for class and conservatism. The flag we see on Tory propaganda and Nazi stickers is hard for us to take on board as a source of pride. We should – this is as much our country as theirs. There are the things we love, *our* nation: a nation of Harry Enfield, curries, Andy Cole, Andy Weatherall, kebabs, Guinness, Paddington Bear, bagels!

SATURDAY NIGHT

The one thing we can say with absolute authority is that the next century is ours. We will inherit this nation. Our generation will be in charge. What shall the flag fly for then? As we stumble onwards popping pills, buying Paul Smith and scraping together a life, perhaps now is the time to start dreaming our dreams. Not just of Saturday night but of our future nation, our continent of Europe. And tomorrow, the new Jerusalem: a golden land that lies just beyond the horizon. We must not let a hatred of nationalism prevent us from genuinely liking each other. It's all about finding ourselves, then our feet, then that frightening beast the ballot box. The twentieth century has definitely left us lost. But we must rise to the challenge of a new identity and a new politic. If we don't, others will.

A LAND FIT FOR HEROES

Beyond the confusion, you can find an inkling of what it's all about. I was born in England, of a Scottish mother. Caucasian by race, C of E by religion. I am from London first, England second, UK third and Europe sometimes. I love my country, for it is a land of good music, good clubs and Bombay duck. It's messy Sunday-morning sessions and Ryan Giggs running down the wing. It's Guinness and a bag of Twiglets. It's happy *Blue Peter* memories and the sound of a kicking bass. This is a land worth fighting for, not leaving to the riff-raff to ruin and pillage. A land with much to love, and plenty to hate. If most of us could be bothered, or knew how to, we would like to change things for the better. The thing is, we seem to have reached a stage where every political avenue has been exposed for its hypocrisy. There are few options left for idealists. Let's face it, anyone who isn't cynical and apathetic has probably no grasp of our reality. Unfortunately, we have to use the system available to us. It's taken thousands of years to get just that far. We must begin to see ourselves not as a counterculture, but as part of the culture. By knowing this, by simply claiming the country as our own, perhaps we could develop a climate where real change is possible, where those who seek power must accept our agenda.

THE NEW JERUSALEM

It's simple things we want, the same things people have wanted for years: social and economic justice; not having to worry if you're sick, old or down on your luck; a roof over your head; a good education for all; peace; a right to diversity, fun and freedom. We want this for ourselves, for our country and for our world. Simple desires, yet hideously complex to achieve. We can start by trying to claim our country, and find the power that enables us to find the answers to make the changes for the better. The alternative is increasing alienation and descent into a disparate land of paranoid people. When we don't give a toss about our fellow countrymen, we don't give a toss when hospitals get closed, when gangs rob cabbies, when Nazis bash Pakis, or when the rights of thousands are dismissed as expendable. The simple realization that most of us will never make enough money to do anything other than skin up and buy trainers should be enough to force us to dream of a golden future. One day, this nation will be ours. Let's think what we want, then see what we can get. We are not alone, we are many.

We are Robin Hood, Twiglets, Linford Christie, King Arthur,

KLF, William Blake, Echobelly, Marmite, Oasis, George Orwell, Irn-Bru, Johnny Rotten, Boudicca and Vimto. We are joy-riders, hooligans, dealers and drunks. We are those who struggle to get a life and those who enjoy themselves despite. We've glimpsed Jerusalem, squinting through half-closed eyes, scrambling messily on a Sunday morn. We must wake from our fantasies, revive our visions and stake a claim on the future. Then ours shall be a golden nation. A land of real hope and true glory. Well, it would be a laugh anyway.

The Face, January 1995 (where it appeared in a far shorter form)

In Search of the Grail

The Dream of the Blue Turtles by Sting is probably the worst album of all time. It is definitely the worst-*titled* album of all time. It seeps with New Age therapy bollocks, with ex-schoolteacher, miserable-git wank. It was the result of a 'dream diary' where dear spiky Sting wrote down his visions from the night before. *The Dream of the Blue Turtles* was apparently a really important one. 'Important' to Sting, that is. As it never revealed that tight trousers and waistcoats were sad, that the Amazonian Indians *want* VHS and that dancing like a trendy Christian when you're not one is a crime, then I think we can safely discount the importance of Sting's dream.

My recent dream, however, was *very* important. The most important thing about my dream was that I remembered it. No memory, me. If I'd kept a 'dream diary' for the last ten years, it would be a sea of blank pages peppered only with the occasional dull sexual fantasy or things like 'the landlord came round saying I was three months late with the rent and threatened to kill me – woke up, and the landlord came round saying I was three months late with the rent and threatened to kill me'. Jung would have ended up in the Post Office if he'd had me as a patient.

Anyway, I'm walking through this forest when I come across this old, derelict cottage. I walk inside and find it fully furnished yet covered in mildew and cobwebs. The sitting-room carpet is sodden and the furniture rotten. On the sofa a man is sitting patiently. He too is covered in cobwebs, his clothes dank from years of neglect. He is dressed like a gentleman from the 1920s, like the apple-headed man of Magritte fame. I wake the man and ask him his name. He tells me. It's C. S. Lewis!

It was a bizarre dream, if you can have such a thing. A quick chat with a pub psychiatrist got to the bottom of it. It was 'the awakening of my dormant spirituality'. This revelation has led to the creation of my forthcoming concept album, *The Dream of Mouldy Lewis* – a musical transubstantiation from the Vimto of a Casio organ to the blood of the London Philharmonic. It also led to a bit of soul-searching. It was all too apparent.

C. S. Lewis dominated my younger years. I lived in Narnia. The Seven Chronicles were my world. They were my passage from the sandals of A. A. Milne to the Doc Martens of Roald Dahl. I stood shoulder to shoulder with Prince Caspian and fought the Last Battle with a plastic sword. I longed to enter the wardrobe a boy and leave a knight, destined for adventure and chivalry. Slaying evil and fighting for the good of Aslan.

When I piece together my early years I find three incidents that mark my transition from blind youth to conscious adult. The first was staring at the TV and realizing that the psychedelic swirl of the BBC logo was in fact a spinning globe. I shouted, 'Look it's the world, it's the world!' but no one listened. The second was lying on the corner of the football pitch at break with a girl who smoked and realizing that really, considering my position in the entirety of the cosmos, I didn't *have* to go back to classes. (Word of advice for any young boys reading this – always hang out with girls who smoke. They're more fun, have all the good ideas and are much, much more likely to put out for a bag of chips and a packet of Polos.)

The third and, to use the jargon, pivotal point was when I was learning to swear. I would hang with the older kids at the bus stop after school, talking about Leatherhead winning the FA Cup, pretending my parents let me go to gigs and explaining why our youth club was the hardest in the world. Every so often I'd try to slip the words 'shit' or 'cock' in to my sentences and, whenever I did, a voice would come into my head along with a small vision. The vision was a lion's head and the voice said, 'Aslan wouldn't like that.' Yes, that fucker Aslan didn't approve of my swearing. He didn't approve of many other things I did either. Just as C. S. Lewis had intended, the chronicles of Narnia had indoctrinated me with a Christian morality. God had come to me not as a white man with a beard, but as a Lion.

This was only understood as an adult when I realized that the C. S. Lewis on a theology documentary I was watching was the same guy who wrote about talking badgers and magical wardrobes. A subsequent delve into the man's background and the true horror of his clever deceit was revealed.

Like most, I struggle with the nonsense of church, the slavery of propriety and the structures of sin. Though now the sleeper has awoken from his mildewed sofa I have been searching a little and now I find myself, as ever, in the delightful search for the Holy Grail.

I do not curse Narnia, or C. S. Lewis. The Lion Aslan that was killed by sinners and rose from the dead may indeed have been a thinly veiled Jesus and the Chronicles of Narnia a fantasy version of the New Testament, but I care not. For what better way to understand that the Bible is just a rewrite of older myths and fables? What better way to form a heart and a head on the universal truths of man? To comprehend such a spirituality is not to give way to the God squad, the fools, the fakes. It doesn't mean you treat Cliff as king and you dance like Sting. The comprehension, the quest for the Grail, is a journey of ennoblement, chivalry, honour, education, empowerment, love and enlightenment. It's also a good laugh.

When George Best lifted the European Cup in 1968, Manchester United's manager, Sir Matt Busby, smiled. That was his grail. Ten years before, in search of that trophy, his young team, 'the Busby Babes', had been wiped out in a plane crash in Munich. After narrowly avoiding death himself, Busby went on his quest. A decade later, his new side beat Benfica at Wembley. Briefly the Grail was his, and what joy there was.

The Grail myth is an enriching one, and as real as any of the utterances of Muhammad or Jove. I recommend it to those who have no religion. It is a class above the raggedy me-isms of modern life. It is also the ideal adulthood to a Narnia childhood. There are two aspects of the Grail: the quest, and the Grail itself. One is about getting what you want out of life and love, honourably. The other is working out what life's all about. The former is the formation of your own goals and morals. The latter is the nice little nagging, philosophical edge to our being.

To sip from the Grail is to sip the vino rouge of Christ's Blood at the last supper. It is to travel through the maze of the Minotaur back through ancient mythology to a time before history. A journey back along the songlines to the point on the African savannah when it suddenly occurred to *homo erectus* to think *who* he was and *where* he was. It was the start of the miracles, the beginning of the terrors: the dawn of man's consciousness.

When reading the stuff of legends – of the Grail, of Arthur, the Green Knight, of the Round Table and all its heroes – you find puzzles, truths and insights that you're unlikely to get in your average John Menzies. Those of you shafted by life, unlucky in love, or just plain mental will find far better advice at Camelot than you will on the psychiatrist's couch. Take it from me. After three wars, one famine, a revolution and a marriage that put Royalty to shame in its messiness, I arrived at my local hospital in need of 'help'.

After a long, laboured talk, I was taught to relax. Under mild hypnosis I was asked to imagine myself in a place of calm, a place of safety and sanctuary. And so I found myself on a large chequered floor in the clothes of a knight, laying down my sword, shield and helmet and kneeling before the stone altar and the lion's head. I was humbled and free. I lifted up my hands, took the Grail and supped the wine therein. I was filled with the peace and love that no quack can deliver.

So go where the dreams take you. If, upon your quest, you have any amusing incidences with witches, dragons or demons, don't forget to record them on your Camcorder and send them to me, Gavin Hills, *The Candid Camelot Show*, left by the lake, a leap of faith at the drawbridge, Camelot, probably Cornwall, maybe Wales, or an outside chance of Essex.

The Idler, July–August 1995

A Song for Europe

Before every match England plays, the team lines up and sings the national anthem. Except it's not, strictly speaking, the English national anthem. 'God Save the Queen' is, in fact, the *British* national anthem. It is the anthem played on royal visits or at Olympic victories. Recently, the English rugby team decided to drop 'God Save the Queen' in favour of the more English 'I Vow to Thee My Country'. For years, the English Commonwealth team has received medals to the tune of 'Land of Hope and Glory'. So should the England football team change the habits of a lifetime and have a new national anthem? And if so, what should it be?

THE CASE AGAINST
For hundreds of years, the English have sung 'God Save the Queen' as the national anthem. Why should we suddenly break with tradition and go changing it? As England is at the centre of the United Kingdom and is home to both Queen and Parliament, it seems only right that we continue to use the British national anthem as our own. It is the oldest national anthem in the world and we should feel proud to sing it. And, on a practical level, at least everyone knows the words.

THE CASE FOR
As England are hosting the European championship next year, it would be nice for the team to go out on the pitch to a tune the whole nation could sing. England has changed in the last few years, and as part of the EEC it would be nice if we could keep hold of our identity as a separate nation. What better way than with a new national anthem? They've done it in rugby and athletics, why not

football? And let's face it, 'God Save the Queen' is a pretty dull tune, and in a country that increasingly is at odds with its royalty, its lyrics aren't really appropriate. It would be great for us to spur on the England team at the start of a match with a song like 'Jerusalem' or even 'You'll Never Walk Alone'. There's no reason why the UK shouldn't keep 'God Save the Queen' as an anthem, but the English have a new one. Even the Queen would probably enjoy a change from that dreadful tune day in and day out.

THE HISTORY OF THE NATIONAL ANTHEM

Ours is the world's oldest national anthem, yet it is probably also the dullest. Billy Connolly once said it was so awful it should be replaced with the theme from *The Archers*. The Queen hears the tune an average of six times a day and has heard it an estimated quarter of a million times in her life! It's a simple tune with only fourteen bars and is within the reach of even the worst musician. Because of its simple nature, it is very hard to pin down the origins of it. The combination of rhythms and melodies have been identified in a number of seventeenth-century dances, including a Christmas carol, 'Remember, O Thou Man', published in 1611; a keyboard piece by John Bull (1619); and a minuet for harpsichord by Purcell posthumously published in 1696.

No one is credited with the words, but it was printed in a songbook called *Harmonia Anglicana* in 1744. The first recorded performance of the then 'God Save the King', according to some, took place at the Drury Lane and Covent Garden theatres on successive nights in September 1745, following Bonnie Prince Charlie's victory at the battle of Prestopans near Edinburgh, until the threat of this young pretender had passed. The Scots have always been a bit uppity over the fact that the anthem was first performed to celebrate an English victory over the Scots.

The words and music of the 1745 version became popular and have lasted, although generally speaking people sing only the first verse. The other verses are full of lovely little bits of bigotry and xenophobia. The second verse includes the lines, '*Scatter his enemies and make them fail/Confound their politicks/Frustrate their knavish tricks . . .*', and has been dropped in recent times for obvious reasons.

Some people say that the original words were actually pro-Scottish Jacobite, but it's generally thought that it was sung to the gladness of King George II. There have, however, been loads of other versions, some very pro-Royalty, and others celebrating the French Revolution appeared throughout the eighteenth century. Typical was this version penned in 1793: '*Long live great guillotine/ Who shaves the head so clean/Of queen or king/Whose power is so great/ That every tool of state/Dreadeth his mighty weight/Wonderful thing!*'

Other countries have also used the tune. At some point, twenty different countries have used it as their official or semi-official anthem. Some of the most famous versions have been from the USA: 'God Save America', 'God Save George Washington' and 'God Save the President'. These days the Yanks sing the words, 'My Country, 'Tis of Thee'. The habit of singing '*der, der, der, Der, Der!*' just before '*Send her victorious*' can be attributed to England fans. Who says we're not creative?

One of the most unusual times the anthem has been booed at Wembley was not, predictably, by the Scots, but by Scousers who attended the 1989 cup final between Liverpool and Everton, and thought it inappropriate after the Hillsborough tragedy.

Wales The Welsh national anthem is sung, funnily enough, in Welsh. The problem is that most of the Welsh football team haven't a clue what the words are. If you watch their lips before an international you'll see the only words they sing are when the crowd roars '*Plaid, Plaid!*'. This is not a reference to a particular sort of checked tweed, but Welsh for 'ours'.

Scotland 'Flower of Scotland' is the Scottish national anthem – and very vindictive it is, too. It's a post-war nationalist folk-song crowing on about a minor victory over the English in 1314. The battle of

low

Bannockburn did indeed send *'proud Edward's army homeward to think again!'* Although, after thinking for a while, Edward's son soon re-invaded and Scotland was under English control by 1333. Hardly something to sing about, especially when you consider that the English were also having to fight the French (aided by those treacherous Scots) at the same time!

THE NEW ANTHEM

There are many ideas about what the English national anthem should be, here are a few favourite options:

'Land of Hope and Glory'   Written in 1902 by A. C. Bensom for the finale of Elgar's 'Coronation Ode', this is the tune that is sung at the last night of the Proms by a load of chinless wonders. Used by the English athletics team, its lyrics are seldom sung as they sound plain daft and are quite hard to remember. Already has a strong football connection as fans sing *'We hate Nottingham Forest, We hate Arsenal, too'*, etc., to it.
Singability: 7/10   Patriotic content: 8/10   Tunefulness: 9/10

'Jerusalem'   William Blake was an English radical. A genius and a patriot, his version of 'Jerusalem' was written in the late-eighteenth century and has been a rallying cry for Englishmen ever since. Used as both a song for schools, trade unions and political parties, its appeal is across the board. It has been used in the past by the group KLF and, more recently, was used by Sky to introduce their FA cup coverage.
Singability: 9/10   Patriotic content: 10/10   Tunefulness: 9/10

'You'll Never Walk Alone'   Originally from the hit musical *Carousel*, it was covered by the popular beat combo of the time Gerry and the Pacemakers. There is great debate about which club's supporters were the first to sing it as a football song, with claims coming from Manchester City, Liverpool, Celtic and even Leicester. The song

has long been connected with Liverpool, and its title appears on the famous Shankley gates, although most clubs sing it. Italian fans sang it after a minute's silence for the Hillsborough victims before league matches in 1989.

Singability: 10/10   Patriotic content: 1/10   Tunefulness: 8/10

'Abide With Me'   The traditional pre-FA-cup hymn. Guaranteed to bring a tear to the eyes of even the most hardened footballing male. Written by H. F. Lyte in the 1830s, what it lacks in poetry it makes up for in pure passion.

Singability: 7/10   Patriotic content: 8/10   Tunefulness: 7/10

'I Vow to Thee My Country'   Will Carling's choice of anthem for the English rugby team. It was also Lady Di's choice of hymn for her ill-fated wedding to the Prince of Wales. The tune is from Holst's 'Planets Suite', and the original words from 'The Last Poem' by Sir Cecil Arthur Spring.

Singability: 7/10   Patriotic content: 9/10   Tunefulness: 6/10

England, June–July 1995

True Blues

There is nothing wrong in supporting Chelsea. Why, some of my best friends support Chelsea. What they choose to do on a Saturday afternoon is their own business. There's actually something quite admirable about people who loyally stand by a club who could, quite conceivably, have Lord Lucan hiding in their trophy room.

There's also nothing wrong in supporting Glasgow Rangers. Many a close relative of mine cheers them on. Their dominance of Scottish football has to be admired, even though their recent performance in Europe does make Manchester United's weak showing look like a glory trail. In fact, there's even nothing wrong about supporting the Ulster side Linfield, apart from the fact that nobody has heard of them. And, more importantly, being a Protestant does not mean you should automatically be labelled a fascist. Hitler, Mussolini and Franco: all Catholics. I rest my case.

What *does* matter, though, is being somebody like Eddie. I met Eddie in Bruges at Chelsea's recent European Cup Winner's Cup quarter-final. Eddie is a True Blue – a follower of Chelsea, Rangers and Linfield, and a young man who has attached himself to the Protestant/Unionist cause to give credibility to his dated racist dogma. To get an idea of how narrow the perspective of people like Eddie is, let's forget the blacks, the Jews, the Pakistanis and even the Fenians. Let's just hear Eddie on the English: 'Well, scousers aren't fucking English, are they? Do you remember the Everton v. Liverpool Cup Final? They booed the national anthem, for fuck's sake! If we were fucking civilized, we'd shoot them as fucking traitors!'

Perhaps this is the real reason why, despite bold attempts to bolster their racist/bigoted credibility, Everton's scummier elements have never been fully included in the True Blue alliance. Geordies or anyone from the North-East also should not apply. 'Middlesborough, Geordies – all that fucking lot. Fucking savages. Take more welfare than the fucking blacks. They're not even part of fucking England. They should be shoved back with all the nasty sweaties.' (Sweaties as in sweaty socks i.e. jocks, the Scottish.)

True Blue Eddie finds no contradiction in denigrating his fellow countrymen and being a staunch defender of the Union. To the likes of Eddie, defending the Union is not about the rights of self-determination, economic well-being or, God forbid, a woman's right to choose abortion. It's about feeling that the IRA are a bunch of wankers and knowing the words to lots of good Proddy songs. 'The Sash My Father Wore' and 'No Surrender' are jolly little sectarian tunes, but there does seem something essentially daft about singing 'We're the Boys from Londonderry' if in fact you come from Slough.

Despite some perceptions of the club, Chelsea *does* have Jewish, black and Asian supporters, even in their occasional Continental forays. Many were evident in Bruges. Their fan-base has altered, though, since the fashionable days of the early Seventies, when they were the Chelsea of the King's Road and pop stars hung out with Peter Osgood. Now they are not so much the side of west London – that dubious honour must go to QPR – but the side of the home counties and the Thames Valley. These days you are more likely to find Chelsea fans from Tunbridge Wells and Slough than you are from Fulham and Putney. It is from these, less cosmopolitan, areas that the white-trash Eddies who have associated themselves with the True Blues come from. This strange awakening of Unionism in the suburbs would be laughable if it didn't have a more sinister side.

After the recent riot during England's friendly match against Ireland at Lansdowne Road, many put the blame on far-right/ extreme-loyalist sympathizers. The BNP, the National Front, C18 and absurdities like the Cheltenham Volunteer Force were blamed for 'organizing' the riot. There were claims by some England followers that they had been supplied tickets by the UDA. While there is little doubt that members and supporters of right-wing movements were involved in the trouble, to say they were capable of organizing it is to elevate them to a status they hardly deserve. All-day drinking, desegregation of the crowd, an impotent Gardi, the background of the Anglo-Irish peace talks, an early goal to Ireland and the 'anything for a laugh' attitude of about half the England supporters at the match combined to ensure it ended in a riot. The right-wing types in attendance encouraged and joined in the whole sorry shambles, but the publicity they achieved from it was largely undeserved. However, over the last ten years sectarianism has crept unchallenged into English soccer. And the promotion of Unionism as bigotry has given new, respectable clothes to old fascists.

Wide-scale, openly racist chanting died out at England matches during the Eighties. While racism now is still far too common in football, it rarely takes the form of whole ends singing evil spear-chucker/wog/Auschwitz nonsense, as was common in the Seventies. Instead, the traditional vague sectarian links of English clubs have become exaggerated. Spurs are still seen as a Jewish club even though probably just as many Jews support the traditionally Greek/Irish Arsenal. Man United are still perceived as Celtic's English cousin because of their big support in Ireland, even though a large number of those Irish fans are Protestant, manager Alex Ferguson is ex-Govan/Glasgow Rangers and George Best has got to be the only player ever to have had his life threatened by the IRA. By the flying of tricolours and the wearing of Celtic hats, Liverpool fans also denoted their sectarian angle against their blue neighbours in a city which was returning Protestant councillors up until the Seventies.

By the 1988 European Championships in Germany, if chants and singing were anything to go by, it was evident that sectarianism had replaced obvious racism at football games. In the match against the Irish Republic in Stuttgart, England fans got on rather well with their Irish counterparts. Many shared the same camping sites, tents even. The bars down town were filled with friendly rivals, as things should be. This despite the small Nazi rally which took place in the town square. There, 'No Pope' stickers were handed out, a black passer-by was chased down the street, and this little song was sung to the tune of 'Sing Hosanna': *'Keep St George in my heart keep me English/Keep St George in my heart I pray/Keep St George in my heart keep me English/So no surrender to the IRA.'* Chorus: *'No surrender, no surrender, no surrender to the IRA!'*, repeated *ad nauseam*. This is a song that has echoed on many a foreign field ever since.

The appeal of anti-IRA jingoism was very obvious. Despite the fact that there has always been a rather surprisingly broad support for a vague Irish unity amongst the English, the IRA are despised. It's not hard to sing anti-IRA songs, but for so many sad ignorant sods this is the start of acceptance of fascist and racist clothing. Idiots like Eddie lap it up.

Sitting in a bar in the backstreets of Bruges before Chelsea's big match, you could spy a rogue's gallery of hoolies, ex-hoolies, thugs and morons. The Belgian police's plan of preventing known trouble-makers getting into their country clearly failed. They did succeed, however, in deporting fathers and sons, old men and several ticket-holding, law-abiding Chelsea fans who had the nerve to try going sightseeing around the town centre before the match. They also managed to blindly baton several of their own supporters and turn a water cannon on a warehouseful of Chelsea 'criminals', none of whom had been charged with anything. Why is it no one seems to be able to get the bad guys any more?

Even of the bad guys, few these days are active, instigating hooligans, even fewer are True Blues, and even fewer of them true Nazis. There were some worrying people about, though. Worrying, ugly people. Ulster and Glasgow accents were in evidence, as was the shaded line between suburban Unionism and Thames Valley fascism. After a few choruses of 'No Surrender' the bar-owner, perhaps thinking that if it had swearing on it the thugs would like it, put on a hardcore-rap record. After a few bars, some nice chaps next to me shouted, 'Put some fucking white music on, you cunt!', then joined their mates in a good old-fashioned '*Sieg heil!*' These chaps are wannabe C18 fascists. And, given that these are supposed to be the master race, C18 are not an attractive crew. Any really effective Final Solution would have cut off their mutant genetic bloodlines years ago.

You want to write off such an obvious bunch of saps. You think that by writing about them you may be giving them undue publicity. The truth is that even at Chelsea and England matches they are a minority of thugs in a minority of hooligans, and if they can't even make headway there, things look pretty bleak for the Fourth Reich. But one wonders how the police can fail to identify and arrest them when everyone with an ounce of savvy can find them without any problems.

The True Blue connection of thug support for Protestant terrorists is real. However, the vast majority of it is a one-way street. Although more reactionary than their IRA adversaries, the UVF were/are an organized terrorist group. Their security procedures do not allow for budding Leatherhead-based loonies to have a tour of duty in West Belfast. Fund-raising gives a few True Blues the feeling that they're playing with the big boys. Yet, like so much of the neo-Nazi claptrap, the reality of their claims is little more than bluff. Don't get me wrong – these guys *are* terrorists. They are terrorists of a more cowardly nature than the IRA they despise so much. These are the fine specimens of British youth that bravely terrorize unarmed Asian families and lone black Britons.

Football no longer provides the big arena for these people to wage an openly racist war. A BNP supporter actually boasted about selling ten copies of his paper outside Glasgow Rangers' ground, Ibrox. Rangers' average gate is 40,000-plus. He did, however, add, 'If everybody who wanted to buy one did, I would have enough to go and live in the Bahamas.' (An odd destination for a racist, it has to be said.) The rivalry between, say, Spurs and Arsenal is based on geography and playing style. Soccer's sectarian battles are based on 600 years of bloody history. Such hatreds are easy to exploit and have given an air of authenticity to some dire, dodgy Chelsea fans.

The trouble needs to be tackled. While nobody should be punished for being a Chelsea, Rangers or even a Linfield fan, it must be clearly understood that thuggy little fascists are latching on to such ties. You could question whether unofficial souvenir stalls outside Stamford Bridge should be selling Rangers T-shirts. And, although no one could doubt that Chelsea chairman Ken Bates abhors racism, some might feel he would be best advised not to use the club programme to air political views. References to dole scroungers, illegal immigrants, 'Brussels wasters' and parasites (from a Bates column last season) could be seen by some as encouraging the Eddies of this world.

The real battle, however, has to be fought by the fans themselves. As the prospects for peace in Northern Ireland look the brightest in twenty-five years, we can hope that this cloak of Unionist respectability is removed from these racist thugs. In the meantime, however, it's time to isolate, repudiate and alienate these ugly second-raters.

The Face, April 1995

Zagreb Blue Boys: An Apology

On 6 September, England play the former Yugoslavian republic of Croatia. In the vain hope that some of their visiting fans might read this, I would like to print the following apology . . .

Riding around with my brother and friend Sylvester a few years ago, we came to find ourselves in the beautiful Croatian capital of Zagreb. Being strangers in town, our first task was to look for accommodation. We were low in money but high in spirits, and we settled on a youth hostel. The building was not picturesque and the view of the chicken-packing factory was not ideal, but our simple room was clean and the three bunk-beds ample for our needs.

Once rested, we left to explore the town. After an exciting jaunt on their marvellous integrated train system, the call went up to quench our thirst in a lovely little baroque bar away from the main town square. There we sat, sipping reasonably priced local orange cordial. As evening fell, eight young gentlemen arrived in the bar, singing, joking and laughing. They plonked a bottle of frighteningly undrinkable vodka down on our table, and proceeded to introduce themselves. They were the Zagreb Blue Boys, followers of Croatia Zagreb FC – the country's leading side after the mighty Hajduk Split.

We spent a fine evening swapping stories about all aspects of the wonderful game of association football. After a large splash of chat, they made a very generous offer. We were asked to play football the next morning in a friendly match at their famous Makasimir stadium! After a few choruses of their club song, we invited everyone back to our hostel. This, I now see, was a mistake.

On entering the hostel room and turning on the light, it became clear that what we thought was a room to ourselves was actually shared with others. The three spare beds in the bunks were taken by large sleeping Germans, who failed to see the humour in us inviting the Zagreb Blue Boys back.

This tense situation was worsened as one of our Croatian friends knocked his head on the main light, rendering it useless. In the blackness, several nationalities groped for direction. After what seemed like an age, the Blue Boys decided to depart. We were left to stumble in the darkness to find a spare bunk for the night. The situation was further exasperated by the queasiness that took hold of my brother. After settling in a top bunk, the evening got the better of him, and he proceeded to be sick all over his EEC partner on the lower tier.

Management were called and we were politely asked to leave the premises. I thought, under the circumstances, it was the least we could do. We took the next train out of town, missing our crucial fixture at the Makasimir.

I know from a subsequent letter that all of the Blue Boys turned out for us the next day. I also know that they were under the impression, due to high-spirited blackguardry on my part, that we played for Manchester United. So if you're out there, Blue Boys – if you're out there, Germans, come to that – I'm sorry. I'm really, really sorry.

England, August–September 1995

White Men Can't Toyi-Toyi!

Black man holds hands with white man as they march in protest down the street. People are chanting, demanding justice. As the protesters reach fever pitch, they start to *toyi-toyi* – make the traditional South African sound of protest. The left leg lifts up, holds crook for a few seconds, then scuttles downwards while the right leg shoots up and repeats the action. A white man at the front of the march is hopelessly out of rhythm. The only thing that is swaying in time is his large pot belly, which flaps over his belt with each lumbering step. The scene is pretty ridiculous and the police are looking nervous. The police are looking *very* nervous, actually, because the protesters *are* the police. Low pay and bad working conditions have sent them out into the streets they used to terrorize. This is the New South Africa, topsy-turvy land, where now even the police have the right to be shat on.

Cape Town, home of the newly elected government of South Africa. Table Mountain scratches the blue skyline, dwarfing the city built by settlers and suffering. From its summit you can view the new Rainbow Nation in all its glory. From up there you can see the skyscrapers of a world financial centre, the pristine chalets of a luxury beach resort, even the compulsory revamped docklands mall complex which it seems all modern cities must have. Look a little further, into the sea, and you'll see Robben Island, where Nelson Mandela whiled away many of his years in prison. There he dreamed of an end to apartheid and a democratic future for all his country's citizens. There he dreamed of freedom and liberty. I find it hard to believe that he ever dreamed of this current scenario.

While I'm in Cape Town, President Mandela is about to celebrate a year in office. He got there as the result of a long struggle. There was no war, no collapsing economy, and no blood baths – save those of the old regime. This is a result that even the most optimistic of commentators would have found laughable and surreal. What they would make of the current shenanigans doesn't bear thinking about.

David Bowie and Iman are in town and round Nelson's presidential palace. They're doing a photo shoot with him for American *Vogue*. Superstar fashion-photographer Bruce Weber is taking the pictures. He wants a grand piano in the shot and spends thousands of dollars sending out for one, only to decide against it. Life has served Nelson an odd slice of pie. Few people in this world can have had such a varied career: enemy of the state, rock smasher, party leader, subject of a Specials hit single, President, statesman, *Vogue* model.

Saturday night and Cape Town is rocking. Down in a large warehouse in the docklands, thousands of young and beautiful beings are crowding in to take drugs and dance. These ravers move to the thumping sounds of 'top UK house DJs' that I've never heard of. The foam is switched on and we could be in Ibiza. This is Africa, yet most of the punters are white. The black club is downtown and rocking to swingbeat. Out clubbing in South Africa, it is tempting to think how segregated everything is. This is, of course, tosh. Apartheid means 'separateness' in Afrikaans. Cosmopolitan cities world-wide, even in my own dear London, have their own clubland separateness. In fact, Cape Town is just like London in many respects, even down to the fish and chips, the ludicrous red plastic Comic Relief noses on all the cars and the late-night queue for Rizlas at garage shops. You can breathe the air in Cape Town though – it's clean and by the sea. So perhaps a sunnier Brighton is a better image. It is South Africa's gay capital, after all.

In the bars in town where the Carling Black Label flows and traveller trash go disco and karaoke, you meet white settlers old and new. There, they say what all ex-pat people say after the briefest of introductions: 'Do you like it here? It's wonderful, isn't it, not what you expected, eh?' It is indeed a beautiful place. No doubt these people genuinely like it here. But you do detect a certain desperation in their voices as they seek your approval. They sound like the brainwashed masses of a religious cult. You get the feeling they want new members to sing their happy songs, live in their fool's paradise, ignoring the real world – a world in which white homes are pretty but smothered in barbed wire, littered with security buttons and labelled with plaques announcing that intruders should expect an armed response.

'They're not embarrassed to say they're South African. It's like it's cool to be a South African. It's like one year on and they don't feel guilty any more. Most of them are still the same old racist shits, though.' So speaks Lance. Lance is a committed, thirtysomething hip-hop manager with hair the size of a gooseberry bush and trousers that don't reach his ankles. Rather like the bold Y-fronts of the New South African flag, Lance is also 'coloured'. Coloured is a peculiarly South African term, and one that was enshrined in apartheid law.

In the old days of divide and rule, the hierarchy went like this. On the top was whitey. Whitey was divided between the Dutch white-trash settler descendants known as the Afrikaaners or Boer, and the old colonial Brits. History, on balance, gives the Brits the upper hand, as we beat them in the Boer War. (Afrikaaners still hold a grudge against the Brits because of this, since we put loads of them in concentration camps.) Next in line come Asians, who are mainly from the Indian subcontinent. Then we have the 'coloureds'. These are mixed-race South Africans, many the result of relationships between Malayan slaves that were imported to the area and local black girls. On the bottom rung are the blacks, and even there we have divisions. First is your Zulu, traditionally favoured by many a white regime, then there's your ANC-supporting average black man, and finally the poor sods who are work-seeking immigrants from countries like Mozambique and Botswana. (These handy terms of racial reference will be used sporadically from now on.)

Anyway, Lance can't believe the Boer have changed overnight. 'I mean, the wealth's still in their hands and that's the real power. I think some of them are so fucked up they want Mandela to screw the country up, even though it will ruin their economy. They just want to say, "I told you so!"' Luckily for coloured Lance, and the other 99.9 per cent of South Africa, the white Boer haven't had a chance to yet.

Lance manages Prophets Of Da City, South Africa's finest hip-hop band. The Prophets are local heroes, Cape Town's own. A posse of blacks and coloureds. Coloureds like DJ Dion, a.k.a. Ready-D, who knew he was coloured from an early age because his parents had to go in front of a tribunal to prove it. 'It was crazy. They did all these dumb tests. They even used to stick a pencil in your hair. If it stayed you were black, if it fell out you were coloured,' he recalls with a wry smile. Dion is a man on a mission. For him, as for the rest of the band, Da Struggle Kontinues. This is the title of their new single. The spelling is not some weird hip-hop affectation, but the Afrikaans spelling. In South Africa 'school' is really spelt 'skool', old or otherwise.

Dion's struggle is a personal one, but it is one that reflects the continuing struggle for justice that is going on through the new South Africa. He grew up in Cape Town's central area, District Six. The area is now barren save for a few police houses and a rather incongruous polytechnic. One lone squatter makes a home in the scrub. 'This used to be the main street. Over there was my aunt's house, and that's where I used to go to school,' Dion points out as we walk through what looks like the proposed site for an NCP car park. 'It was a ghetto, I suppose, but a nice one. Lots of markets and cafés. It was very mixed, lots of different races. My house was over there.'

I stare at a pile of stones and reflect that if this area had been left alone it would have made an ideal Soho-style centre for the new South Africa. Instead, they have the anaemic docklands mall complex. Cape Town could have had soul in its heart – instead it's got Milton Keynes.

When Dion was a young boy, in the late Seventies, letters went around District Six announcing everyone had six months to leave. The apartheid regime had decided that this prime bit of real estate was too good for the darkies, and it was time to get rid of them. District Six was harassed – it wasn't as if they even had anywhere to go. Luckily, fat white boss-guy P. W. Botha solved this tiresome little problem. Flying around in his helicopter, Botha spied an area the other side of Table Mountain. The area was so sandy and so barren that not even the dumbest of settlers had pitched a shack there during the years of white invasion. So good old P. W. decided to send them there.

So Dion and his family and all the rest of District Six were resettled on the Cape Flats, in an area known as Mitchell's Plain. Their old stomping ground was flattened and all the houses bull-dozed. All, that is, except one. Mr Abubakar Brown is a coloured gentleman who stayed to the bitter end. He had lived in District Six since the turn of the century. He remembers it being a holy place, where Muslim and Christian alike used to worship together. He also remembers the nearby fort being a whorehouse. 'They knocked down all the houses until only mine was left,' he recalls. 'The trouble was, it became too dangerous. They put a lot of pressure on me and, anyway, the houses left and right which were supporting my house were demolished, so I had to leave eventually.'

In 1980 Mr Brown 'resettled' in Mitchell's Plain. He is now honorary president of the campaign to get District Six back for its exiled residents. It's a slow and painful process. Many people in South Africa think that now is not the time to rock the boat. 'Mustn't upset whitey' is a hard mind-set to throw off. Coloureds are the filling in South Africa's sandwich, perceived by many as stuck between black and white. Divide and rule worked well. A lot of coloureds still want to hold on to the little advantage they had over the blacks in the last regime. In Cape Town at the last election, swung by the coloured vote, the right-wing National Party had one of its few electoral successes. But for Dion, Mr Brown and the other residents of District Six, da struggle definitely kontinues. Or, to put it another way, 'When you know people actually died so they could just shit in the same toilet as a white man, you know you've got to keep pushing.'

Dion and the boys have the trappings and the beats of black America. The roots of this music clearly lead back to Africa. However, black America's relationship with Africa is something of a confused one. Africa is reinvented and twisted to suit a black American way of thinking. Afrika Bambaataa's Zulu Nation is an odd concept to many non-Zulu blacks in SA, even though many joined it. Yet it's easy to underestimate the inspiration of growing up seeing successful black people in the States, even if it was just in the form of pop stars. The rap scene started early in South Africa, all on import. And, as it proved for so many youths, hip hop was a blessing and an education.

Hip hop's life blood is authenticity. That's what every act seeks to impress on the punters. That's why black kids live it while white kids love it. That's why so many rap acts are posturing prats who wouldn't know a ghetto if they drove through it in their BMW. On the authenticity scale (in which, say, Vanilla Ice and MC Hammer nestle somewhere near the bottom with PJ and Duncan), Prophets of da City are near the tippity-top. The average gangsta rapper may have a good line in Uzis, crack and bitches, but he wouldn't last five minutes in a township like Cape Town's Crossroads. He wouldn't be wearing any flash gold jewellery, only a nice fat burning rubber necklace.

The Prophets aren't hard men, though. They know their politics. It was beaten into them with a policeman's bully club. They're conscious, they know their Biko. Steve *'Cry Freedom'* Biko – the voice of resistance and victim of apartheid. The man who taught that if you free your mind, your country would follow. He helped deprogramme the black mind from one of submission to an educated, achieving, conscious mind. It's his message that the Prophets preach. They take it up and down the country from townships to talkshows. They keep it simple: get a clue, get a life!

Bonny Toun is a correction centre for twelve- to eighteen-year-olds. It holds gang members, thieves and even murderers. The boys here are lucky, because they are not in prison. Prison is a nightmare. 'You have to know your numbers in prison,' muses Shaheen, the Prophets' coloured rapper.

The numbers? 'Yeah, you got to go in as a 27, and act mad so no one will touch you. The 28s'll get you otherwise,' explains black Ramone, the Prophets' very own Bez figure. The numbers are gang slang: 26 is a thief; 27 a murderer; 28 a big man who forcibly buggers other inmates; 30 a fatty who gets buggered. In Bonny Toun they're lucky because the 28s aren't going to get them. They're also lucky because today the Prophets are here to give them a talk. They rap their Afrikaans hit 'Dallah Flet' (roughly translated, 'Go For It'), and the inmates go mental. The youngest inmates get called to the stage for a turn on the mic. There's even an impromptu break-dancing competition.

It's hard to believe that the kids in Bonny Toun are anything more than kids. The only sign that some of them might be anything except angels is the tattoos on the older boys' legs. There are initials like USA and JFK: gang names. Gangs in Cape Town have diabolical names. There's the Junky Funky Kids, the Young Americans, the Ugly Americans, the Rooster Boosters, the Ninja Turtles. There are even running car wars between those who drive Nissans and those who drive Cortinas. It would all be a big joke if you didn't know that young people die every day in these nightmare township gang wars. Six people died on just one night during my visit.

The band offer a credible voice in the midst of all this and, remarkably, it seems listened to. At best, their music is tuneful ragga with tribal beats. An original mishmash which, when done with confidence, creates an atmosphere of empowerment. Cynicism is shot when you see ideals in action. Prophets of da City play a decent tune and have political savvy devoid of posturing. In the tired hip-hop vernacular, respect is due.

During both World Wars, shiploads of black South Africans came and fought for us. Thousands died. The ones that made it home were promised the moon and ended up with just a bicycle, even the crippled ones. During the last years of apartheid, white Thatcher desperately tried to back up the regime. She fought against sanctions and white Norman Tebbit insisted black Mandela was a terrorist. This was wrong. We *owe* South Africa.

Mandela's in charge now. He's there because international sanctions and boycotts crippled the evil apartheid regime into submission. Now the struggle continues. It's the struggle for justice. It's a struggle we should support. We should press for land rights, investment and justice for those for whom apartheid was a robber, a killer and a general 28. We should also look at ourselves, our own politics. Think of the Eighties, of the lame arguments given by the sanction-busters. Think of Mike Gatting and his cricket tour, of Status Quo and Queen playing Sun City. Think of the guilty that remain unpunished. Know in your heart that the struggle continues. We have few heroes left in this world – let's support the ones we've got.

The Face, June 1995

Diary of a Trainer Spotter

Plimmies. That's what they were called. They were black with an elasticated top and a pinky rubber sole. You wore them in gym. They cost a couple of quid from Woolies. Cool didn't come into it. Then along came the Dunlop Green Flash, and innocence was lost. Choice had entered the playground. Life would never be the same again.

For the uninitiated, 'trainer culture' is one of the many signals of the growing Mammon in our society. It sits somewhere between Manchester United's 'Sharp Viewcam' kit and the Lottery. It is part of the descent into a world in which conspicuous wealth is seen as an individual's only true worth. An obvious sign that the country has turned its back on religion and learning and filled the void in its young's lives with the branded motifs of Nike and Adidas. That's as maybe, but all I know is I'd rather be stuck in a lift for eight hours with Anthea Turner and David Mellor than ever be seen in public in a pair of snide Woolies trainers.

If you ignore the shallow veneer of athletic need, trainer culture started in the Seventies with the Dunlop Green Flash. Not a striking trainer, and a complete joke by today's standards, yet an important shoe in the grand scheme of things. For the Green Flash was one of the first trainers to be worn outside of the dusty parquet floor of the school gym. Young herberts wore Green Flash everywhere from kicking balls in the park to hanging around the chip shop waiting for McDonald's to be invented.

Fickleness was soon to set in, however, and by the time the first *Grange Hill* came on our screen, they were already a no-no. They had been replaced with the more expensive, sexier Adidas Samba. In the late Seventies/early Eighties, the Samba was the shoe that launched trainer culture. It was plain black with three simple white stripes. Those who first possessed this shoe felt not as mortals do. They strutted the playgrounds, youth clubs and football terraces like the champions of Troy.

This status was seductive. For the next five years, many young working-class men and women devoted their lives to the pursuit of the perfect trainer. Perfection being defined by exclusivity. Exclusivity being defined not necessarily by price and availability, but by that and the enigma of the right brand. It was the era of the ubiquitous Nike Bruin and the élite football casual classic – the kangaroo-skinned gold flash Diadora Bjorn Borg. It saw a small, simple sports-shoe market blossom into a gold rush for the sole of young Britain.

Beneath the surface of this trainer craze was the underlying erosion of formality in all walks of lives. In jeans and trainers, you feel comfortable, at ease with the modern world. (The army is now relaxing some of its strict uniform rules on its raw recruits, due to the fact that their feet are unaccustomed to the traditional army boot.) On top of this were the old 'Mod' values of innovation and aspiration. Trainers became an accessible sign of status. In a world of unemployment and alienation, you got to feel 'Top Boy' – the new version of 'Ace Face'.

Trainers were not, strictly speaking, the street version of the Porsche or the mobile phone of yuppiedom. While some of their status came from conspicuous expense, most came from a knowledge of what to buy and where. A knowledge unobtainable to those who sought credibility in stocks and shares. Yet, aided by their informality, trainers moved swiftly into the mainstream. Trainer culture is not a strictly British trend, either. There is not a nightclub in the western world where you won't find someone wearing a pair of Adidas Gazelles.

The Gazelle is the trainer that has conquered the West and standardized youth culture to the extent of the blue jean. The Gazelle has had a bizarre life. It was never, as perceived, an 'old skool hip hop' shoe worn by the trainer-conscious Stateside rappers of the early Eighties. That honour goes to the Adidas Shell-toe. No, the Gazelle started to make an impact among Northern football casuals in about 1982. Like the basketball boot, the Converse All-Star, it had a more universal appeal than most trainers. Its simple lines and flat bottom meant it was adopted by skateboarders in San Francisco towards the end of the decade. When skate styles got mixed up with hip-hop styles here a few years back, suddenly it became 'old skool'. It then burst into a variety of colours on sale in the trendy London menswear shop The Duffer of St George – and, soon after, Top Man.

Bung on a pair of Gazelles, some Stüssy trousers and a Ralph Lauren sweatshirt, and you're not going to look out of place whether you're in Milan, Munich or Boise, Idaho. Trainers have had androgyny to help them conquer. They have graced the female fashion press for years. They no longer send the signal 'sporty', but rather 'sussed'. They are a sign of freedom. They seem first choice for Indie Girl. Rave Babe finds them a lot easier to frolic in than laced-up jackboots. Whatever the trend, they appear to go with anything; stick on a posh frock with a nice pair of Vans and you can go down the local, then dine with Dai Llewellyn if needs be.

Trainer culture's only real challenge comes from the recent boom in workwear. City kids like a bit of ruff. There's nothing like wearing the great outdoors on your feet if you live in Mile End. Timberland, Red-Wing [CHK] and Caterpillar all give a rural security to the unsure feet of the mountain-biking/jeep-driving urban masses. This has not gone unnoticed by the likes of Nike and Adidas: the latest lines in trainers are all of the scramble-up-mountains/traipse-through-forests / wade-through-rivers / run-away-from-rogue-bears variety. Strong soles and waterproof uppers seem the order of the day. This is more than a tad sensible. The winter is cruel on the trainer culture. Many are the sleepless nights as one tries to muffle, with pillow on ear, the sound of damp trainers thudding around the tumble-dryer.

Apart from soggy toes in winter, trainer culture has one other major problem. Despite years of growth, since the far-off days of Woolies plimsolls and the Dunlop Green Flash, a good trainer is hard to find. On a recent expedition in search of quality footwear, I was struck by the fact that there was nothing I really wanted. There was the mundane (Adidas, Reebok, Nike), the naff (British Knights, Travel Fox, Hi-Tec), the gauche (Fila, Puma, Tacchini) and the plain absurd (Asics, Airwalk and Northwave).

I ended up buying a pair of Vans low-tops. The same style and brand I first bought over ten years ago. (Flat rubber sole, canvas top – not dissimilar to a certain Dunlop Green Flash, come to think of it.) Except then I was about ten stone lighter and could run for a bus without coughing up my stomach lining.

Spending half my life clad in trainers has singularly failed to prompt me into an active lifestyle. Still, who needs to spend an age working on the ridiculously sculpted torso of a Chippendale? That's what people who don't know what trainers to wear end up doing. That's the key to trainers. They are a symbol of urban suss and knowledge. Not something the clueless can simply buy into or work out. Mammon doesn't come into it.

Guardian, 22 November 1995

My Wonderful Life

They discharged me from hospital the other day. I skipped along the street with a smile on my face and started laughing to myself. I was officially sane, and had a letter to prove it! As with most of life's good news, it was short-lived. The drawbacks were soon pointed out by friends. Sanity had brought with it certain responsibilities. I could no longer murder people at random and claim diminished responsibility. Sympathy would be scant if I went to feed frozen chickens to the lions at London Zoo. And if/when I next take my clothes off in public, my joy would be tampered by the knowledge that this particular perversion could no longer be discounted under the get-out clause of certifiability. Fuck, rumbled at last. The world of reason is not to my liking.

This tragedy of existence is quelled by the current popular culture. Cantona's back. Noel and Liam are rocking. Jarvis and Damon are quipping. From Brighton to Blackpool, something's swinging. I saw Vic and Bob on the telly the other night. Isn't it warming to live in a time of heroes? Things feel real again. We're ditching the synthetic. People prefer cotton to nylon.

I went to a big shop. Apples are back. All sorts of flavours. Not just Golden Delicious, but Cox's Orange Pippins, Russets, Bramleys, Granny Smiths, and some with even older, more mysterious, names. I examined the fine array but neglected to buy. I had plenty of apples. My mum had given me a bag of windfalls. Bruised and worm-ridden yet tasty apples. Harvest was good this year. And the birds didn't get them all as usual. As I crunched the thin, unblemished slices I had cut from these windfalls, I took heart that, unlike the ones in the big shop, they were free fruits from the soil of my youth. The garden of my Action Man.

A quick shufti around my flat revealed one unidentifiable plant that seems destined to survive (even if I water it only once a month) and a yellowing tuffet of chives that were sprouting from a small black plastic Sainsbury's fresh-herb pot. This was my garden, that and the mould in my bathroom.

The rest of the place was full of stereo equipment, TV stuff, computers, modems, a fax, a CDI and the assorted junk of the technological age – binding with wires my hopes and desires.

The Idler, September–October 1995

1996

In the summer of '96, the European Football Championships were held in England, with the national team performing unexpectedly well. A nation held its breath as England beat Spain in the quarter-finals, only to lose the next round to Germany – on penalties, yet again.

Gavin went to all of the matches, of course. He had planned to end his novel *Strings of Life* here at Euro 96 – during an international football championship, as it had begun, but in a world that in many ways was unrecognizable from 1988: new countries, new technologies, new conflicts.

Patriot Games

1995 saw the fiftieth anniversary of the end of the Second World War. An episode in our history which we have all been taught was our finest hour. The passage of time over the fifty years since the war ended has done little to dilute the significance of the event, even to the young. Because the images of Britain during wartime, replayed during the VE Day celebrations, are like the flickering shadows of a former, more honourable world. It is one of a Great Britain where citizens knew who they were and the country knew where it was going. Regardless of the reality behind these images, they represent a legend that still comforts and in some ways cripples us. Because, ingrained somewhere in the psyche of those who weren't singing while the bombs fell, is Britain – like the past, a foreign land.

Britain in 1995 was a nation desperately in search of a new identity to match the power of the one that radiates from the old black-and-white Pathé newsreels and the singalong songs. This is why you had the likes of Michael Portillo and the Tory right hanging on to their Churchillian self-image while the country as a whole fractured and fluctuated around them. That their anti-European, rally-round-the-flag bleating made little impact on people at large suggested that those old tactics are at last going past their sell-by date. People are beginning to realize now that it's nationalism in its many forms that currently scars the world politic; be it Euro-scepticism or ethnic cleansing, at the heart of the Nineties there is a desperate attempt by the lost and the sad to find themselves in the old ideas of what their nation is about. Because at the heart of the Nineties is a search for and coming to terms with self-identity. We are a generation trying to find out who we are.

Yet unknowingly, slowly, we – the alienated, the dire, the down-trodden, the Jarvises and Justines, the junkies and the jelly-literate, the poor sods who invested their beliefs and their hard-earned prejudices in the Eighties – we *are* gaining an identity. Not coherently, not meaningfully, yet blissfully and innocently. We are inventing that key word in Blair-speak – new Britain. The problem is that politics has made itself so narrow and so ignorant that it can only fail to serve the needs of 'the vast majority of normal people in this country'.

Look at Britain today and look at Parliament and you will see two different worlds. And it's no longer just where are the workers, where are the women, where are the black and the young? It's where are the disillusioned, the dope-heads, the independent thinkers, the single parents, the stylish, the sarcastic, the radicals, the reasonable, the everyday folk who make Britain what it is? It is quite possible that in about twenty years the unelected House of Lords will be more representative than the House of Commons. A bunch of aristos could speak for the people more than some squeaky-clean career politicians.

The truth is, the political pursuit of 'the vast majority of normal people in this country' is a lie. The real agenda is the pursuit of the votes of the small percentage of Middle England voters who can swing the next election. These people see themselves as the main-stream, and prick up their ears when they hear phrases like 'the vast majority of normal people in this country'. Yet they are very much of the Old Britain, a people who have not realized their time has gone and that they are no longer 'the silent majority' but a privileged and politically pandered-to minority.

Their numbers get ever smaller. These days, even your mum and dad feel lost! The generation gap is dissolving: youth culture is no longer *youth's* culture. A generation that had grown up with the war was bound to feel ill at ease with Sixties children smoking spliff and dropping hallucinogenics. But E generation and acid generation, far apart? I should coco. The common ground is increasing, and slowly, surely, blissfully, innocently, we are recognizing that our world – not Michael Portillo's – is the real Britain.

Take the last year. Using pop as a barometer, the careless would say it now lacks politics and punch. Yet it's all been there, pumping away in mainstream Britpop. Really *listen* to Blur, Oasis or Pulp. The lyrics are brimming with class politics, passion and injustice. Jungle is a statement in its own right: we're urban, we're black British, we're white British, we're not in the States, we're not in Jamaica – we're here making some noise right now. If you look back at the year again, you'll see opinions there in all fields.

The United Kingdom splits into more than the four home nations. There are different Britains to be found in north London and south London, Glasgow and Edinburgh, or in the Bengali community and the Cypriot; and except for when the idiot rhetoric of bigots whose sense of the nation is stuck in the (mythical) nineteenth century intrudes, they exist side by side as they have done for hundreds of years. The disparate nature of our culture cloaks our genuine connections. And the more our sense of Britishness remains rooted in the fading glories of yesteryear, the more alienated the entire populace becomes. There are many people asking not what their country can do for them, or even what they can do for their country – more just what *is* my country, and do I want any part of it? The answer is that those parts of our country that are worth having have little to do with Michael Portillo. Guinness, Twiglets and jungle on a Sunday morning might not be what built the empire, but they all build a patriot.

Despite its tangled meaning, most of us are actually patriotic in the sense that we love *our* country. For ours is the country we have grown up in, have mates in, and have generally fucked around in for the last few decades. Ignore Portillo and Neo-Labour. *We* are new Britain. Searching for our soul.

The Face, January 1996

Mood-Swings

Another year. Whoop-dee-fucking-doo. I wished they'd sort it out. Religion is rationalized, hierarchies are dissolved and propriety is as archaic as bear-baiting or the idea of a free health service, but still the calendar journeys on, unchallenged by modern man. This tyranny must end. I have enough trouble remembering what day it is, without the complication of months and years zooming by.

The new millennium fills me with mouth bile. May we live for ever on a Friday in the year I left school. This twentieth-century boy will make a bitter twenty-first-century man. I know time waits for no man, but at least some of my dates could turn up. Death is the sound of a ticking clock. The chimes of midnight, direct from Big Ben.

Mood-swings are all the rage. You know what it's like: one day you're fine, the next it's black. It's a kind of post-modern take on having a real character. The other day I was so overwhelmed by optimism and a sense that somehow, now, everything was going to be all right, that I managed to get out of bed without necking a few Nurofen and crying.

Enthusiasm for life always catches me unawares. It's so essentially the *right* way of looking at the world. I have never bought this tortured-artist bollocks. Pain and suffering are not the gift of creative genius. Smiles and chuckles are the highest expressions of the inner man. Someone who has structured their life to achieve happiness and harmony seems to deserve more respect than those who would surrender helpless, crushed, despoiled, torn and overrun. Give me Mrs Merton over Kurt Cobain any day.

Mood-swings are confusing affairs. There's the happy self, the suicidal self, the together self, the wasted self and a whole other load of mental knitting to shock and surprise. If only you could pick the right jumper for the right day. I have often attributed my mood-swings to what gets up my nose. Not just the drugs, but the ether. The wrong record at the wrong time. Eating salad when I wanted chips. Looking at dogs looking at dogs. But maybe it's all just fate. Time, rigid in its certainties, playing out its hand with us travelling neither forward nor back but static, pre-ordained, changing souls. *Hmmm.*

Bits of me keep falling off. It started when I was twenty-one. I had always had a large pinkie-brown jelly-pimple under my arm. It began to hurt. I had somehow managed to pinch it. It went purple, then black and crispy. Eventually, to my amazement, it fell off. I didn't know they did that. It was quite a revelation. I was never really *attached* to the thing – it was unsightly, and lacked glamour. Somehow though, when the jelly-pimple left me, so did the naïvety of my youth. In my over-sensitive, symbolic mind at least. So, as the years have gone by, my hair and jelly-pimples have departed. Not to mention the part of my brain where certainties once lay.

Last week my final jelly-pimple left me. I encouraged it by twisting it daily until eventually the blood-supply stopped. It went purple, then black and crispy. And it fell to the bathroom floor. Now, as I lie in the bath, I focus not on pimples. Like my youth, they have fallen off. Instead I look at the small cluster of verrucas on the big toe of my right foot. Absurd naïvety has been lost. Callous cynicism has set in. Somebody stop the clock.

The Idler, January–February 1996

The Trouble with Boys

Love is never having to say you're insane. As the Greek philosopher Diogenes, the man who invented cynicism, once pointed out, affairs of the heart have always been something of a cerebral minefield. Modern love has a strange new tinge to it, though; mass psychosis appears to be the order of the day. Put simply, we're all going mad.

As for men in particular – well, apparently there's a male crisis. I've read about it – well, read the first few lines about it – in dumb newspapers and even dumber women's magazines. There have even been some hugely dumb TV programmes on the subject. The limp thrust of the argument goes like this: due to female emancipation and changing work patterns, men are no longer born to be the bread-winning head of the family, and so we no longer have a clear role in society. Also since the future favours brains over brawn, there is an elimination of traditional male advantages (discounting Björk and a couple of women Gladiators who shave, men are usually tastier when it comes to a punch-up or picking up hods of bricks). *And* there's the little problem of the falling sperm count; apparently that's to do with ill-fitting Y-fronts, too many shandies, hot baths and female hormones infesting our potatoes and carrots via plastics and pesticides. With our meat being wilted by our two veg, we're apparently spinning into some critical vortex.

Thought through clearly, this argument has to be seen as – and I hope I'm not getting too technical here – *a complete load of bollocks*. I'm a man. My mates are men. Men don't talk or think about this rubbish. Men talk about Oasis or football or nice jumpers. Men think about the weekend, the world's end. Men think about sex, women, other men, farm animals, Austin Allegros or whatever. Crisis! What crisis?

The entire males-in-crisis myth is built on a few old but ridiculous assumptions. One of the most ridiculous is that men actually want, aspire to be, or *like* being the bread-winning head of a household. Despite the perceived domestic revolution, many men still are the bread-winner. And do you know what? It's a pain in the arse, a burden beyond belief. The idea that this weight being shared somehow leaves men lost is a lie. Most young fathers I know would kill to spend more time with their kids.

And if physical strength is becoming redundant in the workplace – so what? For every male muscle redundancy, there's a puny male computer nerd entering employment. Besides, men hated those jobs. Have any of the people who lament the decline of manual labour ever picked up a paving slab, let alone dug coal, or cut steel into sheets? Hard, physical labour is marginally better than unemployment, but few mourn its decline. And it kills men. The Health Education Authority statistics indicate that fewer than 200 men die of testicular cancer a year (be warned, though, testicular cancer is the most common cancer in males under thirty-five). Over 300 die in construction and agriculture.

Like the new man, the new lad and a host of other suspect phenomena, the male crisis is nothing more than a media spin. I blame the male crisis on women's magazines. They've been a factory for female neuroses for years and now they've turned on men. The trouble is, with everyone going mad, anyone who can do a reasonable impression of being sane gets to have a say, regardless of whether what they're saying is true or not. For hundreds of years, human society has worked in the same way. Now as the old, industrial, know-your-place, happy-family world fades, and technology and contraception crumble its edifices away, we are left to work out what to do and how to behave.

And, as is the way in times of uncertainty and chaos, there are those who seek to make money and power from telling the confused what to do; from pro-family politicians to anti-gay clergymen, from women's magazines to MPs who consider *Just Seventeen* to be a force of evil, there is an ever-longer line of ideologues queuing up to stake their claims on our hearts and minds. Yet I, for one, cannot connect the passions of my life with the prose of those who would write the plans for it.

Hundreds of years of therapy, and we're still going mad; how we love a problem in our lives. And how our modern culture, with its enthusiasm for telling people how to look and behave, supplies them. You don't catch bulimia, anorexia, frigidity, post-natal depression, pre-coital trauma et al. biologically; you get infected with them from the pollution in our society. We have a simple choice. We either fall the way of the United States, and sink beneath the sewage of self-obsession and the nauseating preoccupation with the way we look, feel and act. Or we say sod it, and live our lives the best we can.

For years men haven't really given a shit about what they say and do and have generally behaved like dickheads. This was seen as natural male behaviour, as somehow genetic. But it was simple conditioning: we were taught we could get away with it, so we did. Now girls are discovering that, despite not being able to use urinals, they have the ability to be as loud, boorish and imposing as any bloke.

What is becoming obvious is that there is really very little difference between men and women. We have begun to iron out the structures we were fooled into believing were somehow inherent in our make-up. *Really* listen to what men and women say about each other; it's usually the same thing we say about members of the same sex. When men or women prattle on about what the other sex are like, they mean what their last two boy- or girlfriends have been like.

We all play the topsy-turvy game of being dismissive or demanding. This is always directly opposed to the partner's behaviour. So men seek commitment from girls who have none to give, and women seek more sex from men who are offish. It's the human condition, and it's becoming more apparent as society achieves a splash of emancipation. Fact: only 2.6 per cent of our genetic make-up is radically different.

So what's the real deal on men, relationships, sex and all things spunky? Truth to tell, I haven't got a clue. You don't, I don't – and the big *they* don't know either. All there is for sure is a state of confusion. The relationships that surround me fall and rise as waves in the Gulf Stream, a steady, warm current of love and recrimination. The most common cause of break-up? He, she or it is going a bit mad. Sent scatty by the burden of consumer choice.

We live in a land of upgrades, and orgasms that sink battleships. On the one hand, our mortality is confused by our distrust and rejection of the hypocritical values of the past; on the other hand sense, observation and our gut feelings tend to be eroded by sense-less voices and sensual pleasures of our consumer society. So we're left scrambling. Happy in love. Unhappy in fear.

For the last ten years, I've been carried along in life's emotional rapids. At each turn new pleasures were found, old certainties challenged. I've loved, lost and learned. From school disco, to altered states, to altar – each frantic grope or frenetic fuck carrying me one step forward to who knows where. It's made me feel I owned the world, and it's made me feel I should leave it. I'm left with the burden of modern love's cynicism. In fact, it's the post-modern pit: PlayStations, Pulp, personal affairs – it's the same. We're primed to have opinions, not feelings. But for both men and women, the truth lies deep within, untainted by the lie of our lives.

I have never regretted loving anyone, only hurting them. Despite the façade of our shopping-mall feelings, we – men, women, boys, girls and all the shades in between – love, shag and rabbit dumbly on, for the good we do, not the good we receive.

The Face, April 1996

Leatherhead Aggro

'Come and have a go if you think you're hard enough.' 'You're going home in a Saint John's ambulance.' 'You're going to get your fucking head kicked in.' 'We've got sense, we've got brains, we wreck InterCity trains.' 'A-G, A-G-R, A-G-R-O, Aggro!!' How tart the verse of my Leatherhead youth. These were the 'adult' football chants, secret chants that would raise me from child to man.

We had a little gang that would meet in the small overhanging shelter that doubled as the boys' toilets. Every playtime we'd be in the shelter with our green-and-white Leatherhead *FC* scarves, chanting our rites of passage. Our balls were becoming visible, like two baby hedgehogs clinging beneath our walnut dicks. Our first sip of testosterone, and we were already rampant for aggravation. After a little song and a bit of clapping, we'd go and see how high we could piss up the wall in the bogs. Manhood beckoned, and it was going to be fun.

I always had a bit of trouble with the swear words. They were clumsy on my choirboy lips. I loved the word 'aggro', though. Aggro was *smart*. So were turn-ups, boxer jackets and Fred Perrys. For some reason aggro then faded from my life as bovver had from a previous generation.

It popped up again recently, on a wall in the piss-alley that leads to Hackney Central station. As I blandly surveyed the graffiti-infested walls I noticed a faded aerosol stain: 'Tottenham Aggro' (as in *'Tottenham Aggro, Tottenham Aggro, Hello! Hello!'*). Like my memory of the playground, it had been eroded by years of abrasion and smothered by a host of other confusing messages. I found 'Tottenham Aggro' heart-warming. It gave me the goosey tingle of nostalgia.

It was quite a big event as far as the village went. A bus shelter was built. A nice wooden bus shelter. A place to sit while you waited for the infrequent services of the London & Country 416 to Leatherhead. I knew everybody in that village, and they knew me. There wasn't a house where I didn't know the family or mutant pensioner that lived there. Except the big houses, which were villages in themselves. We went to church together, we played Sweet records at the youth club, and we bought rhubarb-and-custards in the only shop. The elders drank together, organized fêtes and protested against the M25, which was due to go straight through our houses. Economic, cultural and political ties were bound in steel cable.

A few days after the bus shelter was erected, there was a scene. I arrived in the morning to catch the bus to school. There was a lot of tutting. I was getting some serious stares. At the back of the bus shelter was 'Gavin' sprayed in Day-Glo pink aerosol. Gulp. I wasn't popular. Neither was my brother. It was my brother that did it, honest. He loved to get me in trouble. What a bastard.

My name was soon joined by other graffiti. Mod hit. Punk hit. Various puppy-love affairs were recorded on its walls. It began to smell of Woodpecker cider, No. 6 and Brut.

The shelter has improved in recent years. Young people no longer live in Surrey villages. The primary schools have closed, and the houses belong to retired couples. People drive Audis. Everywhere's handy for the M25 and the large Asda store. The bus runs once a week to let pensioners cash their Giros. Still, a bit of graffiti remains. My name in pink, and the words 'Leatherhead Aggro'.

The Idler, March–April 1996

Sweet Albion: Euro 96

Twenty-nine years of hurt, plus one of absolute agony as the editor of the official England team magazine. For me, Euro 96 wasn't just a few hot nights this summer, it was the culmination of over a year's work with a side that, up until recently, everybody assured me was the laughing stock of the world.

It was a job that started just after the Dublin riot, continued through the heady 2–1 victory over Japan in last year's Umbro cup, staggered past 0–0 away draws with Norway, and smashed along with some Thais in a Cathay Pacific 747 coming back from Hong Kong. At the start of Euro 96, being editor of *England* was akin to being Ken Bailey, the old flag-waving mascot that you got with the Subbuteo 'fans' set. Although thankfully no one accused me of molesting boys – well, not to my face.

Yet Euro 96 began, with perfect formation, lightning speed and pin-point precision from a team of men unparalleled in the world. Yes, the Red Arrows were the highlight of the opening ceremony. The England team, however, looked lacklustre against Switzerland. The 1–1 draw was, well, what everybody expected from England. Even I had my doubts. At times they did fit the boozed-out, unfit, premiership ponces tag. I kept the faith though, honest. Even when the papers peddled their treason.

With a week until the next England game, I spent my time in a football frenzy. From Nottingham to Manchester to Birmingham to Newcastle, I travelled the country cramming in as much of Euro 96 as I could manage.

I got to see England, my country, as I have never seen her before: as a tourist. You see as I switched from ground to ground, from Germany v. Czech Republic, from Holland v. Scotland, Turkey v.

Croatia and Romania v. Bulgaria, it felt as if I was on the continent. Familiar grounds looked different, surrounding streets bustled with the colours of various nations. You drove around surveying all with a new pair of eyes. And from what I could see, the tournament was raging. Fandemonium, mate, pure fandemonium.

Then came England's matches against Scotland and Holland. The Scots have every right to feel bitter at England's 2–0 victory – that's their job. You couldn't help feel sorry for all the clowns dressed as William Wallace as they made their way back down Wembley way. They arrived as proud Celtic warriors and left as sad men in skirts clutching their free Primal Scream Bannockburn banners.

Still, the English tried to do the Scots a favour by putting on one of the finest displays of football I have ever seen against the Dutch. This was an awesome display against one of the world's finest teams. Even I, with all my faith, was dumbstruck by the match. I found it hard to comprehend what was happening as the team I loved played football the way I love it played. I was in tears by the end of it all. I'm in tears now, when I think of it.

After the Holland match, my world changed. I was suddenly in a land where everyone talked about football and loved the England team. While scum like the *Daily Mirror* wrote xenophobia large, the real country indulged in a warm, positive patriotism unwitnessed in years. It was the flag of St George that was flying, not the burdened Union Jack. There was a cohesiveness about England, a sense of unity amongst its citizens of all shades. I honestly believe that.

Through Spain and Germany, we all celebrated and sobbed *together*. The team was perfect for England. A bunch of perceived yobs who struggled heroically, always with a sense of commitment, fair play and style. Yet, in the end, fortune did not favour the brave. Defeat on penalties by the eventual champions Germany was heart-breaking. Yet, like the pride, the grief was shared. Sweet Albion.

Still, at least now I know we can play, because I remember Euro 96. As Frank Skinner said, 'Football came home, it just couldn't find its keys.'

The Face, August 1996

Death!

He's going to kill me. He's going to take me to the ruins of a bombed-out department block and garrotte me. He's going to poke my eyes out with his umbrella and play marbles with them. Maybe, if I'm lucky, he'll just tail me, then pick me off with an AK-47 as I leave a restaurant tonight. It's going to happen, I'm sure of it. He knows it, I know it.

He knows I'm writing this now. He keeps watching me. I have to keep writing so I don't have to talk to him. And believe me, I will have to talk to him. As soon as I stop writing, he'll swoop like a buzzard. He wants my entrails. I've got to keep writing. He's very close now, passing in front of me, back and forth. Christ, this is scary. I thought, before, when I first met him, that he was a wet blanket, a celery of a man who'd stop his annoying nonsense if I was brash with him. No such luck. The horrible thing is, even though I'm writing this quite manically, I'm *not* being over-sensitive. My life *is* in danger. This man is dangerous. This man is Dubravko Pavlici.

Dubravko is my interpreter. I never wanted him to be, he just is. He intercepted my needs for an interpreter and has chosen to foist himself upon me. Christ, I didn't know what I was doing. How foolish I was. Sitting in the Euro-Club, a sponsored Sarajevan youth club, looking for my arranged interpreter, who'd mysteriously 'gone on holiday'.

The girls in the Euro-Club were having a laugh. They now feel guilty, I can see it in their bullet-hole pupils. They all seep guilt like weeping Madonnas. 'Need an interpreter? Ask Dubravko, he'll do it!' they giggled.

I thought he worked there. No, this was just the girls' little joke.

Dubravko just haunts the Euro-Club, uninvited. A balding, bearded, twenty-five year-old with the physique of John Cleese and the dress sense of a Cheese Ranger. He comes to the Euro-Club to 'help', and to read the large selection of imported foreign magazines. His favourite is *New Scientist*. Before the war, Dubravko was a biology student. There's not a lot of call for this in Sarajevo, these days. So he comes to the Euro-Club, reads foreign magazines, paces, tidies foreign magazines into neat little piles, paces again, then mumbles to himself as he stands by the window staring into the wilderness. Unwittingly, he generally does everything in his power to send people completely hysterical. Nice chap.

When he heard I needed an interpreter, he was delighted. He had a friend. Don't get me wrong, the man speaks English perfectly. In a slow, deliberate manner he can converse in topics as diverse as women's breasts and cosmology.

I was taken in at first. Dull but diligent, I thought. I made the mistake of indulging him, and he took this as a sign of friendship. And, as he keeps telling me, he needs friends. For all his friends had now vanished. 'They vanished,' he says.

We walk the streets of Sarajevo. He talks, I listen. I listen until my ears bleed. It took a while for me to realize the true horror of my acquaintance. On one occasion we made a detour of about two miles, on foot, so he could show me where he used to live. The flats were blasted through years of Chetnik artillery bombardment. Dubravko pointed to the holes with glee. He then showed me the games he played as a child. One was called Mountain Goats. This was basically a version of tag where you can't be caught if you're off the ground. He took me to the place where he played it, and showed me the best places to jump. He had a whole route worked out to evade capture. He insisted I followed him over it. Happy days.

At the end of the first day he followed me home, to my door, 'for friendship's sake'. That evening he followed me to a bar, where he sat with me all evening 'in case I needed anything translated'.

He rings me every morning, he waits outside the house. Things have started to unravel.

He is interested in guns. He is a very good shot, apparently. Has lots of gun magazines. I can go round to his flat and look at them whenever I want. He used to be in the JNA, the old Yugoslavian National Army. He left under a shadow that hovers in my imagination each time I encounter him. I haven't got to the truth yet.

For the mystery is that this is Sarajevo, a city just coming out of the worst siege in modern warfare. They have been under attack for over four years. The Bosnian army is keen for conscripts. They're not that fussy in these parts. They even have one-legged fighters. And here's Dubravko, an excellent shot, a man in love with the gun. He has yet to be called up, and inexplicably has been told that they actually don't *want* him in service. Even when all around they are under a military pressure unheard of in the latter part of the twentieth century.

They know, I know, he knows. Even by the broad Yugoslavian standards, the man is completely and utterly hat-stand. Dangerously so, in fact. This is the man who is my interpreter, my stalker, my reaper. This is the man who tells me where I can get hold of pornography. This is the man I've been hiding from for two days.

I shouldn't have come to the Euro-Club. It was pissing down with rain. It was my only shelter. Now he knows I'm lying, he knows I'm not returning his calls, he knows I haven't left for Dubrovnik. He has, however, just produced an umbrella. He will walk me home with the umbrella, 'for friendship's sake'.

I will surely die.

[This copy was written live in Sarajevo's Euro-Club]

The Idler, November–December 1996

Postcard from Sarajevo

'So we all lost the war. I'm a Muslim, baby, so why don't you kill me?' sung to the tune of 'Loser' by Beck, by a group of teenage girls, ethnicity unknown, strolling along the harbour front in Dubrovnik.

Sarajevo, summer '96. It's ten months since the Dayton Agreement was signed, with the aim of bringing an end to war in the former Yugoslavia. It concluded that Croatia had won, Serbia had lost and that Bosnia-Hercegovina was a high-scoring draw. The last time I left the city – two years ago, after covering the siege for the *Face* – my head was spinning with the sound of gunfire and the smell of burning cars. Even as our Land-Rover dipped over a mountain down the road to safety, I still found myself pursued. This time by the black dogs of depression. The situation seemed hopeless, and I swore I would never go back, except perhaps with a Millennium Falcon.

Yet curiosity – as to how peace had been reached, and whether it could possibly work – carried me back. Two years ago, I was driven around in armoured UN vehicles. Entering this time on a plush commercial coach, Sarajevo certainly seems tranquil enough. The only rat-a-tat-tat to be heard is that of the craftsmen's hammers. They bash out a melodic beat as they mould a new copper dome on to the roof of the old town's mosque. Those with a Ravey Davey bent could find the noise kickin'. Bass is provided by the occasional clap of thunder as the storm clouds break on Mount Igman.

All is action. People strut the highstreet and slouch around the many newly opened bars and restaurants. Shops are full of stock – everything is available from the latest widescreen TV to the most garish of Benetton jumpers. Window-shopping is the order of the day, though. Money is tight and unemployment rife. Customers are either press, aid workers, Mafia or off-duty Nato soldiers. However, prices are stable: everything is in Deutschmarks.

The biggest risk to your personal safety these days is the traffic, which still sprints around as if it were pursued by a squadron of MiG fighters. It stops for neither red light nor oncoming tram. The only thing that brings it to a halt is a fatal crash or the occasional blockade by protesting war veterans who, in possibly their greatest act of courage, form barricades of disabled human bodies, wheelchairs and crutches. Those crippled by war cripple the traffic flow in a vague hope of getting their promised war pension.

Fly-posters advertise a fair cross-section of current Sarajevan life: a yellow tinted Liberali party poster heralds the coming election; a black-and-white photocopy offers a gig by *engleski* band Dodgy; a strange, abstract computer printout inviting you to 'Sex Video Klub SM/fetish/gay'; and this nicely overlapped by an exciting full-colour call to attend 'Iranian Culture Week'. Whether the latter two are connected, I can't quite work out.

Peppered throughout the town there's also the smiling Rodney Trotteresque face of a boy with a machine-gun. This is Sasha, a war hero. A young member of the special forces who, like so many, gave his life for Sarajevo. Like the majority of the so-called Bosnian Muslim army, Sasha wasn't a Muslim. Sasha was just a typical Sarajevan lad – in fact, as was the case with many Bosnian soldiers, he happened to be Serb. The posters advertise a football competition in his memory.

Since I was last here, everything has changed yet nothing has changed. I didn't need the grinning Sasha popping up everywhere to remind me of the recent war. I could still hear it in the back of my head. I found my eyes constantly lifting up to the surrounding hills whence used to cometh the grief. I've returned to see what the peace is like, and still everywhere is the mess those bastards caused. Those who witnessed the damage one IRA bomb did on Manchester earlier in the year might like to get their head around the carnage that four years of bombs, bullets and mortars create. The city is God's ashtray: houses burnt-out butts, towers crumpled fag-packets. All the smart money is in glaziers.

This awkward set plays host to a motley gang of citizens. The visitor can be somewhat thrown by the contrasts. A quick mosey around the block on my first afternoon revealed a pair of Jordanian soldiers wandering down by the river lovingly holding hands, as is the Arab way, like gay lovers with a serious military fetish. A couple of American film directors, in town for one of the six Hollywood films being shot here, sipped coffee in a roadside café, arguing loudly about 'that black guy' in *Pulp Fiction*, neither of them apparently able to remember Samuel L. Jackson's name.

Sarajevo's original citizens are now swamped by outsiders. Many are largely unwanted, refugees who've been herded in from cleansed villages or Designated UN Safe Areas. The rest are those implementing some plan or another. There's the OSCE (Organization for Security and Cooperation in Europe) running around doing lots of important things, none of which I could grasp. Also soldiers from the various countries making up I-FOR (Implementation Force), who look very impressive with lots of exciting tanks and guns yet fail to get respect as they appear to have arrived embarrassingly late for the war. You then have a whole rainbow of NGOs (Non-Governmental Organizations): charity workers ranging from the Serious Road-Trippers to groups of nuns with attitude, many of whom looked like they could give Mike Tyson a good seeing-to. Then there are hundreds of people who are unexplained. These are probably spies for one regime or another, although no one can be sure because in Sarajevo, everybody thinks everybody else is a spy. Sarajevo is spook central. What they hope to find out I don't know – a decent hairdresser, or a kosher source for some pedigree Dalmatian pups, perhaps? Finally, we have the UN. The UN is like a virus that expands at an alarming rate when placed on the petri dish of war and pestilence. Blink your eyes, then there's another department popping up bringing the benefits of bureaucracy to the world's most needy. The UN are *everywhere*. They even have a department that deals with the sewers.

The only organization Sarajevo lacks is Alcoholics Anonymous. It's needed urgently to deal with the hordes of depressive drunks that fill the massed ranks of officialdom. Not to mention the press. All drink Sarajevo dry on a nightly basis. This is one of the few peace dividends.

The war seems to have had little visible effect on the kids who amble around the streets of Sarajevo. They're indistinguishable from kids anywhere else in Europe: lively, belligerent and bored. Down the lido at the edge of town, not a square inch of water is unoccupied. It's a sea of young flesh, and what pool I can spy is looking none too clean. This may be Sarajevo's biggest open sewer. There's a party atmosphere, with all the pool rules being broken. I witness ducking, bombing, running, pushing and untold amounts of heavy petting.

I chat to a group of young lads, trying to glean what they get up to, how they've coped with the war and what the peace is like. My notes read: 'Like swimming', 'Enjoy forming gangs', 'Have fun pushing friends into minefields'.

Much the same as here, really. Save the swimming.

Walking into the town centre, I bump into my old friend Shober. He's a little worse the wear for drink, but looking well. He was demobilized from the Bosnian Army six months back, and has got to be a good two stone heavier than when I last saw him. The peace can be quantified in calories. He tells me he's just back from holiday in Split. Had an affair with a girl from Zagreb: 'Love across the barricades,' he jokes. He's depressed at being back, and I ask why. 'It was great to get out to somewhere *normal*. If you look around you here' – he eyes another bomb-damaged street – 'there's always something reminding you of the war.'

He says Sarajevo, these days, is 'full of strangers'. This is followed by a drunken tale which he swears is true. The flats where he lives are full of refugees ('country people, not *my* people,' he comments).

When they first moved in, one family kept their cow in the lift. Recently, when the electricity was restored, the cow shot up to the tenth floor. The family thought it had been stolen and called the police.

Although parts of Sarajevo do appear to be taking a strangely rural bent, with goats nibbling at patches of roadside grass, there are also signs of a blossoming metropolitan scene. In the town centre you can attend the Sarajevo Film Festival, go clubbing or hang out in the swish new Internet bar. At the Dodgy gig at the Kuk Club (Spiral Tribe are due the week after), we could be at any club in Europe. Except there are more glue-sniffers, and the locals leave at 10.45 due to the 11 p.m. curfew. The band are there because singer Nigel Clark read an enlightening book called *Seasons in Hell* by the *Guardian*'s Ed Vulliamy. Their happy pop seems awkward yet refreshing in such confines, but the audience just shouts for Sex Pistols covers. I even meet my first backpacker, a humble guy called Chris. He seems rather confused as to where he is, and he becomes slightly perturbed when I inform him about the curfew and the fact that there are no campsites, no vacant hotel rooms and that most of the parks are mined.

I've heard it said that Sarajevo is going to become 'the new Prague'. It occurs to me that after four years of war, Sarajevo deserves better than hordes of travellers taking cheap holidays in other people's misery, although I suppose it all adds to the city's integration back into our lovely, liberal West. The universities are making efforts to attract a large input of foreign students in the coming year. And the city has a vibrant young heartbeat that could appeal to those interested in more than just straight education. Musically, Sarajevo seems set to attract some quality bands as well, with both U2 and Massive Attack currently fighting the grey men of management for the right to play there. Even the local indie Radio Zid will soon be joined by a special student radio station which is being set up by some of the younger movers and shakers at the UN. The place has *some* prospects.

The first tourist bus was doing the rounds when I was there. A group of Spanish people, who'd paid over a grand for the privilege, were toured around the city with their video cameras in hand. It's easy to cast them off as macabre voyeurs, but at least they were injecting a large amount of cash directly into the city's economy.

Pondering what tourists could actually *do* in Sarajevo, I visited the museum and persuaded the janitor to make me the first paying guest in over four years. It was fun, but there wasn't that much to see. Most of the exhibits had been stored elsewhere in a safe place. The main things on show were chunks of ancient masonry, which blended in nicely with the newer chunks that had fallen from the mortar-damaged ceiling. Apparently the highlight of the museum used to be its collection of stuffed animals. For the purpose of safety these had been stored in the cellar; unfortunately, this had recently been flooded, and various inanimate Peruvian lemurs and Mexican armadillos were last seen floating off down the drains.

In search of more lively members of the animal kingdom, I pottered over to the zoo. I was out of luck. The zoo had formed part of the no-man's land between the aggressor and the city, and no animals were left. According to the keeper, they'd rescued some of the more exotic animals, such as elephants and tigers, and air-lifted them out. The less glamorous animals, the yaks and their ilk, were simply put down. The wolves and the springbok escaped, and it is suspected that the bison was carved up and sold for steak in the market. No one's going anywhere in the zoo though, because it's all mined. The dodgem cars looked painfully deserted.

Mines are a big problem around the city. Most spare bits of ground – the ones with the longer grass and the three-legged cows – are mined. Removing them is a slow process. They cause the most unlikely problems. Kids tobogganing last snowfall found themselves hurtling skyward instead of downward. The hospital deals with a constant stream of casualties; in Sarajevo, mines still maim or kill an average of three people a week.

The aggressor only left town on 19 March this year, when they finally handed over their stronghold in the heart of the city, Grbav-ica. Walking through the Grbavica district one sees the yellow warning 'Mina' tape criss-crossing the dead ground like a cat's cradle. It still looks much like a front-line war zone. The only improvement the local government has seen fit to make is to change a few street names into useful things like 'the street of the Young Muslims'.

Out on the city limits there are even fewer signs of change. Dobrinja is the old Olympic village. Being surrounded by the aggres-sor on three sides, it was one of the areas worst affected by the siege. Its housing blocks are numbered from one to six. Dobrinja Six is still in the hands of the aggressor, and despite the Dayton Agreement ensuring Bosnia-Hercegovina remains a country in her own right, with no internal borders, one in which citizens are allowed to roam freely within, there's little chance of a day-trip for the residents of Dobrinja's one to five.

The border of what was the front line is marked by devastated buildings and a couple of I-FOR tanks. One of the aggressor's policemen had been shot here the night before, on the junction of William Shakespeare and Gandhi streets. (The names had been chosen in the more optimistic era of the Olympics.) Things were said to be 'tense', but I couldn't tell. I had no interpreter and my vague attempts at communication with locals resulted in the unsurprising discovery that things are 'bad', 'very bad' and 'not good'. A wander over to the aggressor's side of Dobrinja yields even less: I stare and smile at them while they build a new Orthodox church. They sneer at me and direct me back over a minefield.

A young girl from Dobrinja, who I'll call Amra, spoke English with a melancholic, almost rural Irish accent. She was the girlfriend of a friend and her dry wit cheered up many a dinner during my stay, yet it was Amra who needed the cheering. Amra's uncle was in town, scouring the graveyards for the body of his brother. He told her tales. Tales of the concentration camp he was put in, where the aggressors slit the throats of menfolk on a whim, depending on the village they came from. Amra had her own tales, too: of her father sent mad with depression after accidentally shooting his best friend on the Dobrinja front line. She told these stories with a resigned matter-of-factness. The horrors are never far away in Sarajevo. And neither are the culprits.

To the heart of the aggressor. Into the hills and the self-proclaimed Republic of Srpska, the part of Bosnia which, occupied by the Serbian army, has been claimed by the Bosnian Serb's *de facto* leader Radovan Karadžić. Driving along the mountain roads I see that all the barricades and trenches are all still in place, as are the snipers' nests where men saw fit to shoot at civilians. This is where war tourists like the Russian Neo-Nazi Vladimir Zhirīnovsky spent pleasant afternoons sipping back his own brand of vodka and letting a machine-gun rip upon the city below. It feels weird driving through Srpska. I feel nervous, disgusted. This grows when we reach Pale, the aggressor's capital and the closest thing Europe has to a centre for fascism.

It's a backward little ski village, like a glorified Butlin's. The people all look weird, slightly inbred; it appears that cousins have married cousins and possibly some of the farm animals in this (red)neck of the woods. It's Deliverance country, filled with Bosnian Serbs who supported the Serbian army and call themselves 'democrats' when their ideology is more in keeping with the national socialism of Hitler. They believe chiefly in strong government and – laughably – in themselves as some sort of Orthodox master race. It was this conviction which justified their persecution of what they considered Bosnian fundamentalists.

It was people like these, who responded to the Serbian nationalists, who started this whole sorry mess in the first place. Yugoslavia was made up of eleven territories, four of which – Slovenia, Croatia, Bosnia-Hercegovina and Serbia – would be involved in the war. Among these, Serbia had a dominant position somewhat akin to that of England in the UK; moreover, because of historical disputes, it also felt that many of the other territories had land that should be part of a greater Serbia. When the old country began to break up and Slovenia and then Croatia declared independence in the early Nineties, Serbs both in Serbia and other territories rallied to the nationalists led by Radovan Karadžić. When the Croatians broke away, the Serbs invaded the southern part of their country and some of the coast. Shortly after that, 100,000 Bosnians gathered in front of Sarajevo's parliament building in protest against the war. Serbian nationalists shot at them, starting the battle which became the siege.

Karadžić lives here in Pale in a big white house, except of course he can't be found and arrested 'safely' for the war crimes he committed. I mean you'd have to use real force to do that, like half a dozen Woodcraft Folk and a couple of Portsmouth fans. Still, there's a saying in Bosnia now: 'Kill one man and they'll call you a murderer and hang you; kill twenty and they'll let you write a bestseller; kill 100,000 and they'll stick you in the best hotel in Geneva and invite you to a peace conference.' There's evil in Pale, evil and ugliness. And Bosnian Serb nationalists still in power, five miles away from Sarajevo.

In Sarajevo they all have the jitters. This is not helped by the fact that most people spend all day drinking a Turkish coffee so strong that it could be peddled by a Bogotá cartel. Further problems are caused by the migraine-inducing tablecloths the coffeeshops have. These are of the abstract modern kind that look like some six-year-olds have been let loose with highlighting pens. If this wasn't enough, everyone seems hooked on a form of Europop Croatian dance music called Cro-Dance. It has lyrics like *'Zang zang, dumpity dang, everybody pump me!'* Apparently most of the tunes are sung in Croatian, but they are all so over-produced that it comes out as this strange Esperanto whine that could be anything. However, the worst thing the Bosnian people have to endure is their own television. Bosnian TV is Boredom Noir, a genre in its own right.

A quick flick through the channels one night saw the following. Hyatt, the Muslim channel, is showing highlights of the city's buskers, with badly shot footage of one of those dire Peruvian flute bands that have been polluting European cities for years and still not earned enough for their fare home. On the state TV channel BH1, a man is standing by a piano singing Nat King Cole's 'Wonderful World'. He sings in pidgin English and keeps forgetting whole chunks. When the camera switches to a wide shot, it reveals the presenter on a sofa at the side of the studio, reading a book. On Studio 99, the independent, Mafia-run channel, it's a four-hour kids' show from a studio the size of a toilet. A strange fat man with glasses sits with about six children who he encourages to swear to get laughs. Occasionally they put a record on and conga around the room using a strange split-screen effect to make the studio look larger. CPT (Srpska Television) offers an exciting, never-ending news item on progress at the Pale pants factory. They are making the sort of Nora Batty bloomers which only come in one off-yellow-colour synthetic fabric. There's lots of breathtaking footage of Singer sewing-machines stitching up gussets.

The Bosnian people have suffered in so many ways.

Sarajevo at the end of summer 96 is at peace yet slightly maddened. It would not take much for the war to start up again and, depressingly, it seems inevitable that it soon will. The current peace plan, the Dayton Agreement, has at last brought a halt to some of the real horrors. That is an achievement unthinkable a few years back and it should not be underestimated. Still, the plan is tainted by pages of grey areas and the cynical cosmetic fixes of world politics.

Throughout the war there were basically two solutions being pushed by the outside world. One was the Anglo-Franco Euro option which, rather hastily, decided that this should be treated as a simple civil war, and that we should provide aid and push for Bosnia-Hercegovina to be carved up into ethnic regions. The other was the United States' noble plan, which called for Bosnia-Hercegovina to be defended as a country in its own right. Unfortunately, the latter option was backed up only by fine words and a few fighter planes, the former by a huge commitment of ground troops and streams of humanitarian aid convoys.

The callous and pragmatic Euro option held sway until the Serb Nationalist aggressors took the piss with 'safe areas' to such an extent that even mealy-mouthed appeasers like Douglas Hurd couldn't stick to his 'all as bad as each other' rhetoric. When the town Srebrenica fell, with the slaughter of 6,000-plus people, this position finally became untenable.

I find it deeply discouraging that despite the news reports, documentaries and countless top-grade journalistic accounts of the events of the last four years, most people still see the Bosnian war as some sad abstract dispute between a bunch of war-mongering peasant nutters. I've even heard supposed left-wing 'intellectuals' explain that the Serbs have been made scapegoats.

It is in order to counter such apologists that many aid workers and relief organizations like me refer to the 'aggressor' rather than the Serbs. Please, if I give you one thing from this article, let it be this: the Bosnian war was one between a clear aggressor and a clear victim. The aggressor believed in nationalism and totalitarian government. This was a war against fascism and National Socialism. A war against Nazis. And the war is not over, because Sarajevo cannot rest in this current peace.

After Srebrenica fell, we finally made an attempt to stand up to the aggressor. At the end of last summer we bombed the bad guys. It worked. The leaders of all the sides involved were then packed off to Dayton and pressured into an agreement.

But the dynamism of the agreement was then followed by apathy and cynical international PR moves. The Americans finally committed troops which made up part of I-For, a 60,000-strong army of some of the world's best soldiers. However, it soon became apparent that this iron fist was to be given the kid-glove treatment as Bill Clinton and, to a lesser extent, John Major both had short-term electoral ambitions and didn't want any body bags turning up. So despite a mandate they decided not to press home their advantage and enforce a lasting peace. They let war criminals like Radovan Karadžić and General Miladic go unapprehended and did little to dismantle the aggressor's military and political structures. History will judge how many of our soldiers' lives this saves in the long run, or what further atrocities this leads to.

Why care about Bosnia? I don't really know. They share our sense of humour, I suppose, and they managed to feed their pets throughout the war. That should be enough. If not try this. The siege of Sarajevo lasted from 2 May 1992 to 26 February 1996. Over these 1,395 days, 10,615 people were killed, including 1,601 children. Over 50,000 were injured. It was the longest siege in the history of modern warfare. We stood by and watched.

The aggressor is now dormant and we have a peace, of sorts. To paraphrase a liberal Serb (yes, they do exist), Vuk Drašković, in a recent letter to a Belgrade newspaper: 'That peace is neither right-eous nor base. It's woven from blood and tears, from illusions and deceits, from ideological and Mafia-backed nationalism, and from severe wounds that will not be able to heal for a long time to come. But in the end such a peace is the only outlet, the only hope and chance, that our future generations of unborn will not come into a world that resembles our own. So that those children yet to be brought into the world do not experience the life we have had, Serbia tomorrow must not resemble the Serbia of today. Changes are critical, pressing changes to the very foundation of our nation. The social system, ideology ... the system of values, everything that caused this cataclysm, this harm to the people, the country, the culture, and morals – all this we must change.'

Sadly, if this has any chance of succeeding we must defeat outright those who perpetrated these crimes, arrest those responsible and crush their apologists. It's not easy, but neither is tobogganing down a minefield.

The Face, October 1996

Top of the Git Parade

Sometimes things aren't good. They aren't good in the same way winter isn't good. Sometimes you find yourself in a bleak realm where rays of sunshine are fading memories from times past. You become what's known as a miserable git. That tag is one I suffer. People have got so used to it that I now have to use it on all official forms.

My current misery has been hanging in the air for some time now. It clouds me in its sulphur and rubs all sores with salt. It is a result of a certain inborn suffering called love. L-o-v-e. No birds sing or angels cry when I spell that word out. No, my heart sinks, the tears well in my eyes and I rush for a pint of Strongbow to fill my hollow soul. Except even the relief of alcohol is unavailable as the tax demands arrive and the rent arrears its fearful face.

I'm in 50p land. I always seem to have just about 50p on my self-pitying personage. Not enough for a bus, just enough for baked beans and an onion. I wisely always invest in a 25p reverse forecast on the dogs at the next available dog race. They never win. They never do when you're in 50p land.

The wife doesn't understand me. She doesn't think I really love her. The girlfriends understand me. They think I really love the wife. My friends think I'm barmy in whatever actions I take. Except, of course, the one who decided to go off with the wife. I search for solutions but find myself trapped in a maze of rather uninspiring depression. I thought the up-side of emotional decay was at least you got a few novels completed or had an exhibition at the Serpentine gallery. So far I've managed to scrawl 'modern life is rubbish' on a notepad. And even that's not original, Blur beating me by a couple of years.

Still, could be worse eh? Great relief that is. Yes, technically it can always get worse. Death and disability could rain down. No such luck, though. I'm left with the mundane melancholy of the broken-hearted, destined to live my life as lead player in the lyrics of a thousand second-rate love songs. I would willingly swap my technical advantages to be the man or woman who has the dubious distinction of the person that suffers the most. The relief in knowing I was absolved from human duties would be help enough to bear the pain. I, however, like Leyton Orient, like the Rolling Stones, like John fucking Major, I must soldier on.

The real rub of run-of-the-mill heartbreak depression is that you have to carry on. You go to work, you make your phonecalls and you smile the odd smile down the pub. Yet all is tedious struggle as poor-me drains your energy, debilitating your personality into that of a bitter, broken man. I always thought that life's decision was a choice between pain and drudgery. I never thought I'd end up with both.

Another turgid day drags its hours through and thus a woeful week plods on. I keep telling myself things must get better but the certainty of this perceived wisdom is slipping from mere reassuring thought to a fanatical absolute. Things *must* get better. The failure for them to do so is just so awful to contemplate that I would be forced to commit that most drastic of options: take responsibility for my own actions.

The Big Issue, 1996

Weekend Warrior

They say men join the French Foreign Legion to forget. This may also be true of 'C' Company 4th (Volunteer) Battalion Royal Green Jackets. But I was convinced that girls found men more attractive in uniform.

I'd telephoned a number on a television ad. They'd sent me an information pack full of smiling squaddies in exotic locations. This was followed by a letter inviting me along to a drill evening at my local infantry company. So I sauntered along and stood in a London hallway with a brace of young hopefuls, staring at ageing posters warning of the battle plans of the Soviet empire. I was soon taken into an office to fill out forms and ask questions of a man dressed as a sergeant.

The first question came easy enough. If I join, how do I get out? 'You're a volunteer. You leave when you like. You take your kit back to the store and you're out,' he replied, in a manner that suggested he answered this particular question every five to ten minutes. I filled out the forms, went to a medical, was security-checked and swore allegiance to the Queen. I was in. Five minutes later I had a gun in my hand. Except it wasn't a gun, it was – 'and don't you ever fucking let me hear you call it otherwise' – a rifle. An SA-80 assault rifle, the standard British army issue. Either 'one of the most accurate weapons in the world', or 'a ridiculous Government white elephant that weighs too much, jams all the time and all but fell to bits during the Gulf War', depending on who you listen to. It was like being a seven-year-old and being handed your older brother's mountain bike. You had to appear grateful but knew you weren't mature enough to handle it.

Ten minutes later I was doing press-ups; punishment for not

using the correct safety procedures on my rifle (not that I had any idea what they were). I'd be doing a lot of these punishment press-ups in the coming months: press-ups for doing something wrong; press-ups for other people doing things wrong; press-ups to help me get fit to do, er, more press-ups. Two hours later I was lying pissed in the mess, supping back the cheapest pint this side of Scarborough, chatting nonsense with my mates. So odd, so quickly.

There are two things that shock you. The first is the formality. The only people who use the term 'sir' in civilian life are police constables addressing offending male motorists. Suddenly addressing those above you by their correct titles and showing them due respect does not come naturally. Still, it's easy enough to learn because everybody is above you when you're a recruit. The second shocker to nonchalant novices such as me is fitness. The first three-mile run left me near-crippled. It took me more than a week to be able to walk properly. I was later to realize this was just a little stroll.

I'd joined the aforementioned 4th (Volunteer) Battalion Royal Green Jackets, a London-based infantry unit and part of the Territorial Army. Training takes place one night a week, at weekends and at least a fortnight a year. They're either civilians pretending to be soldiers at the weekend, or soldiers pretending to be civilians during the week, depending on how you view such things. Some in the regular army, and the public, view the TA as a bunch of part-timers. Many in the TA view the regular army with bafflement, amazed that anybody would want to do this job full-time.

Meanwhile, increasing numbers of the TA are actually ex-regulars who've either left of their own accord or been part of the mass redundancies that have taken place over the past ten years. TA soldiers now serve in all of the British army postings, with more than a hundred currently in Bosnia.

The TA is one of the few parts of the British army the Government would like to expand. Apart from economic reasons, there is an argument that its troops are actually more able to perform some of the duties of the modern soldier. A civilian background, as opposed to an institutionalized army one, is desirable in a position where contact with the public is a daily occurrence. You can't always go by the book at a checkpoint in Sarajevo. I was to find TA battalions claiming their soldiers are more rounded than the regulars and can talk about more than 'sex, football and killing people'.

As a recruit I was subjected to four weekends of training. The aim was to teach me how to become a rifleman. The first weekend I was bundled into a hall in Putney with about seventy others, issued kit, placed in a section of nine people, then trundled off in a lorry to a wood in Pirbright, near Guildford, in the heart of stock-broker Surrey.

It was mid-January and the coldest night for fourteen years; ideal weather to be lying under a tree tucked up in a sleeping-bag. The term 'sleeping-bag' was to prove an oxymoron though, as we never got more than a couple of hours' sleep in more than four weekends. The recruit plan is simple; deprive them of sleep, run them till they drop, have a go at them and see how they react.

It's called character-building. Or is it soul-destroying? We were taught how to camouflage ourselves, various ways to walk, crawl and shuffle, how to hear and listen in the dark and how to move in section. It was all about being not seen or heard – something very hard to adapt to when you're the sort of person who starts singing to yourself when things fall a bit quiet.

Our section leader and mentor for the weekends was Corporal Dahliwell, a man capable of being both demonic and endearing. He kept his distance, shouted and swore at us, but we knew he was on our side. Those he led were many and varied: a female maths student from UCL, an ex-Para recruit who worked for an ad agency, a Waitrose shelf-packer, an ex-submariner, a Post Office security adviser, a banker, a canoe instructor and an unemployed guy. We were a pretty unimpressive-looking bunch, truth be told.

The section was split into two teams called Charlie and Delta, and within that you had a battle partner. They watched your back, and ensured you always had somebody boiling water for tea while you were shaving. That was the theory, at least. I found my partner not of my choosing. It was an arranged marriage, and the tensions soon became obvious. One thing that becomes apparent in training is that there's absolutely no point in complaining. Nothing will come of it. It only adds to the self-awareness that you are, by choice, doing something absolutely bloody ridiculous when you could be at home, in the warm, with a beer, snuggled up watching telly.

Weekend one finished with a splash. I plummeted off a rope on the assault course through ice and into a water obstacle. I was the only one to achieve this honour. I was awarded the nickname Splasher. This was the first of many nicknames I received including: Head-butter, Techie, Professor, and – my personal favourite – Super-Gav.

Throughout the training, a subtle indoctrination went on. You weren't entering the British Army or the TA, you were becoming a volunteer rifleman in the family of the Royal Green Jackets. The regiment is all. Formed in 1966, the Royal Green Jackets are an amalgamation of several London rifle brigades. The regiment, in its previous incarnations, has always been ground-breaking, being the first to use rifles as opposed to muskets. In the American wars against the Indians and the French, along with the Peninsula campaign against Napoleon and the Spanish, it adopted radical new battle tactics. Instead of marching into battle like the Guards, in rows, wearing big red jackets, they engaged the enemy by skirmishing on the flanks. They wore green jackets for camouflage. They played the enemy at their own game, adopting their tactics when appropriate. They pioneered the buddy system now used throughout the army.

Officers were always obliged to fight, walk and eat with their men. They taught their soldiers to be 'a thinking rifleman'. You were to do 'everything that was necessary and nothing that is not'. Tales of battle honours were told late at night by the glow of bonfire. We had the most Victoria Crosses and the smartest soldiers.

The Regimental Sergeant-Major gave lucky recruits sips of brandy while proclaiming his love of the regiment. Our battalion had just come first, second and third in the Courage Trophy, a competition between all London TA units. Much was expected of us.

On the second weekend I found myself in hospital under surveillance after morning PT turned into some sort of Marx Brothers routine. While being carried over somebody's shoulder I cracked my head on the head of somebody else, who was being carried the other way. After regaining consciousness I was carried on a relay race only to be dropped, on my head, on the ground. I don't remember much after that. There was a bit of claret, a bucket of vomit and the next thing I know some neurosurgeon is inspecting me. The things one does for Blighty.

By the third weekend we many were becoming we few. Some had jumped, others were pushed. I was delighted to find my 'buddy' had found he couldn't take the pace. My happiness was short-lived, as he was soon replaced by my new battle partner, Mr Blobby. Now Mr Blobby was a sweet enough guy. Outside the army I'm sure he'd have been fine. He certainly had something, as this was his third season as a recruit. He'd failed every time (and he was to fail again this time).

What made matters worse was that things were getting a bit serious now: we had an enemy! Our orders told us of a vicious group of terrorists out to destabilize the very heart of our society. The Pirbright Trotskyite Workers' Liberation Front were out to get us! And get us they did. Despite the best-laid plans of Corporal Dahliwell, our midnight reconnaissance patrol behind enemy lines did not go at all well. Our section spent a good couple of hours stumbling through the undergrowth in search of the PTWLF. Night-sights allow the viewer to see in the dark. And we did spot the enemy a couple of times. The trouble is, though, that after a night or so without sleep and an exhausting day your mind starts playing tricks on you. With my night-sights I not only saw the enemy positions but a couple of magic tigers and a handful of pixies.

Before we knew it, instead of finding the enemy, the enemy had found us. Rifles sounded, flares went up, smoke blinded us. We shot at anything, including each other. People fell over. Guns jammed. We all ran off. As 'a thinking rifleman' I thought the only sensible course of action to take was to shoot all the officers and defect to the Trotskyites. Unfortunately my coup was unsuccessful.

Our leaders had their revenge the next day by giving us a bit of NBC warfare training. NBC stands for Nuclear Biological Chemical. It has to be said that this training was slightly on the optimistic side. Still, there's nothing like dressing up in a green boilersuit, slipping on a gas mask and some rubber gloves, putting your heavy backpack on, then going for a march. Especially if at the end of it you get shoved in a room full of CS gas and told to remove your respirator. Your eyes burn and you start to choke. This is followed by a quick exit to throw up.

NBC isn't the nastiest bit of training you have to do. That honour has to go to sword drill. In sword drill the veneer of modern warfare is stripped away. You fix your sword to the end of your rifle. You charge at things and try to kill them. After all, killing is what it's all about. Over the months of being a recruit a change came over me. I had lost nearly one and a half stone. Army PT instructors make excellent personal trainers for those who find work-outs a tad too trying. I was slimmer, bolder, rougher, tougher. Mentally, I was more alert, with my addled memory gearing up for its first input of retainable information since my O levels.

It would be wrong to say I was enjoying myself, though. It was, by and large, hellish. By weekend four I was actually very worried about what they'd expect from me. Nerves were twitchy and my stomach was anxious. It's abundantly clear when you're doing things wrong or right in the army.

Reputations lasted as long as the next battle exercise or physical test. This was the most meritocratic work environment I'd ever been in. You couldn't just bluff your way through and brown-nose where necessary. While sexism and racism were apparent, they were of the blatant sort and essentially superficial. While other regiments may be different, the Royal Green Jackets appeared to represent London as a whole. I saw more black and Asian faces in the ranks in four months than I've seen in journalism in ten years. Liberal niceties may not exist, but I can say in honesty that there are friendships and appointments within the army that are far more colour-blind than those in the media.

On weekend four I felt I was getting the hang of things: the hang of important things, like how you actually go about killing people during a war. The PTWLF were on the prowl again. We were to attack their positions. It went like clockwork. We crawled among them like panthers, then ripped them to shreds. Well, we slunk exhausted up a hill, posted a grenade in their bunker then wasted about sixty rounds of ammunition on them. I promptly ballsed up by killing myself, failing to check a body for booby-traps. Still, it made me feel proud to go down in a sea of communist blood.

There were moments towards the end when I actually felt I could cut it as a Royal Green Jacket, a thought that hadn't really entered my head before. I began to see soldiering as some sort of communion with nature. I was living and reacting like an animal. My life was fight or flight.

There was one moment on duty, when the dawn started to rise. I stared at the canopy of the forest, spun out like a raven-coloured cobweb above my head. The birds were beginning to wake. Then, as morning opened like Venus from the shell, a bomb went off. It was five in the morning and we were being 'bumped', army lingo for being attacked. I saw enemy, I shot at enemy. Got my gear together and with pack on back I fled with the others.

Then we were sent on a three-mile run in full kit, carrying rifles and LAWs. LAW stands for Light Anti-Tank Weapon. And when anything is described as 'Light' in the army you can be sure it weighs the same as a small family car. All thoughts of awe at nature's wonder depart when you're on the verge of collapse. All you think about is the end. These are the kind of runs that sort out the mice from the men. This jog was the last leg of an intersection competition that had been running throughout the training weekends. We were nine seconds short of getting the overall first prize. I soon found the Nietzschian within me. I directed my anger at failure towards the weakest member of the section, the bastard who'd cried off half-way through the run because he had 'sore feet' and left me half crippled carrying the LAW. Revenge was a dish served tepid when we later 'lost' some of the offending recruit's kit, leaving him liable for cost. Nasty? You bet. *C'est la guerre*.

After completing the initial four months of training, recruits are said to have passed 'phase one' and are accepted by their battalion for six months. In that time they have to complete a hideous two-week Combat Infantrymen's training course at Catterick, north Yorkshire. Of all the initial recruits less than 15 per cent go on to pass at Catterick and gain the prize of a green beret.

The question, then, has to be asked: why do they want to do it? You are paid, but as part-time jobs go you might be better off at Burger King. My income from the TA didn't even cover the gym bills I was paying to keep fit for it. One theory has it that all men, and some girls, like to run around playing at soldiers, but that doesn't seem to be the real motivating force within the volunteers. They aim to be professional. I found few of the gun-nutter-military-fetish types you might imagine frequent such an establishment. If anything, there was a social etiquette that any gun/war talk was frowned upon.

I think the reason most people volunteer is the essential otherness of it all. You're stuck in a completely different environment to your usual one, doing very challenging things with a cross-section of people you do not encounter in your everyday life. It's a great leveller and a unique tool for finding out something about yourself. Some of it, like my first aid instruction, was genuinely useful. Other parts, like what to do in the event of a nuclear attack, less so.

The army life lacks its obvious old benefits. Its offer of showing you the world is less relevant these days when for £250 you can holiday in Goa or Mombasa. And the old pull of Queen and country fades as those young people with a sense of civic duty queue up for work with VSO or Oxfam. It can't even offer you a job for life any more.

What it does give you is something different: a pride I had never felt before. It also blessed me with a pleasure I have never experienced. It was a feeling so ecstatic that, if bottled, would corrupt mankind for ever. It was the feeling of throwing off my blistering boots and rancid camouflage gear, then sinking my body into a hot bath knowing the whole gruelling affair was over. God was in his heavens and Pirbright was free from communism.

Observer, 26 May 1996

Urban Commandos

DPM is this season's khaki. Khaki was last season's citrus. Citrus was the season before's denim. What went on before that, I neither know nor care. Suffice to say that every suave bod around town has spent the last year bowling around in a pair of camouflage trousers. A stranger to these shores might easily fall under the misapprehension that the kids here were revolting. From Soho to Sauchiehall Street, a trendy militia has been formed. The Winter Palace remains untouched, but the Camden Palace is full of the blighters.

As fashion trends go, the camouflage craze looks set to have some longevity. It has always been a bit of a hardy perennial in the fashion market. Scummier skinheads were big on 'jungle greens' in the Seventies, and Katherine Hamnett did her own high-fashion take in the early Eighties. Public Enemy fought the power in some nice Arctic combat outfits, which later became very big on the German techno scene. In recent times, all sorts of camouflage combinations have been popping up on the catwalk, in clubs, and even on East 17. Top Shop have their own range for cadets, and Sign of the Times are still churning out the gear to the senior ranks. Yep, camouflage or, to give it the correct name, Disruptive Pattern Material (DPM), is on the up.

It's not that hard to work out why DPM trousers are so popular. Although fashion's fickle lottery is responsible for most of our stylish whims, there are reasons why some things succeed and others don't. The key long-term trend in fashion since the advent of the blue jean in the Fifties has been practicality and comfort. Most of the things we wear are either sportswear or workwear or designer imitations thereof, clothes designed with function in mind: polo-shirts, sweat-shirts, desert boots, jeans. MA1 flying jackets, trainers, biker jackets, hiking boots, deck shoes, yachting jackets – you name it. Fashion designers have simply stolen – sorry, 'been inspired by' – items that have functional design. And the most functional designer of all is the military.

The forces have to ensure their clothing has all the best aspects of both workwear and sportswear. It must be hard-wearing, yet versatile, allowing the wearer to run, abseil, hike, climb and, of course, kill people. The result is that when you put on a pair of combat trousers you feel genuinely reassured by them. They feel tough, and the pockets are in the right place. Simple things, yet a world away from the feeling you get when you slip on the average pair of designer strides.

The other thing that the military has to think about is making sure its troops are not seen, and shot, by the enemy, thus the lovely coloured splodges on their Disruptive Pattern Material – yet the design still has to be distinctive enough to ensure you don't shoot any of your own troops. And, unsurprisingly, it must alter for different terrains. Hence DPM comes in a vast variety of shades, colours and patterns. Function *and* variety: the ideal choice for the Nineties fashion consumer.

Camouflage was actually invented not by the military but by hunters who had to stalk their prey, and copied the animals' own markings to avoid detection. All very back-to-nature. The military didn't need to learn the art of camouflage until later, as all fighting used to take place at close quarters on open ground. It wasn't until muskets became rifles at the end of the eighteenth century that soldiers started to cam it up, gradually abandoning their old coloured uniforms for more sensible khaki.

Camouflage patterns as we know them today first appeared during the First World War thanks in part to developments in the art world at the time. The British and French armies employed painters to design their camouflage, and Franz Marc, an avant-garde artist serving as a cavalry man in the German army, used techniques from modern art to create his abstract patterns. In a letter written in 1916, he explains that his latest military tarpaulins 'chart a development from Manet to Kandinsky'. A few years later Pablo Picasso, on spotting a camouflaged cannon in Paris, was to claim, 'It is we who have created that.' He was right.

Before the late Seventies, the vast bulk of civilian DPM sales was to labourers who had been buying it as cheap, durable workwear since the end of the Second World War. Military surplus wear had been worn by hippies in the Sixties, but it was more popular in America than Britain, and camouflage was rarely seen anywhere. Then British punks adopted it as a striking bit of anti-fashion, and it's been coming and going ever since.

So when you next put on your combat pants, remember you're not just pulling on your trousers but slipping into years of history, of cubism and Kandinsky, of function and comfort, of Katherine Hamnett and Top Shop. And hey, be careful out there.

The Face, December 1996

1997

On 1 May the Labour Party won a general election for the first time since 1979. Gavin and his brother Fraser held a party on election night, and when each of the big Tories went down, they wrote their name on a rocket and shot them up into the sky. Michael Portillo, Gerry Hayes, David Mellor: they all went up in flames over Hackney that night. It was a time of optimism, a new start.

Gavin didn't publish a great deal of journalism in the first four months of 1997. He had been to Beirut with Miranda Sawyer as the new presenters of the BBC's *Rough Guide* TV series to film a pilot. He went to do his jungle training with the Territorial Army in Belize. He went to do a travel piece in Iceland, a place he found exhilarating. He was looking forward to working on his novel. On 17 May he celebrated his thirty-first birthday. Afterwards, he went to Cornwall with friends for a few days' break.

Belize: Carry On up the Jungle

The clues were there. I should have realized weeks before, when I saw a picture in the paper of a squaddie with a rasher of bacon strapped on his head. He had a demented smile, and a skull-burying worm living in his scalp. The bacon had been put there by doctors to tempt the tubby little worm out. 'I can feel him having a disco in my head every night!' commented the young private. The poor man had just come back from Belize in Central America. He was part of the advanced guard in a British Military operation known as Exercise Native Trail. An exercise *I* had agreed to go on, of my own free will, as part of my role as a volunteer in the Royal Green Jackets reserves.

Exercise Native Trail had sounded very enticing, the name conjuring up images of happy army folk ambling through the jungle on a glorified nature walk. I'd thought it was going to be the ideal winter break. A couple of weeks wondering at the marvels of the rainforest and tanning myself on the white sands of Belize's Caribbean atolls. I did not expect to find myself attempting to lie motionless in a muddy puddle overnight in the middle of the jungle waiting to ambush suspected drug-traffickers. Especially while I was desperately trying to suppress the urge either to swipe at the numerous insects and snakes who saw me as a nice evening snack or scratch my inflamed fungal-infested scrotum, which was throbbing like a thirsty dog. Still, you live and you learn. And Exercise Native Trail was one big learning curve.

Belize lies just south of Mexico due east of Guatemala. It's an English(ish)-speaking country, more Caribbean than Central American. Sparse in population, heavy in jungle, it consists of a mainland about the size of Wales and a large barrier reef which includes numerous islands, cays and atolls. It was once British Honduras, an anarchic colony founded by pirates and loggers. Although independent since 1981, the British army hung around due to the fact that Guatemala always laid claim to the territory. Now British troops are there primarily to support and train the Belizean army, the BDF (Belize Defence Force). That, and to educate young innocents like me in the black arts of jungle warfare.

The jungle is not the natural terrain of those in the reserve forces. Territorial Army folk rarely go anywhere more exotic than the Brecon Beacons or Pirbright. Yet now, post-cold war, with the regular army scaled down and stretched beyond breaking point, the reserve forces are increasingly being used to fill the gaps. It's now essential all reserves are trained to a higher standard, so as to produce soldiers of a sufficient quality to paper over the cracks that are appearing in most full-time regiments. With the regular army spread thinly amongst its commitments in Northern Ireland, Bosnia, Cyprus and a host of other jolly places around the world, training opportunities in the likes of Belize can't be filled as easily.

It was previously thought that reserve forces weren't up to training in harsh terrains like the jungle, and in some ways Exercise Native Trail was a bit of an experiment. Still, I didn't feel like a guinea-pig – more like a suckling pig at a bar mitzvah.

It took three days to get to Belize from Britain. The RAF VC10 'Spirit of St Jude' was cursed by engine trouble. We moved like a crippled frog, hopping at first to Newfoundland and then, croaking in little leaps, through the States. Upon each landing we were greeted by the reassuring sight of the local emergency rescue service flashing around our wings. This was all very exciting and did mean I had a chance to visit airports I had previously only dreamed about. However, our delayed arrival in Belize meant that we had little time to acclimatize.

On debarkation, I immediately tried to find someone in charge to explain that I'd really only come for the rum and cokes. Before I knew it, though, I was slung on a truck and carted up-country to the thick Belizean hooly: the heart of darkness. What Conrad had taken months to do was achieved in hours. And the heart it did sink.

I'd assumed, in my stupidity, that my time in the jungle would be spent in a nice little ethnic house on stilts, rather like Treetops Game Lodge in Kenya, or the stockade that the Swiss Family Robinson used to live in. You know, a place with a large veranda to sup your G&Ts on, and a rainbow-coloured parrot squawking on a post. I was severely disappointed. Accommodation was basic; in fact, if it had been any less basic we would have had to take a second look at evolutionary theory to check man really had moved on since the chimpanzee. For our living quarters were trees. Trees that, on a good day, we could sling a hammock in between. Trees that were on top of a hill so steep that, every time I climbed it, a channel was carved into its side by the river of sweat that waterfalled from my bulging brow.

Our only concession to civilization was the digging of a hole in the ground affectionately called a 'shit pit'. The thrill of this extravagant luxury turned out to have been short-lived when I realized it had been dug a mere metre or two from my section's hammocks. Apart from the obvious problem of the smell, there was the farting morning chorus as first light illuminated a platoon's worth of hairy squaddie arses as they unloaded down the hole. Still, there would come times when I would look fondly back on this rancid area as a veritable palace.

For the purpose of the exercise we were placed in platoons. Platoons consist of three sections. In our case we had one section from the Honorable Artillery Company (yuppies), one from the Parachute regiment (thugs) and lastly a section comprising of our happy gang from the Royal Green Jackets (a mixture of yuppies and thugs). We were all under the command of a selection of top-notch Jungle Warfare Instructors (always referred to as the JWIs – the army *loves* initials). The JWIs were largely from the SAS. You knew they were from the SAS by their lack of regimental beret or insignia on their person, by their tall, well-built bodies, by their thousand-yard stares and by their dry sarcastic voices saying things like 'It's only a *little* walk' or 'Don't step on the crocodiles, it tends to make them angry.'

Amongst army folk the SAS, always pronounced 'Sas' not 'S-A-S', are rarely referred to directly. They're always given more enigmatic tags. People say things like, 'He's a special lad' or 'That's a boy from Hereford.' Hereford, to me, is a small market town near the Welsh border. I assumed for the first couple of days that our JWI commander had a keen interest in farming. I only later realized that Hereford is also home to the SAS. My small talk on the problems with the modern dairy herd had been entirely wasted.

The first thing the JWIs taught me was how to navigate in the jungle. Well, they tried. To get 'home' was easy – I simply followed my nose. For anything else I required handy bridle paths or nature trails to steer my way through such a sprawling mass of flora and fauna. I needed signposts and big flashing lights saying 'This way to the small rock at grid 603–450'. But no. Maps of the area are, at best, just vague impressionistic paintings, the sort of things medieval monks drew for their kings. I kept looking for markings saying 'There be dragons,' all I found were reference points like rivers. These would helpfully appear and disappear by the hour depending on the weather and the mood of the gods.

All you can do in the end is look at a compass, set a bearing, then soldier religiously on in a set course, counting your footsteps to work out how much ground you've covered. It's a thankless, confusing task, because the second thing that the JWIs taught me was that *everything* is against you in the Belizean jungle. Just to get a mere kilometre from our little faecal-smelling home would take a day of hard grind.

Your problems start with the jungle: a dense forest of plant, tree and creeper. This is one big weeding problem. Travelling through it is like being half an inch high and having to make your way through Michael Heseltine's hair. And, unlike most lost-world-explorer types, you can't simply hack through it. The British army does not hack. It doesn't saw or break either. This is not for any great ecological reason but for tactical ones. To do so would leave a trail, a sign the enemy could follow. You *manoeuvre* through the jungle. Where necessary you tie back the foliage with string, untying when departing.

All this wouldn't be so bad, but the trees and plants of the jungle aren't busy lizzies and willows, they're evil things designed to maim and torture humble humans. There's the White Sap tree, whose ooze can blind you if you're not careful. Then there's the Wait-A-While plant that hooks you with barbs that dig in further the more you struggle. However, I soon found out that the real villain of the piece is the aptly named Bastard Tree. (And yes, it is called that, even in Mayan.) It's a thin, blackish tree with a scaly trunk covered in more spines than a porcupine.

The Belizean jungle covers a vast mountainous area. You are always either panting up a hill or rolling down one. It's all one big shock to the system for a London lad. When it rains the whole jungle floor turns to slippery mud. Keeping hold of your footing is a difficult task, especially when at calf level you have numerous vines, roots and other natural tripwires. Many a time I was sent tumbling. And each time, you can bet that this unlucky soldier gripped a steadying hand right on to the trunk of a Bastard Tree. I still tweezer a new set of needles out of my palm every night.

If the plants don't get you, the animals do. The jungle is home to an A–Z of everything that slithers, flaps, stings and bites. It soon became apparent they were all after me; mosquito, moth, caterpillar, jaguar, tarantula, scorpion and snake. The snakes were particular fun. They had a great knack of doing just enough to freak you out.

On my first patrol, a highly poisonous Coral snake appeared, then disappeared under the leaves on the forest floor. I would have preferred it if he'd told me where he was going. His whereabouts wriggled in my mind throughout my stay. Thoughts of snakes were only diminished by attacks from flies that sounded like chainsaws.

They'd dive on you, attach themselves to your clothing and try to bury in. I don't know why they bothered – various insects, parasites and fungi had already got to my skin. Within days I had become an all-you-can-eat buffet for every creepy-crawly in the neighbourhood.

If all this wasn't enough, a few days in, and just as I was getting used to it, Winston introduced a whole new metaphysical enemy to frighten me. Winston is a local man who's lived in the jungle most of his life and is employed by the British Army as a tracker. In passing conversation he informed me of the twelve-foot-high spirits that live in the trees, a mad woman who lives in the water and a curious half-man/half-monkey that screams at you late at night. Normally I'd be sceptical of such things but, there in the madness of the jungle, it all seemed very plausible. I did not sleep well.

Winston had his uses, though. He was an expert on jungle survival. He'd always be pulling out a selection of edible fruit, roots and leaves from the undergrowth. I tried all of his various offerings and they all tasted much the same: a kind of strange blend of gooseberries, celery and potato. Bland as they were, they were infinitely more tasty than army rations. These were distributed in box-form under the pointless name of Menu A. Pointless, because if there was a menu B, C or D, we never got to see it. There are only so many boil-in-the-bag beef stews and dumplings a man can take. Within days I was fantasizing about fry-ups and curries. That's of course when I wasn't fantasizing about being out of the jungle.

We marched in the mud, we ate in the mud, we slept in the mud. We patrolled, we recced positions, we learned to fight at close quarters. I seem to remember spending most of my time struggling through the undergrowth up large hills with a rifle in my hand, a Bergen on my back, a water pouch around my neck and webbing and ammunition around my waist. For some reason our destinations always had food-based names, Pork Chop Hill, Guacamole Bridge, Meat and Two Veg Valley, that sort of thing. This was a cruel joke to play for those on Menu A.

What made things worse though was that no matter how hard you were trying to give your peak best, there was always some SAS guy ahead of you carrying twice the weight you were, sauntering away as if this was just a stroll around the playground. The SAS are the prefects of the army. They're the goody-two-shoes who do everything right. They always follow the drills they've been taught and they don't cut corners. It's not just that they're physically stronger than the normal army, they're more intelligent, too. It's sickening, really. Still, they can't be that clever. Nobody with an ounce of nous would spend more time in the jungle than they really had to. They'd been there for months.

A lot of the time we were there we were on what is known as 'harsh regime'. This means that, for tactical reasons, noise has to be kept to a minimum, there are to be no fires or cigarettes, no lights at night, certainly no rubbish left behind, bowels are to be evacuated only in a plastic bag to be carried with you. When on harsh regime you have to be on guard for an hour during dusk and dawn – the most likely times of an enemy attack. You must be ready to move straight away so all your kit is packed away.

The annoying thing is you don't get a chance to sling your hammock up in the daylight. It's a hard task at the best of times, but fumbling around in pitch-blackness trying to ensure a comfy kip was near impossible. Many a night I spent clinging for dear life on skew-whiff bedding that sloped like the red route at Klosters. A random element in hammock-slinging was the fact that a lot of the trees in the jungle are completely rotten. It was always a moment of great drama when I jumped in the sack at night awaiting the crack of nearby timber.

What kept me sane throughout my stay in the jungle was the folks in my section, nine others, all reservists, many ex-regular soldiers but all from quite diverse backgrounds. My battle partner was Corporal T, a Metropolitan police firearms instructor who, rather interestingly, had *no interest in guns or gun people*. There were two lawyers in the section as well as a printer, a carpenter, a drugs-and-alcohol counsellor and Corporal Stress – a sexually-transmitted-disease expert in a leading London hospital. 'I must see about twenty cocks and ten arses a day,' he mused, in one of the exercise's quieter moments.

Humour was retained throughout, encouraged by our leader, Sergeant Major Dave T, a veteran of many a jungle campaign from Brunei to Borneo. On non-harsh-regime nights Dave would invite us all to his hammock for a 'bring-a-candle party'. Dumb as it sounds, these parties were the highlight of the day. We'd sit in a circle, ging-gang-gooley style, light a candle as a substitute bonfire and pass around a cup of coffee. Dave would keep us entertained as he told tales of how he single-handedly defeated communism, the IRA and any Military Policeman you care to mention.

Towards the end of the exercise people were falling out; with the elements, with nature and with each other. A certain regimental friction had developed between the Green Jackets and the Paras. And between both of them and the HAC. Meanwhile, the enemy we were supposed to be fighting was somewhere out there running drugs across the border. I had a personal battle of my own. I had developed crotch rot, a fungal infection around the scrotum which feels as if somebody has swiped a machete between one's legs. I had also caught a hacking cough that was doing the rounds. Worst of all I was starting to smell, I mean, *really* smell. The sort of smell you find if you mix milk with seafood and leave by a radiator for a week.

And it wasn't just me who was smelling, the whole of my section was producing a hum that was even more offensive than the nearby hole of a thousand menu As. The only up-side was that the insects we attracted on arrival were now having second thoughts. Even mosquitoes have some standards.

The final part of our duties was an ambush, a big surprise party for the destabilizing drug runners of some strange-sounding cartel. We were to trek out to a rendezvous point, get into position, then wait.

When the pretend bandits went past, we were to open fire. It sounds rather dramatic and exciting when you say it like this, in reality it's a rather demanding endurance test. We schlepped out *en masse*, in the nearest to silence we could manage, and battled our way through the rainforest. On arrival we were placed in position, and there we waited. Time passes slowly when you're not having fun.

I was positioned on my belly in the remnants of a puddle. Plants tickled my face and arms. To my left Corporal Stress lay languid. He had the expression of a bloodhound in mourning. For Corporal Stress is a nicotine addict of the first order and this was harsh regime. His agony was my only source of comfort as we sat through the cold, wet night. Listening to the scream of howler monkeys and the deep rasp of the big cats. Twitching at every contact of plant on face, thinking this was the spider, the snake or scorpion that had decided tonight was my night.

Dawn rose with the distant crackle of gunfire and cries in Spanish out in front. We opened fire. My SA-80 rifle had got through three magazines' worth before it was time to evacuate. And boy, did we evacuate. Skipping and scurrying back to our base carrying our injured by improvised stretcher. It was hard it was furious it was fun, because this was the end of the exercise and we were sprinting back to something called sanity.

Our shackles of suffering were soon removed. We were alive and elated in a way only those who've escaped something so soul-sapping can be. For this is the feeling, the reason why people put themselves through such pains: the addictive drug of completion. We climbed in the trucks, finally heading for where I wanted to go in the first place. And so it was: white sands, a fountain of rum and cokes and one extra element – a whole load of ripping yarns about wrestling snakes, slotting drug-dealers and the trauma of my scrotum.

Everybody should be forced to serve their country in this manner. Well, not everybody, just people like Sting. I think a few weeks of jungle-training will help him see the light. Nature is not our friend. We do not need to protect the rainforest from man. We need man to be protected from the rainforest.

And if, some time in the future, Her Majesty's Army is called upon to defend some Commonwealth jungle or another, I tell you I'm not going. Not unless they send with me a bargain bucket of weed-killer and enough concrete slabs to patio the whole godforsaken lot.

Unpublished feature written for the *Daily Telegraph*, 1997

Days of Being Wild

There's a feeling in youth, a feeling of immortality. It leads you on to conviction, strength and love. And foolishness. Football in the Eighties, the football of my youth, was pure foolishness. On one level it is summed up by the victory of Wimbledon over Liverpool in the 1988 FA Cup final. The Cup final was important in those days, before the Premiership usurped *everything*. It was also the only live televised game of the year. A special day.

Don't get me wrong. Wimbledon won deservedly. I think it was Lawrie Sanchez who scored. There was the romance of the underdog in their victory and it was greeted with the same outpouring of joy and emotion that is now reserved for any Manchester United hiccup. Yet this also represented the triumph of footballing philosophy that had turned the game into dishwater. Nominally called 'the long-ball game', it was, in layman's terms, 'hoof it up the park and hope'. It was to football what Thatcher was to the economy. It was Conservatism in action. And boy, did it help the small business.

Brighton used it to reach the Cup final in 1983. Graham Taylor used it with great success at Watford, so did Steve Coppel at Crystal Palace. Even the big boys played that tactic. The England team under Bobby Robson had it as cornerstone to their play. But for the hand of God, it may have lifted them the ultimate trophy in Mexico 86. There was some artistry around, too. The likes of Kenny Dalgliesh and Glenn Hoddle did their best to pierce the bland high ball. Yet even such masters as they have their memory tarnished by the grey fog of apathy that surrounded the game in the Eighties.

Now Premiership soccer is one of the world's leading television sports. Everyone wants a slice. The worldwide sales of Manchester

United's merchandising will soon outstrip that of any other club on the planet. Players from all round the world flock to our league to play at clubs that only ten years ago were virtual wastegrounds. English football has gone from being total bollocks to total football.

Along with this recent boom has come wave upon wave of nostalgia. Everyone from Bobby Moore to Brian Clough has been trawled through. Yet no one has touched the Eighties in all its mundaneness. Until recently. Now matches have started appearing on UK Gold. In the coming months we may be in for a feast of tight silky tops, outrageous bubble perms, awful bleached highlights and a few non-hoofing highlights like Ricky Villa shuffling past the Man City defence to win Spurs the Cup in 81.

Yet as I sat checking out a United v. Liverpool re-run, I found myself looking at the crowd, not the game. Just as I did as a youth, come to think of it, because whatever was happening on the pitch was never going to be as exciting as what was going on around you. For when you talk of football in the Eighties, you don't *really* talk of football, you talk of everything *but* the game. The teams, matches and players – Spurs, Man City, Wimbledon, Liverpool, Glenn Hoddle, Norman Whiteside, Alan Hansen – are merely hooks, reference points that lead the mind on to songs, clothes, trains and, of course, *the off*.

It's hard to work out whether there isn't something stupid about being nostalgic about a decade that gave us Bradford, Heysel and Hillsborough. Yet youth stays in your mind for ever. And nothing takes residence in the grey cells like the feeling of fear. And fear goes with ecstasy like victory with defeat. On that front, the Eighties youth had it all. It is up to those who had first-hand experience in these matters to bear witness. Strut with me now down our first memory lane, that of witness A and the station incident:

'I remember going to Euston Station after a match with a bunch of lads. We were bowling round in a group nominally looking for the lads from the other side. This was the bread and butter of Eighties soccer. There was a lot of walking around in big gangs thinking you were something special. I turned a corner into a side road, then milled for a while. There was a lot of milling in those days.

'The next scene I've played through my mind several times since then. A guy in front of me turned to look at me. He was wearing an Ellesse beanie hat, a mauve Fila tracksuit and Nike trainers. In a matter of seconds, though, he was joined by a mob of about fifty bounding down the street. I had found the other side's firm. The first guy reached for his pocket, then his arm came swinging down on my chest. I took a step back just at the right moment. The blade only nicked me. It did, however, cut a neat slice down my recently purchased black Demob coat.

'There followed a noise, a primal scream from a hundred mouths. It was off. I ran backward and forward with the chaotic tides of violence. They ran us, then we ran them, and so on. They chucked dustbin lids and bottles at us, we threw CS gas at them. I say "we" rather presumptuously. I was in a state of shock and simply copying everyone else's dance moves. Most incidents like this were brief – this went on far too long. People were getting hurt. Ears were going missing. I was delighted to see the police turn up and call an end to it. I think everybody was, really. It was like that most weeks, though, come to think of it.'

Odd as it seems, many who cut their teeth on Eighties soccer find the modern game missing something. They see football as something they can no longer relate to, as something that lacks substance and soul. They see a game without the violence: a game minus the adrenalin of destruction they were weaned on.

It was put to me that you get a more authentic atmosphere watching football down the pub than you do at a ground these days. You can stand up, swear and brawl with the opposition while consuming gallons of your favourite alco-pop. Many miss the time when the burning issue in ground catering was whether you robbed the till or touched the burger van. What passes for a riot these days is, frankly, pitiful. If a fat drunk runs on the pitch because his team has scored there are questions about it in Parliament. Not like the Eighties. In those days, riots were riots.

Witness B remembers a cup quarter-final between Millwall and Luton. 'It was like everyone knew there was going to be this huge off. There were people from every London club going up there. Even ICI guys (Millwall's big rivals) were turning up for a laugh. It was Millwall's most important away match in years. The stakes had risen so high by then. It was the peak of the casual thing. Every firm was jockeying for number-one slot. Millwall had a reputation for fighting with the police, which is possibly the hardest thing you can do. Everyone was up for it that night.

'The first thing I remember seeing when we got to Luton was some guy crossing the road and smacking a copper in the mouth. It was just mayhem from then on. The bit everyone remembers is when the mob ran on to the pitch chasing the police. It looked good on TV. I managed to get my jeans caught on the fence, though, so I didn't quite make it. You can see me dangling in the background in the footage. I'm wearing a red Next jacket. (Next was cool for about a week, honest.)

'Outside afterwards it was just crazy. The police were getting run everywhere. As our train left all you could see was burning cars. All I remember thinking was, "I hope my Mum doesn't see me on the TV."'

It's remarkable to think how far football has come in so few years. You'll rarely see a policeman inside a ground today. Now you have stewards with little to do. There are no hordes of opposing fans baying at each others' throats any more. A new steward's job involves telling people to sit down if they are standing up, or to be quiet if they are singing. Occasionally they have the excitement of ejecting someone for litter-dropping or swearing. Such is stewarding.

While few see this as a lamentable situation, there are some things you can be slightly tearful about – like turning up on match day and getting a ticket at the turnstile; like turning up on match day without any money and bunking over a turnstile; like turning up at Wembley and slipping the turnstile operator your watch so he'd let you in the cup final. You could do that when they had terracing. Now you have to spend the first half-hour of any match trying to find seat 398, row Q, block 45, upper McDonald's stand. And you're sat next to somebody from Morgan Grenfell who's asking you what the side in red is called. Football's new fans are resented because they weren't there during the fighting. How many face-painted fools in Euro 96 had done their national service?

Witness C explains the turmoil that three lions on your chest used to mean: 'It was the European Championships in Germany. Euro 88. We were in Düsseldorf, due to play Holland the next day. There were a few of us chilling out by the train station. We hadn't got anywhere to stay so we'd simply put our gear in lockers and gone on the piss. Germany was playing in Cologne that day. After that match about 2,000 German hoolies had got on to the train to Düsseldorf to have a pop at the England.

'We weren't expecting this onslaught. There were only about fifty of us around the station area all in all. We ran at first. The Germans were firing flare-guns and chucking gas at us. We were hopelessly outnumbered and in a dead end. I remember thinking, this is it. There was no need for a conscience in this situation. We had little choice but to stand and fight. Soon we were having a crack at them. It was exhilarating. We chased them around the block, by which time other England fans had arrived, and the police. "World War Three," the *Sun* headline read the next day.'

Three places hold the truth of Eighties football, not tales of bravado and blagging. First Heysel with its thuggery and stupidity, then Bradford and the flames of neglect, finally Hillsborough. Realistically, it's quite hard to argue football in the Eighties was better than football now but, like punk rock, it had its moments. It *was* rubbish, in an era that will always be referred to in rather grave tones. This was English football's nadir and we were fools, herded like cattle and treated like sheep.

If football now is consumer-led, those who don't like it have nobody to blame but themselves. It's hard to take people bleating on about commercialism in the game when already this year I have received three books written by moaning, weren't-really-hooligans-honest geezers. It's a bigger market than Ryan Giggs duvets. Football-wise, I think the game now is much better, although I don't really know for sure; I couldn't tell you who scored the best goal in the 84/85 season or who won Player of the Year in 87. My mind was elsewhere.

What I can tell you with conviction is that West Ham were the only firm to take each end of Stamford Bridge simultaneously. I know because I bore witness. In fact, it is my shame that I was witnesses A, B and C. Well, not exactly me. A younger, dumber, me. A guy who I can't really look in the eye any more. Another me, who filled the back of my mind with vivid memories stretching from Stanley Park to Southampton. He dressed pretty well, I seem to remember. All mouth and nice trousers, he got beaten up a few times and deserved it. He got arrested a few times and deserved that even more. Still, I don't remember him doing anything particularly wrong. I do remember him having a lot of fun and adventure. Maybe I'm being too easy on him. If I ever see him on the news again, though, I'm shopping him to the hooligan hotline. It will be good publicity for when the book comes out.

To have been an Eighties football hooligan is a bit like having been a Maoist in the Sixties. You know you were wrong, but you also know it seemed right at the time. Like youth, it felt complete and enduring. Let us never mention this again.

Arena, March 1997

Happiness

An osprey, winged by a hunter's arrow, rides the hot air that rises from the Gulf Stream waters. It flies in circles, unable to navigate with the burden of the disability. Flutter hard, you handsome eagle. Spread those damaged wings. Swoop for fish in loch or bay. Nourish your birdie tum-tum. The bird is Britain. I am an arse. Satire is deaf.

I have reached a stage in my life where I think, on balance, I . . . How do I explain? I spend all my money on Pringles, cocaine, Regaine and strangely coloured underwear. The term 'going out' now means a trip to somebody else's sofa. Maybe I should go and play war in the garden – that used to make me happy. Still, mustn't grumble. Whinging, however, is a must, as I gradually replace self-loathing/pity with a persona of giddy yet false promises and possibilities.

I've been studying rather sad people to learn how to be happy. Pushing your tongue to the top of your mouth apparently creates some happy juice in your brain. So do the complex sugars of fruit juice. Such facts should be spread to all the miserable hordes. I'm not up on the true medical nature of these facts, or indeed whether or not they work. I only know that, having researched and then experimented with them, I have, as a result, found myself a considerably happier person. You just thrust your tongue into the squidgy bit at the top of your mouth and drink fruit juice. Not at the same time – that would lead only to misery and despair. Just do it, and you become happy; happy becomes you. Happy.

There are other methods, too. Laughter is the best medicine. Not for everything (chicken soup is good for colds) – mainly for depression. Laugh a real laugh, and happy juice floods the cranial cheese. Force a smile, a real crow's-foot smile: again, happiness is yours.

The real, guaranteed bliss is achieved only when you have earned the art of fooling your subconscious. Masquerade your emotions into a beloved bean-feast and suddenly your life is one of great happiness. Every day, in every way, I'm getting happier and happier. The subconscious has no eyes, no ears and no ego. Feed your dormant demon the deification of happy-bunny world. It sups it like caviar. Or perhaps like a nourishing fish in a birdie tum-tum.

So it is all as simple as shrimp. The happy shrimp. The wise shrimp. The pink shrimp.

Everything is fine, in theory. In practice, it is perfection. The methods of happiness are jewels from Jehovah. Eels from God. Try it. Sit on the sofa. Relax, let the mind wander whither it wants. Guide the ghouls to the graveyard and let Mr Happy run riot. Listen to his wisdom: why write, why work, why worry, why vote, why love, why dream, why die, why dead? I'm happy, therefore the money goes on brightly coloured pants, powders of perfection, bald-people hair-care products and quality crisps.

I wouldn't be surprised if, with this amount of happiness in my life, I'll soon burst, splattering the carnage of my happiness over an unsuspecting public. Not with this much happiness.

The Idler, March–April 1997

Tom Hodgkinson chose this piece to read at
Gavin's funeral in Headley on 29 May 1997

Facing the Enemy

Fraser Hills on loss, anger and the death of a brother

I've read the stories, seen the body and washed the T-shirt, and I still don't know what to write. I know what I don't want to write – some 'I knew him best and hurt the most' rant about changing his nappy, teaching him how to walk, wank, write, teaching him about gigs, terraces and Bjorg Élites. It's not a competition, and at this moment I can't cut myself in half for you all to see. I have come to terms with the fact that my life will never be the same again, which helps me deal with any desire to set myself an emotional target.

I'm sitting on a rocky beach in Spain, face to face with my enemy. It's my holiday, and I've been crying since five or six this morning. I'm glad the afternoon sun is so hot, because it's drying my tears and the snot on my face, and depriving that bastard of some sustenance.

I've always been an angry man. Now I've finally got something to direct my anger at, and it's covering two-thirds of the planet. I want revenge for the death of my brother. Why is there no 'other driver' or likely lad I can be angry with? Or better still, why can't I make my way to one of the war zones he visited and fight for democracy, every enemy death a tribute? All I have is this vast expanse of water in front of me, waving.

It's beating me. It's dodged my punches and kicks, and it now ignores my vicious, spitting abuse and carries on waving powerfully. Half-way up the cliff to my right is a home-made diving-board overlooking the water and poking out like a cheeky stiffy, turned on by the swell. I decide I'm going to get my revenge, I'm going to show the bastard. As I start clambering the cliff, a sick, nervous feeling comes washing over me, and combined with the man-on-a-mission natural rush, I start feeling possessed and paranoid.

So here I am, at the end of a slippery plank, head full of meaning and symbolism, ready to challenge the sea head to head. Futile, macho bollocks.

Wood, air – and now water slapping me, stinging me, submerging me and holding me to ransom under its surface. I open my eyes, and for a second expect to see Gavin swimming towards me with a cheeky smile and a fishy tale, telling me to get back to the surface, to stop being such a mug. Part of me wants to stay under looking for him, or proving to the sea that I can, and that it's not going to have me. I come back up and look around, expecting the world to have been holding its breath, too. My partner Becky waves, but everyone else is more interested in Jackie Collins than in me. As I bob about in the waves, I still can't understand why I'm allowed to swim to the shore and he wasn't, why this sloppy killer has the right to pick and choose who it murders.

The day after my brother drowned, I took loads of his most cherished possessions, put them in a hold-all, and with friends went to the spot where Gavin fell. We all wrote our goodbyes and put them in with the rocks weighing the bag down and, with everybody holding me, I swung around and threw it as far out into the sea as I could. Earlier in the day my mum had made everybody promise to hold on to me as I threw the bag. Perhaps she really does know me better than I know myself, as I would gladly have followed him into the deep.

Fraser Hills
The Idler, July–August 1997